MO
DE
RN

JÉRÉMY BALLESTER – BRIAN BOCLET – JEAN-MARIE LANIO
OLIVIER MAGNE MOF – THOMAS MARIE MOF – PATRICE MITAILLÉ

THE BIG BOOK OF BAKING & VIENNOISERIE

· TO ·
OUR ·
· REA
DERS

DEAR READER

This book will introduce you to, or help you rediscover, a wide variety of viennoiserie and other baked goods, along with their origins, history, production process, and the ingredients used to make them.

In these pages, to guide you as effectively as possible in preparing the recipes, we have provided a set of steps throughout the book on hydrating, kneading, fermenting, resting and baking times, temperatures, etc.
However, as we know, when it comes to this profession, it is not an exact science—but this is what makes it so interesting and varied. It is also why you may need to adapt these various directions to your geographical location, to your equipment, and to the ingredients at your disposal. Our viennoiserie recipes usually call for bread flour (T65) and strong flour. Bread flour (T65) typically contains between 10.5% and 11.5% protein, whereas strong flour generally has a higher protein content, ranging from 12.5% to 13.5%.

As far as fermentation methods are concerned, when the same product can be made using different pre-fermentations (levain or fermented dough), we have suggested the one we feel is the most appropriate.
When it comes to levains, we use ones without salt. These are refreshed the day before for products to be made immediately, and the same day for those produced for later on. Discover how to prepare them on pages 8–9. In addition, the fermented dough used in the recipes corresponds to the surplus from the previous day's recipes that contain butter and sugar (croissant dough, brioche, Viennese bread, etc.).

All that is left to do now is to wish you happy reading and success with these authentic, traditional, and innovative recipes, whether they are simple or complex . . .

STEP-BY-STEP DIRECTIONS AND BASICS

SPECIAL BREADS

REGIONAL BREADS

BREADS OF THE WORLD

CLASSIC VIENNOISERIE

CONTENTS

MODERN VIENNOISERIE

VIENNOISERIE FROM AROUND THE WORLD

FANCY VIENNOISERIE

SWEET BAKED GOODS

LAMINATED DOUGH

STEP BY STEP

DIREC TIONS • AND • • BAS ICS • •

STIFF LEVAIN

BY USING DIFFERENT TYPES OF FLOURS (BUCKWHEAT, EINKORN, SPELT, KHORASAN WHEAT) TO MAKE A STIFF LEVAIN, YOU CAN CREATE PREPARATIONS WITH DIFFERENT FLAVORS.

INGREDIENTS PREFERMENT

Rye flour (T170)	500 G (1 LB 1 5/8 OZ)
Water at 30°C (85°F)	650 G (1 LB 7 OZ)
Honey	10 G (3/8 OZ)

Combine all the ingredients.
Ferment at 30°C (85°F) for 24 to 48 hours.

FOR THE FIRST FEEDING

Preferment	550 G (1 LB 3 3/8 OZ)
Bread flour (T65)	500 G (1 LB 1 5/8 OZ)
Water at 30°C (85°F)	75 G (2 5/8 OZ)

Combine all the ingredients.
Ferment at 30°C (85°F) for 12 hours.

FOR THE SECOND FEEDING

First feeding	500 G (1 LB 1 5/8 OZ)
Bread flour (T65)	500 G (1 LB 1 5/8 OZ)
Water at 30°C (85°F)	250 G (8 3/4 OZ)

Combine all the ingredients.
Ferment at 25°C (75°F) for 12 hours.

FOR THE THIRD FEEDING

Second feeding	500 G (1 LB 1 5/8 OZ)
Bread flour (T65)	500 G (1 LB 1 5/8 OZ)
Water at 30°C (85°F)	250 G (8 3/4 OZ)

Combine all the ingredients.
Ferment at 25°C (75°F) for 12 hours.

FOR THE FINAL LEVAIN

Third feeding	500 G (1 LB 1 5/8 OZ)
Bread flour (T65)	1 KG (2 LB 3 3/4 OZ)
Water at 30°C (85°F)	500 G (1 LB 1 5/8 OZ)

Combine all the ingredients.
Ferment at 25°C (75°F) for 1 to 2 hours, then at 3°C (35°F) for 12 hours.

At this stage, you can use the levain, but it will have a low acidity level. It will develop more character over time as it stabilizes.
If you take care of your levain properly, you will be able to keep it going and use it forever:
For subsequent feedings, proceed in the same way as for a final levain (1 kg/2 lb 3 3/4 oz levain + 2 kg/4 lb 6 oz flour + 1 kg/2 lb 3 3/4 oz water).
If the levain loses its flavor and acidity, feed it with French T80 flour (available online) or 3 parts bread flour mixed with 1 part whole-wheat flour.

LIQUID LEVAIN

AS WITH A STIFF LEVAIN, YOU CAN USE DIFFERENT TYPES OF FLOUR TO MAKE LIQUID LEVAIN TO VARY THE FLAVOR OF YOUR PREPARATIONS.

INGREDIENTS PREFERMENT		
Rye flour (T170)	**500 G (1 LB 1 5/8 OZ)**	Combine all the ingredients. Ferment at 30°C (85°F) for 24 to 48 hours.
Water at 30 (85°F)	**650 G (1 LB 7 OZ)**	
Honey	**10 G (3/8 OZ)**	

FOR THE FIRST FEEDING		
Preferment	**500 G (1 LB 1 5/8 OZ)**	Combine all the ingredients. Ferment at 30°C (85°F) for 12 hours.
Bread flour (T65)	**500 G (1 LB 1 5/8 OZ)**	
Water at 30°C (85°F)	**500 G (1 LB 1 5/8 OZ)**	

FOR THE SECOND FEEDING		
First feeding	**500 G (1 LB 1 5/8 OZ)**	Combine all the ingredients. Ferment at 25°C (75°F) for 12 hours.
Bread flour (T65)	**500 G (1 LB 1 5/8 OZ)**	
Water at 30°C (85°F)	**500 G (1 LB 1 5/8 OZ)**	

FOR THE THIRD FEEDING		
Second feeding	**500 G (1 LB 1 5/8 OZ)**	Combine all the ingredients. Ferment at 25°C (75°F) for 12 hours.
Bread flour (T65)	**500 G (1 LB 1 5/8 OZ)**	
Water at 30°C (85°F)	**500 G (1 LB 1 5/8 OZ)**	

FOR THE FINAL LEVAIN		
Third feeding	**1 KG (2 LB 3 1/4 OZ)**	Combine all the ingredients. Ferment at 25°C (75°F) for 3 hours, then at 8°C (45°F) for 12 hours. For subsequent feedings, proceed in the same way as for a final levain (1 kg/2 lb 3 1/4 oz levain + 3 kg/6 lb 10 oz flour + 3 kg/6 lb 10 oz water).
Bread flour (T65)	**3 KG (6 LB 10 OZ)**	
Water at 30°C (85°F)	**3 KG (6 LB 10 OZ)**	

PREPARING THE DRY BUTTER

This step involves using a rolling pin, as shown in the photographs on the facing page, or a dough sheeter, to make the butter the perfect shape and texture for preparing laminated dough. The French term for the block of butter is *beurrage*.

The size of the butter should correspond to the width of the dough and half of its length.

To be sure of a high-quality laminated dough, it is important that, when the butter is removed from the refrigerator, it has a consistency that is about the same as that of the dough.

In general, depending on the butter used, the ideal temperature should be between 12 and 16°C (55 to 60°F).

For this reason, the advice is to prepare the butter beforehand and, if possible, to store it in a refrigerator set at the right temperature, between 8 and 12°C (45 to 55°F).

1

2

3
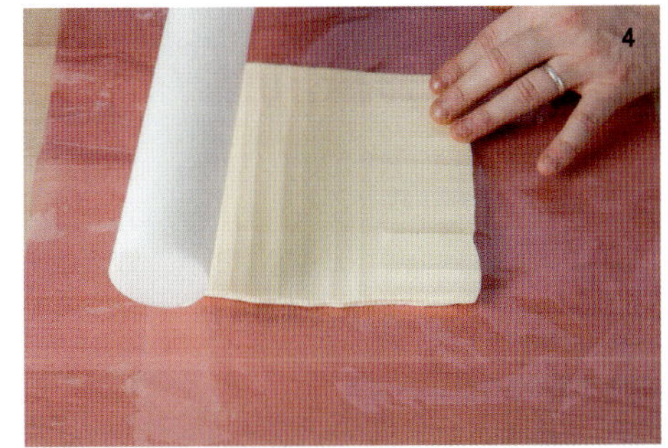
4

5
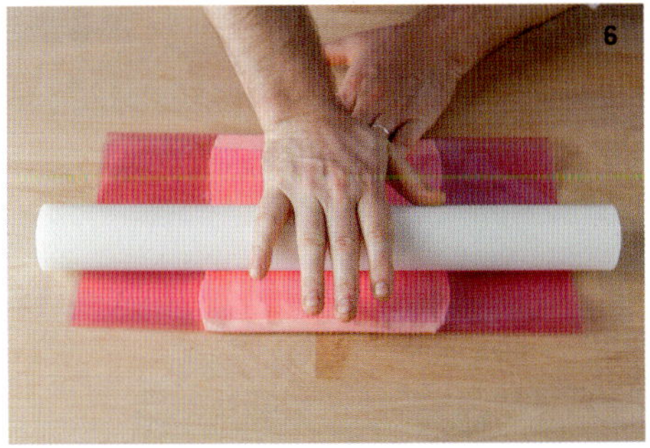
6

7

8

9

10

ENCASING THE BUTTER (*BEURRAGE*)

The first stage for making the initial layers in laminated dough involves encasing the butter in the dough.
It is important to make sure that the dough and butter are perfectly aligned **(1)**. Neither the dough nor the butter should protrude over an edge during this stage **(2, 3)**, otherwise the laminated dough may not turn out evenly. Cutting the folded edges of the dough **(4, 5)** will reduce the elasticity of the dough on the sides and makes it easier to stretch the dough **(6, 7, 8)**.

1

2

3

4

5

6

7

8

TURNS (*TOURAGE*)

Referred to in French as *tourage*, which can be loosely translated as "turns," this technique is essential for creating laminated dough, which can be used, for example, to make puff pastry. It is important to gently roll out the dough in stages to achieve delicate, thin layers of butter and dough. There are four types of turns, which are sometimes called folds, for creating between nine and twenty-seven layers of butter. The choice of a particular turning method should be directly related to the final thickness of the laminated dough and the desired brittleness of the finished product. A thick dough with few layers of butter will inevitably cause the butter to leak out during baking, resulting in a dry product.

However, a thin dough with too many layers of butter can lead to crushing the layers of dough and butter, resulting in a thin, ill-defined pastry.

In general, the turns are performed in succession, with no resting between each turn; however, the exception is for the three single-turn method, for which it is advisable to rest the dough for at least 30 minutes between the second and third single turns.

To make a single turn, the length of the dough should be three to three-and-a-half times its width.

For a double turn, the length of the dough should be four to four-and-a-half times its width.

TWO SINGLE TURNS

These turns will result in nine layers of butter. When applying pressure, it should be light. This method is recommended for products that require a final thickness of between 2 and 3 millimeters thick, such as for miniature viennoiseries.

ONE SINGLE AND ONE DOUBLE TURN

These turns will result in twelve layers of butter. You should apply moderate pressure. This method is recommended for products requiring a final thickness of between 3 and 3.5 millimeters (about ⅛ inch). It is a common, all-purpose method.

TWO DOUBLE TURNS

These turns will result in sixteen layers of butter. You should apply moderate pressure. This method is recommended for products requiring a final thickness of between 3.5 and 4.5 millimeters (about $^{3}/_{16}$ inch), such as *pains au chocolat* and *couques*.

THREE SINGLE TURNS

These turns will result in twenty-seven layers of butter. You should apply significant pressure. This method is recommended when you want to obtain crumbly products, for example, or when incorporating a larger amount of butter.

2 SINGLE TURNS

1 SINGLE TURN AND 1 DOUBLE TURN

2 DOUBLE TURNS

3 SINGLE TURNS

TRADITIONAL LAMINATED DOUGH

KNEADING INGREDIENTS

Bread flour (T65)	**1 KG (2 LB 3 ¼ OZ)**
Water	**430 G (15 ⅛ OZ)**
Salt	**25 G (⅞ OZ)**
Cold unsalted butter, previously melted	**150 G (5 ¼ OZ)**

TURNING (*TOURAGE*)

Dry butter *(see page 10)*	**800 G (1 ¾ LB)**

METHOD

BASE TEMPERATURE	46 to 50°C (115 to 120°F).
INCORPORATE	In a stand mixer, mix all the kneading ingredients in the bowl.
INITIAL MIX	On speed 1 for about 6 minutes.
CONSISTENCY	Firm dough.
WEIGHT	One 1.6-kilogram (3 lb 8 ½-oz) dough piece.
REST	At 3°C (35°F) for at least 2 hours.
TURN	Encase the dry butter in the dough **(1, 2, 3)**. Make two single turns **(4 to 7)**.
REST	At 3°C (35°F) for at least 4 hours.
TURN	Make two single turns **(4 to 7)**.
REST	At 3°C (35°F) for least 4 hours.
TURN	Make one single turn **(4, 5)**.
REST	At 3°C (35°F) for about 12 hours.

1
2
3
4
5
6
7

INVERTED LAMINATED DOUGH

KNEADING INGREDIENTS

Strong flour	**400 G (14 OZ)**
Bread flour (T65)	**600 G (1 LB 6 ⅛ OZ)**
Water	**600 G (1 LB 6 ⅛ OZ)**
Salt	**25 G (⅞ OZ)**

KNEADED BUTTER (BEURRE MANIÉ)

Dry butter	**1 KG (2 LB 3 ¼ OZ)**
Strong flour	**150 G (5 ¼ OZ)**
Bread flour (T65)	**150 G (5 ¼ OZ)**

FOR THE KNEADED BUTTER

In a stand mixer fitted with a paddle attachment, mix all ingredients until smooth. Set aside at 3°C (35°F).

METHOD

BASE TEMPERATURE 46 to 50°C (115 to 120°F).
INCORPORATE In a stand mixer, mix all the kneading ingredients in the bowl.
INITIAL MIX On speed 1 for about 6 minutes.
CONSISTENCY Medium-firm dough.
WEIGHT One 1.6-kilogram (3 lb 9 ⅜-oz) dough piece.
REST At 3°C (35°F) for at least 1 hour.
TURN Encase this water dough (*détrempe*) in the kneaded butter **(1, 2)**. Make one double turn **(3, 4, 5)** and one single turn **(6, 7)**.
REST At 3°C (35°F) for at least 4 hours.
TURN Make one double turn **(3, 4, 5)** and one single turn **(6, 7)**.
REST At 3°C (35°F) for about 12 hours.

1
2
3
4
5
6
7

QUICK LAMINATED DOUGH

KNEADING INGREDIENTS

Bread flour (T65)	**1 KG (2 LB 1 3/4 OZ)**
Water	**500 G (1 LB 1 5/8 OZ)**
Salt	**25 G (7/8 OZ)**
Frozen, diced dry butter	**800 G (1 3/4 LB)**

METHOD

BASE TEMPERATURE	46 to 50°C (115 to 120°F).
INCORPORATE	In a stand mixer, mix all the kneading ingredients in the bowl.
INITIAL MIX	On speed 1 for about 3 minutes.
CONSISTENCY	Firm dough.
WEIGHT	One 2.3-kilogram (5 lb 2-oz) dough piece.
TURN	Make two single turns **(1 to 5)**.
REST	At least 2 hours at 3°C (35°F).
TURN	Make two single turns **(6 to 9)**.
REST	At least 2 hours at 3°C (35°F).
TURN	Make one single turn **(6, 7)**.
REST	About 2 hours at 3°C (35°F).

1
2
3
4
5
6
7
8
9

VIENNESE LAMINATED DOUGH

	KNEADING INGREDIENTS
Bread flour (T65)	**1 KG (2 LB 3 1/4 OZ)**
Milk	**400 G (14 OZ)**
Eggs	**110 G (3 7/8 OZ)**
Salt	**20 G (3/4 OZ)**
Superfine sugar	**40 G (1 3/8 OZ)**
Cold unsalted butter, previously melted	**200 G (7 OZ)**

	TURNING (*TOURAGE*)
Dry butter	**800 G (1 3/4 LB)**

METHOD

BASE TEMPERATURE	46 to 50°C (115 to 120°F).
INCORPORATE	In a stand mixer, mix all the kneading ingredients in the bowl.
INITIAL MIX	On speed 1 for about 6 minutes.
CONSISTENCY	Firm dough.
WEIGHT	One 1.8-kilogram (3 lb 14 1/2-oz) dough piece.
REST	At 3°C (35°F) for at least 2 hours.
TURN	Encase the dry butter in the dough **(1, 2, 3)**. Make two single turns **(4 to 7)**.
REST	At 3°C (35°F) for at least 4 hours.
TURN	Make two single turns **(4 to 7)**.
REST	At 3°C (35°F) least for at 4 hours.
TURN	Make one single turn **(4, 5)**.
REST	At 3°C (35°F) for about 12 hours.

1

2

3

4

5

6

7

VIENNESE FERMENTED DOUGH

KNEADING INGREDIENTS

Strong flour	**1 KG (2 LB 3 ¼ OZ)**
Water	**275 G (9 ¾ OZ)**
Milk	**275 G (9 ¾ OZ)**
Salt	**18 G (⅝ OZ)**
Superfine sugar	**100 G (3 ½ OZ)**
Yeast	**30 G (1 OZ)**
Unsalted butter	**150 G (5 ¼ OZ)**

METHOD

BASE TEMPERATURE	48 to 52°C (120 to 125°F).
INCORPORATE	In a stand mixer, mix all the kneading ingredients in the bowl.
INITIAL MIX	On speed 1 for about 3 minutes.
KNEAD	On speed 2 for about 8 minutes.
CONSISTENCY	Medium-firm dough.
DOUGH TEMPERATURE	At 23°C (75°F).
BULK FERMENT	For about 45 minutes, then at 3°C (35°F) for 12 hours.

FLAKY BRIOCHE DOUGH

KNEADING INGREDIENTS	
Strong flour	**1 KG (2 LB 3 ¼ OZ)**
Eggs	**420 G (14 ¾ OZ)**
Milk	**100 G (3 ½ OZ)**
Salt	**18 G (⅝ OZ)**
Superfine sugar	**40 G (1 ⅜ OZ)**
Yeast	**30 G (1 OZ)**
Unsalted butter	**250 G (8 ¾ OZ)**

FINAL KNEADING	
Superfine sugar	**80 G (2 ⅞ OZ)**
Viennese fermented dough *(see page 28)*	**300 G (10 ½ OZ)**

BASE TEMPERATURE 50 to 54°C (115 to 120°F).
INCORPORATE In a stand mixer, mix all the kneading ingredients in the bowl.
INITIAL MIX On speed 1 for about 7 minutes.
INCORPORATE Add the final kneading ingredients.
KNEAD On speed 1 for about 7 minutes, then on speed 2 for 1 minute.
CONSISTENCY Medium-firm dough.
DOUGH TEMPERATURE At 23°C (75°F).
BULK FERMENT For about 40 minutes, then at 1°C (35°F) for 12 hours.

CHOUX PASTE

INGREDIENTS	
Water	**250 G (8 ¾ OZ)**
Salt	**4 G (⅛ OZ)**
Superfine sugar	**8 G (¼ OZ)**
Unsalted butter	**100 G (3 ½ OZ)**
Strong flour	**150 G (5 ¼ OZ)**
Eggs	**225 G (8 OZ)**

Bring the water, salt, sugar, and butter to a boil.
Add the flour, then use a spatula to stir and dry the mixture over high heat.
In a mixer fitted with a paddle attachment, gradually add the eggs and mix until smooth.

ALMOND CREAM

INGREDIENTS

Almond flour	**250 G (8 ¾ OZ)**
Superfine sugar	**250 G (8 ¾ OZ)**
Unsalted butter, softened	**250 G (8 ¾ OZ)**
Eggs	**225 G (8 OZ)**
Rum (optional)	**25 G (⅞ OZ)**

In a stand mixer fitted with the paddle attachment, mix the almond powder with the superfine sugar, and butter. Gradually add the liquid ingredients and combine. Set aside at 3°C (35°F).

PASTRY CREAM

INGREDIENTS

Milk	**1 KG (2 LB 3 ¼ OZ)**
Eggs	**200 G (7 OZ)**
Superfine sugar	**200 G (7 OZ)**
Custard powder	**90 G (3 ⅛ OZ)**
Vanilla bean	**1** (optional)

In a saucepan, heat the milk (with the scraped vanilla bean, if using). Blanch the eggs and sugar, then add the custard powder. Mix the two preparations and boil for 1 minute. Cool in a blast chiller. Set aside at 3°C (35°F).

CHOCOLATE STICKS

INGREDIENTS

Milk chocolate couverture (35%)	**700 G (1 LB 8 3/4 OZ)**
Almond praline	**700 G (1 LB 8 3/4 OZ)**
Chopped toasted almonds	**350 G (12 3/8 OZ)**

Place a 40 × 30-cm (15 1/2 × 11 3/4-inch) stainless steel frame on an aluminum baking sheet lined with parchment paper, or on a silicone mat.
Melt the milk chocolate. Add the almond praline and chopped almonds, then mix.
Pour the chocolate mixture into the frame. Set aside at 3°C (35°F) for at least 1 hour.
Cut the chocolate from the frame, then cut according to the product/s to be made. Set aside at 3°C (35°F) until ready to use.

NEUTRAL SYRUP

INGREDIENTS

Water	**1 KG (2 LB 3 1/4 OZ)**
Superfine sugar	**1 KG (2 LB 3/14 OZ)**

In a saucepan, bring the water and sugar to a boil.
Set aside at 3°C (35°F).

• S P
E C I
A L •

• B R
E A D
S • •
• • •

BAGUETTE WITH SEEDS

MAKES 6 LOAVES

KNEADING INGREDIENTS

Bread flour (T65)	**1 KG (2 LB 3 1/4 OZ)**
Water	**650 G (1 LB 7 OZ)**
Salt	**19 G (5/8 OZ)**
Yeast	**7 G (1/4 OZ)**
Liquid levain	**100 G (3 1/2 OZ)**

FINAL KNEADING

Seed Mix	**200 G (7 OZ)**
Sesame seeds	**22 G (3/4 OZ)**
Brown flaxseeds	**22 G (3/4 OZ)**
Golden flaxseeds	**22 G (3/4 OZ)**
Millet seeds	**22 G (3/4 OZ)**
Poppy seeds	**12 G (3/8 OZ)**
Water	**100 G (3 1/2 OZ)**
Bassinage water	**AS NEEDED**

FOR THE SEED MIX

In a convection oven at 200°C (390°F), lightly toast the seeds for 15 minutes. Submerge the seeds in water. Set aside at 3°C (35°F).

METHOD

BASE TEMPERATURE 56 to 60°C (135 to 140°F).

INCORPORATE In a stand mixer with a C-shaped or spiral dough hook attachment, mix the flour and water in the bowl.

INITIAL MIX On speed 1 for about 3 minutes.

AUTOLYSIS At least 1 hour.

INCORPORATE Add the salt, yeast, and liquid levain.

KNEAD On speed 1 for about 8 minutes, then on speed 2 for 1 minute.

INCORPORATE Add the toasted seed mixture, then the bassinage water in a fine stream, if necessary.

CONSISTENCY Soft dough.

DOUGH TEMPERATURE 23°C (75°F).

BULK FERMENT About 1 hour, then at 3°C (35°F) for 12 hours.

FOLD TO DEGAS After 1 hour of bulk fermentation.

WEIGHT Six 300-gram (10 1/2 oz) dough pieces.

PRESHAPE Oval.

REST About 45 minutes.

SHAPE Baguette; place the baguettes on a floured linen proofing cloth, seam side up.

FINAL PROOF About 1 hour.

SCORE One slash.

BAKE In a deck oven at 250°C (480°F) for about 20 minutes.

COOL On a wire rack

SESAME BAGUETTE

MAKES 6 LOAVES

KNEADING INGREDIENTS

Bread flour (T65)	**1 KG (2 LB 3 ¼ OZ)**
Water	**650 G (1 LB 7 OZ)**
Salt	**19 G (⅝ OZ)**
Yeast	**7 G (¼ OZ)**
Liquid levain	**100 G (3 ½ OZ)**

FINAL KNEADING

Sesame seeds	**120 G (4 ¼ OZ)**
Water	**50 G (1 ¾ OZ)**
Bassinage water	**AS NEEDED**

FOR THE SESAME SEEDS

In a convection oven at 200°C (390°F), lightly toast the sesame seeds for 15 minutes. In a mini food processor, lightly process 40 g (1 ⅜ oz) of the toasted sesame seeds.

METHOD

BASE TEMPERATURE 56 to 60°C (135 to 140°F).
INCORPORATE In a spiral mixer, mix the flour and water in the bowl.
INITIAL MIX On speed 1 for about 3 minutes.
AUTOLYSIS At least 1 hour.
INCORPORATE Add the salt, yeast, and liquid levain.
KNEAD On speed 1 for about 8 minutes, then on speed 2 for 1 minute.
INCORPORATE Add the toasted sesame seeds, processed toasted sesame seeds, and 50 grams (1 ¾ oz) water, then add the bassinage water in a fine stream, if necessary.
CONSISTENCY Soft dough.
DOUGH TEMPERATURE 23°C (75°F).
BULK FERMENT About 1 hour, then at 3°C (35°F) for 12 hours.
FOLD TO DEGAS After 1 hour of bulk fermentation.
WEIGHT Six 300-gram (10 ½ oz) dough pieces.
PRESHAPE Oval.
REST About 45 minutes.
SHAPE Baguette; place the baguettes on a floured linen proofing cloth, seam side up.
FINAL PROOF About 1 hour.
SCORE A long slash and three herringbone slashes on the top of the baguette.
BAKE In a deck oven at 250°C (480°F) for about 20 minutes.
COOL On a wire rack.

COUNTRY-STYLE BAGUETTE

MAKES 6 LOAVES

KNEADING INGREDIENTS

Bread flour (T65)	**850 G (1 LB 14 OZ)**
Rye flour (T170)	**150 G (5 ¼ OZ)**
Water	**700 G (1 LB 8 ¾ OZ)**
Salt	**18 G (⅝ OZ)**
Yeast	**6 G (3/16 OZ)**
Fermented dough	**250 G (8 ¾ OZ)**

FINAL KNEADING

Bassinage water	**AS NEEDED**

METHOD

BASE TEMPERATURE	62 to 66°C (145 to 150°F).
INCORPORATE	In a spiral mixer, mix all the kneading ingredients in the bowl.
INITIAL MIX	On speed 1 for about 3 minutes.
KNEAD	On speed 1 for about 8 minutes.
INCORPORATE	A trickle of bassinage water, if necessary.
CONSISTENCY	Soft dough.
DOUGH TEMPERATURE	23°C (75°F).
BULK FERMENT	About 1 hour, then at 3°C (35°F) for 12 hours.
FOLD TO DEGAS	After 1 hour of bulk fermentation.
WEIGHT	Six 35-gram (11 ¾-oz) dough pieces.
PRESHAPE	Oval.
REST	About 45 minutes.
SHAPE	Pointed baguette; place the baguettes on a floured surface, seam side up.
FINAL PROOF	About 1 hour.
SCORE	Four slashes.
BAKE	In a deck oven at 250°C (480°F) for about 20 minutes.
COOL	On a wire rack

HERRINGBONE BAGUETTE REVISITED

MAKES 5 LOAVES

KNEADING INGREDIENTS
REGULAR BREAD DOUGH

Strong flour	**1 KG (2 LB 3 1/4 OZ)**
Water	**650 G (1 LB 7 OZ)**
Salt	**18 G (5/8 OZ)**
Yeast	**10 G (3/8 OZ)**
Fermented dough	**200 G (7 OZ)**

TO FINISH

Poppy seeds	**AS NEEDED**

METHOD

BASE TEMPERATURE	50 to 54°C (120 to 130°F).
INCORPORATE	In a spiral mixer, mix the flour and water in the bowl.
INITIAL MIX	On speed 1 for about 3 minutes.
AUTOLYSIS	30 minutes.
INCORPORATE	Add the salt, yeast, and fermented dough.
KNEAD	On speed 2 for about 7 minutes.
CONSISTENCY	Medium-firm dough.
DOUGH TEMPERATURE	23°C (75°F).
BULK FERMENT	About 45 minutes.
WEIGHT	Five 200-gram (7-oz) dough pieces and five 150-gram (5 1/4-oz) dough pieces.
PRESHAPE	Oval.
REST	About 30 minutes.
SHAPE	Shape the 200-gram (7-oz) dough pieces into 60-centimeter (23 1/2-inch)-long baguettes and place them on a linen proofing cloth, seam side down. Use a transfer board to flatten the baguettes. Using a pastry cutter, make nine herringbone slits along the length, each 11 centimeter (4 1/4 inches) long. Widen the slits. Shape the 150-gram (5 1/4-inch) dough pieces into 35-centimeter (14-inch)-long baguettes. Using scissors, cut each of these baguettes diagonally into nine pieces. Moisten the surface of each dough piece, then roll in the poppy seeds. Insert a poppy-covered dough piece into each slit in the whole baguettes.
FINAL PROOF	About 1 hour 30 minutes.
BAKE	In a deck oven at 250°C (480°F) for about 15 minutes.
COOL	On a wire rack.

RUSTIC BAGUETTE

MAKES 6 LOAVES

KNEADING INGREDIENTS

Bread flour (T65)	**850 G (1 LB 14 OZ)**
Whole-wheat einkorn flour	**150 G (5 ¼ OZ)**
Water	**650 G (1 LB 7 OZ)**
Salt	**20 G (¾ OZ)**
Yeast	**6 G (3/16 OZ)**
Liquid levain	**150 G (5 ¼ OZ)**

FINAL KNEADING

Bassinage water	**AS NEEDED**

METHOD

BASE TEMPERATURE	62 to 66°C (145 to 150°F).
INCORPORATE	In a spiral mixer, mix all the kneading ingredients in the bowl.
INITIAL MIX	On speed 1 for about 3 minutes.
KNEAD	On speed 1 for about 8 minutes.
INCORPORATE	A trickle of bassinage water, if necessary.
CONSISTENCY	Medium-firm dough.
DOUGH TEMPERATURE	23°C (75°F).
BULK FERMENT	About 1 hour 30 minutes, then at 3°C (35°F) for 12 hours.
FOLD TO DEGAS	After 1 hour 30 minutes of bulk fermentation.
WEIGHT	Six 300-gram (5 ¼-oz) dough pieces.
PRESHAPE	Oval.
REST	About 1 hour.
SHAPE	Baguette; place the baguettes on a floured linen proofing cloth, seam side up.
FINAL PROOF	About 1 hour.
SCORE	Diamond pattern.
BAKE	In a deck oven at 250°C (480°F) for about 20 minutes.
COOL	On a wire rack.

CHRISTMAS BAGUETTE

MAKES 8 LOAVES

KNEADING INGREDIENTS

Bread flour (T65)	**750 G (1 LB 10 ½ OZ)**
Rye flour (T170)	**250 G (8 ¾ OZ)**
Water	**680 G (1 ½ LB)**
Salt	**22 G (¾ OZ)**
Yeast	**5 G (3/16 OZ)**
Liquid levain	**300 G (10 ½ OZ)**

FINAL KNEADING

Chestnut paste (pâte de marron)	**80 G (2 ⅞ OZ)**
Ground cinnamon	**2 G (1/16 OZ)**
Orange, zest only	**1**
Candied orange, chopped	**150 G (5 ¼ OZ)**
Candied ginger, chopped	**150 G (5 ¼ OZ)**

METHOD

BASE TEMPERATURE 62 to 66°C (145 to 150°F).

INCORPORATE In a spiral mixer, mix all the kneading ingredients in the bowl.

INITIAL MIX On speed 1 for about 3 minutes.

KNEAD On speed 1 for about 5 minutes, then on speed 2 for 2 minutes.

INCORPORATE On speed 1, add the chestnut paste, ground cinnamon, and orange zest. When the dough is smooth, add the candied orange and ginger.

CONSISTENCY Medium-firm dough.

DOUGH TEMPERATURE 23°C (75°F).

BULK FERMENT About 45 minutes, then at 3°C (35°F) for 15 hours.

FOLD TO DEGAS After 45 minutes of bulk fermentation.

WEIGHT Eight 300-gram (5 ¼-oz) dough pieces.

PRESHAPE Oval.

REST About 30 minutes.

SHAPE Baguette; place the baguettes on a linen proofing cloth, seam side up.

FINAL PROOF About 1 hour.

PREBAKE PREP Place the baguettes on a sheet of parchment paper and sprinkle with flour.

SCORE One slash and fancy-cut herringbone cuts.

BAKE In a deck oven at 250°C (480°F) for about 22 minutes. Adjust the oven temperature to 210°C (410°F) for the final 10 minutes.

BENOÎTONS

MAKES 50 LOAVES

KNEADING INGREDIENTS

Rye flour (T85)	**750 G (1 LB 10 ½ OZ)**
Bread flour (T65)	**250 G (8 ¾ OZ)**
Water	**700 G (1 LB 8 ¾ OZ)**
Salt	**22 G (¾ OZ)**
Yeast	**20 G (¾ OZ)**
Fermented dough	**300 G (10 ½ OZ)**
Liquid levain	**300 G (10 ½ OZ)**

FINAL KNEADING

Dried currants	**800 G (1 ¾ LB)**
Green anise seeds	**5 G (3/16 OZ)**

METHOD

BASE TEMPERATURE 70 to 74°C (160 to 165°F).
INCORPORATE In a stand mixer, mix all the kneading ingredients in the bowl.
INITIAL MIX On speed 1 for about 3 minutes.
KNEAD On speed 1 for about 3 minutes, then on speed 2 for 1 minute.
INCORPORATE On speed 1, add the dried currants and green anise seeds.
CONSISTENCY Soft dough.
DOUGH TEMPERATURE 23°C (75°F).
BULK FERMENT About 1 hour.
FOLD TO DEGAS After 1 hour of bulk fermentation.
SHAPE Stretch into a 30 × 75-centimeter (12 × 29 ½-inch) rectangle.
CUT TO SIZE Cut the dough in half lengthwise.
Cut into 15 × 3-centimeter (6 × 1 ¼-inch) sticks.
Place the sticks on baking sheets lined with parchment paper.
FINAL PROOF About 1 hour.
BAKE In a deck oven at 250°C (480°F) for about 15 minutes.
COOL On a wire rack.

BUCKWHEAT CROWN

MAKES 5 LOAVES

KNEADING INGREDIENTS

Bread flour (T65)	**400 G (14 OZ)**
Whole-grain buckwheat flour	**400 G (14 OZ)**
Whole-wheat flour (T150)	**200 G (7 OZ)**
Water	**650 G (1 LB 7 OZ)**
Salt	**21 G (3/4 OZ)**
Yeast	**12 G (3/8 OZ)**
Fermented dough	**250 G (8 3/4 OZ)**
Liquid levain	**250 G (8 3/4 OZ)**

METHOD

BASE TEMPERATURE	68 to 72°C (154 to 162°F).
INCORPORATE	In a stand mixer, mix all the kneading ingredients in the bowl.
INITIAL MIX	On speed 1 for about 3 minutes.
KNEAD	On speed 1 for about 3 minutes, then on speed 2 for 1 minute.
CONSISTENCY	Medium-firm dough.
DOUGH TEMPERATURE	23°C (75°F).
BULK FERMENT	About 1 hour.
WEIGHT	Five 430-gram (15 1/8-oz) dough pieces.
PRESHAPE	Shape into balls.
REST	About 15 minutes.
SHAPE	Rings; place them in floured rattan bannetons seam side up.
FINAL PROOF	About 1 hour.
SCORE	Five slashes.
BAKE	In a deck oven at 250°C (480°F) for about 35 minutes, gradually lowering the temperature.
COOL	On a wire rack.

FLUTED CROWN WITH QUINOA SPROUTS

MAKES 3 LOAVES

QUINOA SPROUT LEVAIN	
Rye flour (T70)	**50 G (1 ¾ OZ)**
Quinoa flour	**50 G (1 ¾ OZ)**
Stiff levain	**5 G (³⁄₁₆ OZ)**
Quinoa sprouts	**200 G (7 OZ)**
Water at 12°C (55°F)	**100 G (3 ½ OZ)**

KNEADING INGREDIENTS	
Bread flour (T65)	**900 G (1 LB 15 ¾ OZ)**
Water	**600 G (1 LB 6 ⅛ OZ)**
Salt	**20 G (¾ OZ)**
Yeast	**8 G (¼ OZ)**
Quinoa sprout levain	**405 G (14 ¼ OZ)**

FOR THE QUINOA SPROUT LEVAIN

In a stand mixer, beat all ingredients on speed 1 for 4 minutes. Let ferment at room temperature for 12 hours.

METHOD

BASE TEMPERATURE 55 to 60°C (130 to 140°F).

INCORPORATE In a spiral mixer, mix all the kneading ingredients in the bowl.

FIRST MIX On speed 1 for about 3 minutes.

KNEAD On speed 2 for about 5 minutes.

CONSISTENCY Medium-firm dough.

DOUGH TEMPERATURE 23°C (75°F).

BULK FERMENT About 1 hour 15 minutes.

WEIGHT Three 450-gram (15 ⅞-oz) dough pieces and three 200-gram (7-oz) dough pieces.

PRESHAPE Shape the 450-gram (15 ⅞-oz) dough pieces into balls. Shape the 200-gram (7-oz) dough pieces into ovals.

REST About 15 minutes.

SHAPE Shape the 450-gram (15 ⅞-oz) dough pieces into rings. Roll out the 200-gram (7-oz) dough pieces into 70 × 10-centimeter (27 ½ × 4-inch) ovals. Place the rolled-out dough on a surface and shape into pentagons by folding each side over itself. Overlap the two ends, making sure to tuck the last one underneath and seal. Place the rings over the pentagons, then seal all the ends.

FINAL PROOF About 25 minutes.

FINISH On the baking mat, sift flour over the dough.

BAKE In a deck oven at 240°C (465°F) for about 20 minutes.

COOL On a wire rack.

FLOWER CROWN

MAKES 1 LOAF (1.65 KG/3 LB 10 OZ OF DOUGH)

KNEADING INGREDIENTS

COUNTRY-STYLE BREAD DOUGH

Bread flour (T65)	**800 G (1 ¾ LB)**
Whole-wheat flour (T150)	**100 G (3 ½ OZ)**
Rye flour (T170)	**100 G (3 ½ OZ)**
Water	**650 G (1 LB 7 OZ)**
Salt	**20 G (¾ OZ)**
Yeast	**5 G (3/16 OZ)**
Fermented dough	**150 G (5 ¼ OZ)**
Stiff levain	**150 G (5 ¼ OZ)**

FINAL KNEADING

Bassinage water	**AS NEEDED**

METHOD

BASE TEMPERATURE	56 to 60°C (135 to 140°F).
INCORPORATE	In a spiral mixer, mix all the kneading ingredients in the bowl.
INITIAL MIX	On speed 1 for about 3 minutes.
KNEAD	On speed 1 for about 8 minutes, then on speed 2 for 2 minutes.
INCORPORATE	A trickle of bassinage water, if necessary.
CONSISTENCY	Medium-firm dough.
DOUGH TEMPERATURE	23°C (75°F).
BULK FERMENT	About 1 hour 30 minutes.
WEIGHT	One 1.3-kilogram (2 lb 14-oz) dough piece and one 350-gram (12 3/8-oz) dough piece.
PRESHAPE	Form into a ball.
REST	About 20 minutes.
SHAPE	Roll out the 350-gram (12 3/8-oz) dough piece into a 34-centimeter (13 ½-inch)-diameter disk. Using a plain 6-centimeter (2 ⅓-inch) round pastry cutter, cut around the edge of the dough disk to make a flower shape. Shape the 1.3-kilogram (2 lb 14-oz) dough piece into a 32-centimeter (12-inch)-diameter ring. Place the 350-gram (12 3/8-oz) flower in the bottom of a 37-centimeter (14 ¼-inch)-diameter ring-form banneton and dust lightly with rye flour, then turn the ring over. Cut out the center of the disk and fold the petals over the ring.
FINAL PROOF	At 5°C (40°F) for about 12 hours.
FINISH	On the baking mat, sift a dusting of flour over the crown.
BAKE	In a deck oven at 250°C (480°F) for about 50 minutes, gradually lowering the temperature.
COOL	On a wire rack.

ANCIENT WHEAT FLOWER RING

MAKES 3 LOAVES

KNEADING INGREDIENTS

Ancient Vanilnoir whole-wheat flour (T150)	**1 KG (2 LB 3 ¼ OZ)**
OR other whole-wheat ancient wheat flour	**1 KG (2 LB 3 ¼ OZ)**
Water	**650 G (1 LB 7 OZ)**
Yeast	**6 G (3/16 OZ)**
Salt	**20 G (¾ OZ)**
Liquid levain	**250 G (8 ¾ OZ)**
Bassinage water	**AS NEEDED**
Oil	**AS NEEDED**

METHOD

BASE TEMPERATURE	55 to 60°C (130 to 140°F).
INCORPORATE	In a spiral mixer, mix all the kneading ingredients in the bowl.
INITIAL MIX	On speed 1 for about 3 minutes.
KNEAD	On speed 1 for about 5 minutes, then on speed 2 for 3 minutes.
DOUGH TEMPERATURE	23°C (75°F).
BULK FERMENT	About 1 hour, degas, then 2 hours at 3°C (35°F).
FOLD TO DEGAS	After 1 hour of bulk fermentation.
WEIGHT	Three 700-gram (1 lb 8 ¾-oz) dough pieces and three 250-gram (8 ¾-oz) dough pieces.
PRESHAPE	Shape into balls.
REST	15 to 25 minutes.
SHAPE	Using a rolling pin, roll out each 250-gram (8 ¾-oz) dough piece to the size of a flower pastry cutter. Let rest for 5 minutes. Using the pastry cutter, cut out flowers, transfer to a linen proofing cloth, then lightly oil the petals. Form each 700-gram (1 lb 8 ¾-oz) dough piece into a ring, incorporating the flower scraps. Place the rings on top of the oiled dough, make cuts in the center of each dough and fold over to seal to the ring.
FINAL PROOF	About 30 minutes.
PREBAKE PREP	On the baking mat, sift a dusting of flour over the ring.
BAKE	In a deck oven at 240°C (465°F) for 35 to 45 minutes.
COOL	On a wire rack.

CHESTNUT BREAD

MAKES 4 LOAVES

KNEADING INGREDIENTS

Bread flour (T65)	**900 G (1 LB 15 ¾ OZ)**
Chestnut flour	**100 G (3 ½ OZ)**
Chestnut paste (pâte de marron)	**150 G (5 ¼ OZ)**
Water	**650 G (1 LB 7 OZ)**
Salt	**21 G (¾ OZ)**
Yeast	**10 G (⅜ OZ)**
Fermented dough	**200 G (7 OZ)**
Stiff levain	**200 G (7 OZ)**
Unsalted butter	**70 G (2 ½ OZ)**

METHOD

BASE TEMPERATURE 56 to 60°C (135 to 140°F).

INCORPORATE In a stand mixer, mix all the kneading ingredients in the bowl.

INITIAL MIX On speed 1 for about 3 minutes.

KNEAD On speed 2 for about 5 minutes.

CONSISTENCY Medium-firm dough.

DOUGH TEMPERATURE 23°C (75°F).

BULK FERMENT About 2 hours.

WEIGHT Four 350-gram (12 ⅜-oz) dough pieces and four 200-gram (7-oz) dough pieces.

PRESHAPE Shape into balls.

REST About 20 minutes.

SHAPE Reroll the 350-gram (12 ⅜-oz) dough pieces.
Roll out the 200-gram (7-oz) dough pieces into 17-centimeter (6 ¾-inch)-diameter disks.
Lightly oil the center of the disks, then place the balls on the disks, seam side up. Fold the edges of the disks toward the center to enclose the 350-gram (12 ⅜-oz) dough pieces.
Place the dough pieces in floured rattan bannetons, seam side up.

FINAL PROOF About 1 hour 30 minutes.

SCORE An "X" cut.

BAKE In a deck oven at 230°C (445°F) for about 35 minutes, gradually lowering the temperature.

COOL On a wire rack.

SQUASH BREAD

MAKES 5 LOAVES

KNEADING INGREDIENTS

Bread flour (T65)	**900 G (1 LB 15 3/4 OZ)**
Rye flour (T170)	**100 G (3 1/2 OZ)**
Water	**600 G (1 LB 6 1/8 OZ)**
Salt	**20 G (3/4 OZ)**
Yeast	**7 G (1/4 OZ)**
Cooked squash puree	**370 G (13 OZ)**
Fermented dough	**150 G (5 1/4 OZ)**
Stiff levain	**150 G (5 1/4 OZ)**
Turmeric	**5 G (3/16 OZ)**

FINAL KNEADING

Pumpkin seeds	**200 G (7 OZ)**
Dried cranberries	**200 G (7 OZ)**
Water	**66 G (2 3/8 OZ)**

COOKED SQUASH

Winter squash	**400 G (14 OZ)**
Olive oil	**15 G (1/2 OZ)**

FOR THE COOKED SQUASH PUREE

Wash the squash, cut it in half, and remove the seeds. Brush with the olive oil and place it on a baking sheet lined with a silicone mat. Bake in a convection oven at 150°C for about 30 minutes. Puree the squash in a food processor. Set aside at 3°C (35°F).

FOR THE CRANBERRIES

Soak the dried cranberries in the water for at least 2 hours.

METHOD

BASE TEMPERATURE 56 to 60°C (135 to 140°F).

INCORPORATE In a spiral mixer, mix all the kneading ingredients in the bowl.

INITIAL MIX On speed 1 for about 3 minutes.

KNEAD On speed 2 for about 4 minutes.

INCORPORATE The pumpkin seeds and soaked cranberries on speed 1 until the dough is smooth.

CONSISTENCY Soft dough.

DOUGH TEMPERATURE 23°C (75°F).

BULK FERMENT About 1 hour 30 minutes.

WEIGHT Five 500-gram (1 lb 1 5/8-oz) dough pieces.

PRESHAPE Shape into balls.

REST About 20 minutes.

SHAPE Using a rolling pin, press the dough pieces through the middle into six equal sections. Place the dough pieces in round floured rattan bannetons.

FINAL PROOF At 5°C (40°F) for about 12 hours.

BAKE In a deck oven at 250°C (480°F) for about 30 minutes.

COOL On a wire rack.

DRIED FIG AND PRUNE BREAD

MAKES 1 LOAF

KNEADING INGREDIENTS	
Bread flour (T65)	**700 G (1 LB 8 ¾ OZ)**
Wheat-wheat flour (T150)	**200 G (7 OZ)**
Whole-grain buckwheat flour	**100 G (3 ½ OZ)**
Water	**750 G (1 LB 10 ½ OZ)**
Salt	**25 G (⅞ OZ)**
Yeast	**5 G (3/16 OZ)**
Stiff levain	**200 G (7 OZ)**

FINAL KNEADING	
Bassinage water	**AS NEEDED**
Pitted dried figs	**200 G (7 OZ)**
Pitted prunes	**200 G (7 OZ)**

METHOD

BASE TEMPERATURE 56 to 60°C (135 to 140°F).

INCORPORATE In a stand mixer, mix all the kneading ingredients in the bowl.

INITIAL MIX On speed 1 for about 3 minutes.

KNEAD On speed 2 for about 4 minutes.

INCORPORATE A trickle of bassinage water, if necessary, followed by the figs and prunes.

CONSISTENCY Medium-firm dough.

DOUGH TEMPERATURE 23°C (75°F).

BULK FERMENT About 2 hours.

SHAPE Fold the dough into fourths and roll out to a 22 × 38-centimeters (8 ¾ × 15-inch) dough piece. Place it on a floured linen proofing cloth, seam side up.

FINAL PROOF At 5°C (40°F) for about 12 hours.

SCORE Diamond pattern.

BAKE In a deck oven at 250°C (480°F) for about 50 minutes, gradually lowering the temperature.

COOL On a wire rack.

FLAKY BREAD ROLLS

MAKES 31 LOAVES

KNEADING INGREDIENTS

Bread flour (T65)	**1 KG (2 LB 3 ¼ OZ)**
Water	**540 G (1 LB 3 OZ)**
Salt	**18 G (⅝ OZ)**
Yeast	**10 G (⅜ OZ)**

TURNING (TOURAGE)

Dry butter	**360 G (12 ⅝ OZ)**

TO FINISH

Salt flakes	**AS NEEDED**
Unsalted butter	**100 G (3 ½ OZ)**

FOR FINISHING

Heat the unsalted butter to obtain a brown butter.

METHOD

BASE TEMPERATURE 56 to 60°C (135 to 140°F).

INCORPORATE In a stand mixer, mix all the kneading ingredients in the bowl.

INITIAL MIX On speed 1 for about 3 minutes.

KNEAD On speed 1 for about 3 minutes.

CONSISTENCY Firm dough.

DOUGH TEMPERATURE 23°C (75°F).

WEIGHT One 1.56-kilogram (3 lb 7-oz) dough piece.

PRESHAPE Oval.

BULK FERMENT About 1 hour.

PRESHAPE Degas the dough piece, forming it into a rectangle.

REST At 3°C (35°F) for about 2 hours.

TURNING (TOURAGE) Encase the dry butter in the dough. Make two single turns.

REST At 3°C (35°F) for about 45 minutes.

CUT TO SIZE Using a dough sheeter, roll out the dough to a thickness of 3.5 millimeters (⅛ inch).
Cut into thirty-one 3.5 × 26-centimeter (1 ⅜ × 10 ¼-inch) rectangles.

SHAPE Roll the rectangles up along a long edge.
Place the flaky rolls in 6.5-centimeter (2 ⅝-inch)-diameter molds.

FINAL PROOF At 27°C (80°F) for about 2 hours.

FINISH Lightly sprinkle the rolls with the salt flakes.

BAKE In a deck oven, without steam, at 230°C (445°F) for about 20 minutes.

FINISH Brush the rolls with the brown butter.

COOL On a wire rack.

OAT BREAD

MAKES 5 LOAVES

KNEADING INGREDIENTS

Bread flour (T65)	**800 G (1 ¾ LB)**
Oat flour	**200 G (7 OZ)**
Water	**700 G (1 LB 8 ¾ OZ)**
Salt	**21 G (¾ OZ)**
Yeast	**6 G (3/16 OZ)**
Fermented dough	**200 G (7 OZ)**
Stiff levain	**200 G (7 OZ)**

FINAL KNEADING

Bassinage water	**150 G (5 ¼ OZ)**

TO FINISH

Old-fashioned oats	**AS NEEDED**

METHOD

BASE TEMPERATURE	56 to 60°C (135 to 140°F).
INCORPORATE	In a stand mixer, mix all the kneading ingredients in the bowl.
INITIAL MIX	On speed 1 for about 3 minutes.
KNEAD	On speed 2 for about 6 minutes.
INCORPORATE	A trickle of bassinage water.
CONSISTENCY	Medium-firm dough.
DOUGH TEMPERATURE	23°C (75°F).
BULK FERMENT	About 1 hour, then at 3°C (35°F) for 12 hours.
WEIGHT	Five 450-gram (15 ⅞-oz) dough pieces.
SHAPE	Bâtard (no preshaping).
FINISH	Moisten the surface of the bâtards, then roll them in the old-fashioned oats.
SCORE	One slash.
	Place the bâtards in greased 18 × 8 × 8-centimeter (7 × 3 ¼ × 3 ¼-inch) loaf pans.
FINAL PROOF	About 1 hour 30 minutes.
BAKE	In a deck oven at 250°C (480°F) for about 35 minutes, gradually lowering the temperature.
COOL	On a wire rack.

SPELT BREAD

MAKES 3 LOAVES

KNEADING INGREDIENTS

White spelt flour	**500 G (1 LB 1 ⅝ OZ)**
Whole-wheat spelt flour	**500 G (1 LB 1 ⅝ OZ)**
Water	**700 G (1 LB 8 ¾ OZ)**
Salt	**22 G (¾ OZ)**
Yeast	**2 G (1/16 OZ)**
Fermented dough	**200 G (7 OZ)**
Stiff levain	**300 G (10 ½ OZ)**

FINAL KNEADING

Bassinage water	**AS NEEDED**

METHOD

BASE TEMPERATURE	56 to 60°C (135 to 140°F).
INCORPORATE	In a stand mixer, mix all the kneading ingredients in the bowl.
INITIAL MIX	On speed 1 for about 3 minutes.
KNEAD	On speed 1 for about 6 minutes, then on speed 2 for 3 minutes.
INCORPORATE	A trickle of bassinage water, if necessary.
CONSISTENCY	Medium-firm dough.
DOUGH TEMPERATURE	24°C (75°F).
BULK FERMENT	About 2 hours.
WEIGHT	Three 700-gram (1 lb 9-oz) dough pieces.
PRESHAPE	Shape into balls.
REST	About 45 minutes.
SHAPE	Lightly flour the surface of the dough pieces with rye flour. Using your fingertips, press the dough to make creases on the surface. Place them in floured rattan bannetons, seam side up.
FINAL PROOF	At 5°C (40°F) for about 12 hours.
SCORE	No scoring needed, because the creases will open on their own.
BAKE	In a deck oven at 250°C (480°F) for about 40 minutes, gradually lowering the temperature.
COOL	On a wire rack.

EINKORN BREAD

MAKES 3 LOAVES

KNEADING INGREDIENTS

Whole-wheat einkorn flour	**1 KG (2 LB 3 ¼ OZ)**
Water at 50°C (120°F)	**800 G (1 ¾ LB)**
Salt	**30 G (1 OZ)**
Einkorn levain	**600 G (1 LB 6 ⅛ OZ)**

METHOD

BASE TEMPERATURE	85 to 95°C (185 to 205°F).
INCORPORATE	In a stand mixer, mix all the kneading ingredients in the bowl.
INITIAL MIX	On speed 1 for about 3 minutes.
KNEAD	On speed 1 for about 4 minutes.
CONSISTENCY	Soft dough, gelatinized.
DOUGH TEMPERATURE	30°C (85°F).
BULK FERMENT	About 1 hour 30 minutes.
WEIGHT	Three 800-gram (1 ¾-lb) dough pieces.
SHAPE	Gently shape into balls. Place the balls in floured bannetons, seam side up.
FINAL PROOF	About 45 minutes.
BAKE	In a deck oven at 250°C (480°F) for about 45 minutes, gradually lowering the temperature.
COOL	On a wire rack.

KAMUT WHEAT BREAD

MAKES 6 LOAVES

KNEADING INGREDIENTS

White Khorasan flour	**600 G (1 LB 6 ⅛ OZ)**
Whole-wheat Khorasan flour	**400 G (14 OZ)**
Water	**800 G (1 ¾ LB)**
Salt	**21 G (¾ OZ)**
Yeast	**5 G (3/16 OZ)**
Fermented dough	**200 G (7 OZ)**
Stiff levain	**200 G (7 OZ)**

FINAL KNEADING

Bassinage water	**AS NEEDED**

METHOD

BASE TEMPERATURE	60 to 64°C (140 to 145°F).
INCORPORATE	In a stand mixer, mix all the kneading ingredients in the bowl.
INITIAL MIX	On speed 1 for about 3 minutes.
KNEAD	On speed 1 for about 6 minutes, then on speed 2 for 1 minute.
INCORPORATE	A trickle of bassinage water, if necessary.
CONSISTENCY	Soft dough.
DOUGH TEMPERATURE	23°C (75°F).
BULK FERMENT	About 1 hour 30 minutes.
WEIGHT	Six 350-gram (12 ⅜-oz) dough pieces.
PRESHAPE	Shape into balls.
REST	About 20 minutes.
SHAPE	Form into triangles and place them in floured rattan bannetons, seam side up.
FINAL PROOF	At 5°C (40°F) for about 12 hours.
SCORE	Triangle pattern.
BAKE	In a deck oven at 250°C (480°F) for about 30 minutes, gradually lowering the temperature.
COOL	On a wire rack.

SOURDOUGH BREAD

TO BE SOLD UNDER THE NAME OF *PAIN AU LEVAIN* OR "SOURDOUGH BREAD," BREAD MUST BE MADE FROM A SOURDOUGH LEVAIN WITH A MAXIMUM POTENTIAL OF HYDROGEN (PH) OF 4.3 AND AN ENDOGENOUS ACETIC ACID CONTENT OF 900 PPM (PARTS PER MILLION), ACCORDING TO ARTICLE 3 OF THE FRENCH BREAD LAW OF SEPTEMBER 13, 1993.

MAKES 3 LOAVES

KNEADING INGREDIENTS

Stone-ground light whole-wheat flour (T80)	**1 KG (2 LB 3 ¼ OZ)**
Water	**800 G (1 ¾ LB)**
Salt	**25 G (⅞ OZ)**
Stiff levain	**400 G (7 OZ)**

FINAL KNEADING

Bassinage water	**AS NEEDED**

METHOD

BASE TEMPERATURE	60 to 64°C (140 to 145°F).
INCORPORATE	In a spiral mixer, mix the flour and water in the bowl.
INITIAL MIX	On speed 1 for about 3 minutes.
AUTOLYSIS	About 1 hour.
INCORPORATE	Add the salt and stiff levain.
KNEAD	On speed 1 for about 8 minutes.
INCORPORATE	A trickle of bassinage water, if necessary.
CONSISTENCY	Medium-firm dough.
DOUGH TEMPERATURE	24°C (75°F).
BULK FERMENT	About 2 hours.
WEIGHT	Three 700-gram (1 lb 8 ¾-oz) dough pieces.
SHAPE	Bâtard (no preshaping).
REST	About 15 minutes on the baking sheet to let the seams seal well. Place the dough pieces in floured rattan bannetons, seam side up.
FINAL PROOF	At 13°C (55°F) for about 12 hours.
SCORE	One slash.
BAKE	In a deck oven at 250°C (480°F) for about 50 minutes, gradually lowering the temperature.
COOL	On a wire rack.

CORN BREAD

MAKES 4 LOAVES

SCALDED CORN FLOUR

Corn flour	**250 G (7 OZ)**
Water at 100°C (210°F)	**250 G (7 OZ)**

KNEADING INGREDIENTS

Bread flour (T65)	**750 G (1 LB 10 1/2 OZ)**
Scalded corn flour	**500 G (1 LB 1 5/8 OZ)**
Corn puree	**150 G (5 1/4 OZ)**
Water	**450 G (15 7/8 OZ)**
Salt	**21 G (3/4 OZ)**
Yeast	**5 G (3/16 OZ)**
Fermented dough	**200 G (7 OZ)**
Stiff levain	**200 G (7 OZ)**

TO FINISH

Cornmeal	**AS NEEDED**

FOR THE SCALDED CORN FLOUR

The day before, mix the corn flour and boiling water in a food processor. Cool, then set aside at 3°C (35°F).

METHOD

BASE TEMPERATURE 56 to 60°C (135 to 140°F).

INCORPORATE In a stand mixer, mix all the kneading ingredients in the bowl.

INITIAL MIX On speed 1 for about 3 minutes.

KNEAD On speed 2 for about 6 minutes.

CONSISTENCY Medium-firm dough.

DOUGH TEMPERATURE 23°C (75°F).

BULK FERMENT About 1 hour, then at 3°C (35°F) for 12 hours.

WEIGHT Four 500-gram (1 lb 1 5/8-oz) dough pieces.

SHAPE Bâtard (no preshaping).

FINISH Moisten the surface of the bâtards, then roll them in the cornmeal.

SCORE Sausage cut.
Place the bâtards in greased 18 × 8 × 8 centimeters (7 × 3 1/4 × 3 1/4-inch) loaf pans.

FINAL PROOF About 1 hour 30 minutes.

BAKE In a deck oven at 250°C (480°F) for about 35 minutes, gradually lowering the temperature.

COOL On a wire rack.

FIR-TREE HONEY BREAD

MAKES 3 LOAVES

HONEY-RYE LEVAIN

Rye flour (T85)	**200 G (7 OZ)**
Water at 12°C (55°C)	**200 G (7 OZ)**
Honey	**75 G (2 5/8 OZ)**
Liquid levain	**10 G (3/8 OZ)**

KNEADING INGREDIENTS

Bread flour (T65)	**800 G (1 3/4 LB)**
Water	**450 G (15 7/8 OZ)**
Salt	**22 G (3/4 OZ)**
Yeast	**10 G (3/8 OZ)**
Honey-rye levain	**485 G (1 LB 1 1/8 OZ)**

FINAL KNEADING

Bassinage water	**AS NEEDED**

FOR THE RYE LEVAIN

The day before, in a stand mixer, mix the rye flour (T85), 12°C (55°F) water, honey, and liquid levain. Ferment at 24°C (75°F) for 12 hours.

METHOD

BASE TEMPERATURE 56 to 60°C (135 to 140°F).

INCORPORATE In a stand mixer, mix all the kneading ingredients in the bowl.

INITIAL MIX On speed 1 for about 3 minutes.

KNEAD On speed 2 for about 5 minutes.

INCORPORATE A trickle of bassinage water, if necessary.

CONSISTENCY Medium-firm dough.

DOUGH TEMPERATURE 23°C (75°F).

BULK FERMENT About 1 hour 15 minutes.

WEIGHT Three 480-gram (1 lb 1-oz) dough pieces and three 120-gram (4 1/4-oz) dough pieces.

SHAPE Shape the 480-gram dough (1 lb 1-oz) pieces into balls and the 120-gram (4 1/4-oz) dough pieces into teardrops.

REST About 20 minutes.

SHAPE From each 120-gram (4 1/4-oz) dough piece, make a row of seven dough balls of decreasing size. Using a rolling pin, roll out the balls widthwise. Arrange the balls on a lightly floured linen proofing cloth, with the largest one closest to the edge. Pinch both sides of the largest ball, lift slightly, and pull toward the edge. Repeat with all the other balls, moving them closer to the previous one to create a fir-tree shape. Shape the 480-gram (1 lb 1-oz) dough pieces into teardrops and place them on these fir trees, seam side up.

FINAL PROOF About 1 hour.

FINISH On the baking mat, sift flour over the dough.

BAKE In a deck oven at 240°C (465°F) for about 30 minutes, gradually lowering the temperature.

COOL On a wire rack.

WHOLE-WHEAT BREAD

THE TERM "WHOLE-WHEAT BREAD" CAN ONLY BE USED TO REFER TO BREAD MADE WITH "WHOLE WHEAT" OR "INTEGRAL WHEAT" FLOUR, OBTAINED EITHER BY GRINDING THE WHOLE WHEAT GRAIN, OR BY COMBINING ALL THE PRODUCTS OF THE MILLING PROCESS.

MAKES 5 LOAVES

KNEADING INGREDIENTS

Whole-wheat flour (T150)	**1 KG (2 LB 3 ¼ OZ)**
Water	**820 G (1 LB 12 ⅞ OZ)**
Salt	**23 G (⅞ OZ)**
Yeast	**2 G (1/16 OZ)**
Whole-wheat levain	**400 G (7 OZ)**

METHOD

BASE TEMPERATURE	58 to 62°C (135 to 145°F).
INCORPORATE	In a spiral mixer, mix all the kneading ingredients in the bowl.
INITIAL MIX	On speed 1 for about 3 minutes.
KNEAD	On speed 2 for about 5 minutes.
CONSISTENCY	Medium-firm dough.
DOUGH TEMPERATURE	23°C (75°F).
BULK FERMENT	About 1 hour 30 minutes.
WEIGHT	Five 440-gram (15 ½-oz) dough pieces.
PRESHAPE	Shape into balls.
REST	About 20 minutes.
SHAPE	Make short bâtards and place them on a linen proofing cloth, seam side down.
FINISH	Sift flour over the bâtards.
SCORE	Sausage cut.
FINAL PROOF	At 10°C (50°F) for about 12 hours.
BAKE	In a deck oven at 250°C (480°F) for about 40 minutes, gradually lowering the temperature.
COOL	On a wire rack.

SANDWICH BREAD

MAKES 5 LOAVES

SCALDED WHEAT FLOUR

Strong flour	**160 G (5 ⅝ OZ)**
Water at 100°C (212°F)	**320 G (11 ¼ OZ)**

KNEADING INGREDIENTS

Strong flour	**840 G (1 LB 13 ⅝ OZ)**
Scalded wheat flour	**480 G (1 LB 1 OZ)**
Milk	**290 G (10 ¼ OZ)**
Salt	**20 G (¾ OZ)**
Superfine sugar	**110 G (3 ⅞ OZ)**
Yeast	**35 G (1 ¼ OZ)**
Unsalted butter	**50 G (1 ¾ OZ)**

FOR THE SCALDED WHEAT FLOUR

The day before, in a stand mixer, mix the wheat flour and boiling water. Cool, then set aside at 3°C (35°F).

METHOD

BASE TEMPERATURE 50 to 54°C (120 to 130°F).

INCORPORATE In a stand mixer, mix all the kneading ingredients in the bowl.

INITIAL MIX On speed 1 for about 3 minutes.

KNEAD On speed 2 for about 8 minutes.

CONSISTENCY Firm dough.

DOUGH TEMPERATURE 23°C (75°F).

BULK FERMENT About 15 minutes.

WEIGHT Five 175-gram (6 ¼-oz) dough pieces.

PRESHAPE Shape into balls.

REST About 45 minutes.

SHAPE Degas the dough pieces, then make a single turn. Roll out in the other direction to form long rectangles. Roll up the dough pieces lengthwise, then place them two by two in greased 18 × 8 × 8-centimeter (7 × 3 ¼ × 3 ¼-inch) sandwich loaf pans.

FINAL PROOF About 1 hour 45 minutes.

BAKE In a deck oven at 185°C (365°F) for about 25 minutes.

COOL On a wire rack.

GASCON SOURDOUGH CORN BREAD REVISITED

MAKES 4 LOAVES

SCALDED CORN FLOUR

Corn flour	400 G (14 OZ)
Water at 65°C (150°F)	650 G (1 LB 7 OZ)

KNEADING INGREDIENTS

Bread flour (T65)	600 G (1 LB 6 ⅛ OZ)
Scalded corn flour	1.05 KG (2 LB 5 OZ)
Water	100 G (3 ½ OZ)
Salt	21 G (¾ OZ)
Yeast	30 G (1 OZ)
Stiff levain	200 G (7 OZ)

FINAL KNEADING

Toasted millet seeds	200 G (7 OZ)

TOASTED MILLET SEEDS

Millet seeds	120 G (4 ¼ OZ)
Water	80 G (2 ⅞ OZ)

TO FINISH

Chestnut leaves or cabbage leaves	AS NEEDED

FOR THE SCALDED CORN FLOUR

The day before, in a stand mixer, combine the corn flour and 65°C (150°F) water. Cool, then set aside at 3°C (35°F).

FOR THE SEEDS

In a convection oven at 200°C (390°F), lightly toast the millet seeds for about 15 minutes. Submerge the seeds in water. Set aside at 3°C (35°F).

METHOD

BASE TEMPERATURE 64 to 68°C (145 to 155°F).

INCORPORATE In a stand mixer, mix all the kneading ingredients in the bowl.

INITIAL MIX On speed 1 for about 3 minutes.

KNEAD On speed 2 for about 6 minutes.

INCORPORATE Measure out 1.2 kilograms (2 lb 10 ⅜ oz) of dough and mix in the toasted millet seeds.

CONSISTENCY Medium-firm dough.

DOUGH TEMPERATURE 23°C (75°F).

BULK FERMENT About 30 minutes.

WEIGHT Four 350-gram (12 ⅜-oz) dough pieces containing millet seeds and four 200-gram (7-oz) dough pieces of plain dough.

PRESHAPE Shape into balls.

REST About 20 minutes.

SHAPE Reshape the 350-gram (12 ⅜-oz) dough pieces. Roll out the 200-gram (7-oz) dough pieces into 17-centimeters (6 ¾-inch)-diameter disks. Lightly oil the center of the disks, then place the balls on the disks, seam side up. Fold the edges of the disks toward the center to enclose the dough pieces. Place straight into four 16-centimeter (6 ¼-inch)-diameter casseroles lined with chestnut or cabbage leaves.

FINAL PROOF About 45 minutes.

SCORE Star shape.

BAKE In a deck oven at 250°C (480°F) for about 35 minutes, gradually lowering the temperature.

COOL On a wire rack.

RYE BREAD

THE TERM "RYE BREAD" CAN ONLY BE USED TO REFER TO BREAD MADE WITH A MIXTURE OF WHEAT FLOUR AND RYE FLOUR IN WHICH "THE PROPORTION OF WHEAT FLOUR MUST BE LESS THAN OR EQUAL TO 35 PERCENT OF THE MIXTURE OF THE TWO FLOURS (MINIMUM 65 PERCENT RYE FLOUR)."

MAKES 4 LOAVES

SPONGE LEVAIN

Rye flour (T85)	**325 G (11 1/8 OZ)**
Water at 24°C (75°F)	**210 G (7 3/8 OZ)**
Yeast	**1 G (1/32 OZ)**

KNEADING INGREDIENTS

Rye flour (T85)	**325 G (11 1/8 OZ)**
Bread flour (T65)	**350 G (12 3/8 OZ)**
Water	**530 G (1 LB 2 5/8 OZ)**
Salt	**18 G (5/8 OZ)**
Yeast	**12 G (3/8 OZ)**
Sponge levain	**536 G (1 LB 2 7/8 OZ)**

FOR THE SPONGE LEVAIN

The day before, in a stand mixer, combine the rye flour, 24°C (75°F) water, and yeast.
Ferment at room temperature for 1 hour 30 minutes, then at 10°C (50°F) for 12 hours.

METHOD

BASE TEMPERATURE 68 to 72°C (155 to 160°F).
INCORPORATE In a stand mixer, mix all the kneading ingredients in the bowl.
INITIAL MIX On speed 1 for about 3 minutes.
KNEAD On speed 1 for about 3 minutes, then on speed 2 for 1 minute.
CONSISTENCY Medium-firm dough.
DOUGH TEMPERATURE 23°C (75°F).
BULK FERMENT About 30 minutes.
WEIGHT Four 440-gram (15 1/2-oz) dough pieces.
PRESHAPE Shape into balls.
REST About 15 minutes, seam side up.
SHAPE Using a rolling pin, gently roll out the four sides of the balls, then fold them over each other to form pavés. Place them on a linen proofing cloth, seam side up.
FINAL PROOF About 45 minutes.
FINISH On the baking mat, sift flour over the dough.
SCORE Diamond pattern.
BAKE In a deck oven at 250°C (480°F) for about 45 minutes, gradually lowering the temperature.
COOL On a wire rack.

RYE BREAD
WITH DRIED FRUIT

MAKES 6 LOAVES

KNEADING INGREDIENTS

Rye flour (T170)	**500 G (1 LB 1 5/8 OZ)**
Rye flour (T85)	**500 G (1 LB 1 5/8 OZ)**
Water at 65°C (150°F)	**950 G (2 LB 1 1/2 OZ)**
Salt	**25 G (7/8 OZ)**
Fermented dough	**420 G (14 3/4 OZ)**
Stiff levain	**420 G (14 3/4 OZ)**

FINAL KNEADING

Raisins	**150 G (5 1/4 OZ)**
Water	**50 G (1 3/4 OZ)**
Dried apricots	**150 G (5 1/4 OZ)**
Dried figs	**150 G (5 1/4 OZ)**
Prunes	**150 G (5 1/4 OZ)**

FOR THE DRIED FRUIT

Soak the raisins in the water.
Coarsely chop the apricots, figs, and prunes.

METHOD

BASE TEMPERATURE 95 to 105°C (205 to 220°F).

INCORPORATE In a stand mixer, mix all the kneading ingredients in the bowl.

INITIAL MIX On speed 1 for about 3 minutes.

KNEAD On speed 1 for about 3 minutes, then on speed 2 for 1 minute.

INCORPORATE On speed 1, add the dried fruit.

CONSISTENCY Sticky dough, gelatinized.

DOUGH TEMPERATURE 35°C (95°F).

BULK FERMENT About 2 hours.

WEIGHT Using a bowl scraper, place six 550-gram (1 lb 3 3/8-oz) dough pieces in greased 18 × 8 × 8-centimeter (7 × 3 1/4 × 3 1/4-inch) bread pans.

FINISH Smooth the surface of the dough pieces with a dampened hand.

FINAL PROOF About 1 hour 15 minutes.

BAKE In a deck oven at 250°C (480°F) for about 1 hour, gradually lowering the temperature.

COOL On a wire rack.

HEALTHY
PUMPKIN SEED AND CRANBERRY BREAD

THE INGREDIENTS USED IN THIS BREAD—PUMPKIN SEED OIL AND CRANBERRIES—MAKE IT A PARTICULARLY HEALTHY LOAF. MADE WITH RYE FLOUR AND WHEAT FLOUR, IT IS RICH IN FIBER, MINERALS, AND VITAMINS. ADDING PUMPKIN SEEDS AND FLAXSEEDS PROVIDES ESSENTIAL FATTY ACIDS. CRANBERRIES ARE AN EXCELLENT SOURCE OF POWERFUL ANTIOXIDANTS.

MAKES 6 LOAVES

KNEADING INGREDIENTS

Bread flour (T65)	**900 G (1 LB 15 ¾ OZ)**
Rye flour (T170)	**100 G (3 ½ OZ)**
Water	**650 G (1 LB 7 OZ)**
Salt	**21 G (¾ OZ)**
Yeast	**8 G (¼ OZ)**
Liquid levain	**200 G (7 OZ)**

FINAL KNEADING

Bassinage water	**70 G (2 ½ OZ)**
Pumpkin seed oil (bassinage)	**70 G (2 ½ OZ)**
Dried cranberries	**125 G (4 ⅜ OZ)**
Brown flaxseeds	**60 G (2 ⅛ OZ)**
Pumpkin seeds	**60 G (2 ⅛ OZ)**
Water	**120 G (4 ¼ OZ)**

TO FINISH

Pumpkin seeds	**AS NEEDED**

FOR THE SEEDS

In a convection oven at 150°C (300°F), lightly toast the flaxseeds and pumpkin seeds for 15 minutes. Submerge the seeds in the water and set aside at 3°C (35°F).

METHOD

BASE TEMPERATURE 54 to 58°C (130 to 135°F).

INCORPORATE In a stand mixer, mix all the kneading ingredients in the bowl.

INITIAL MIX On speed 1 for about 3 minutes.

KNEAD On speed 2 for about 6 minutes.

INCORPORATE On speed 1, add the water, then the pumpkin seed oil in a thin stream. Add the cranberries and seed mixture.

CONSISTENCY Soft dough.

DOUGH TEMPERATURE 23°C (75°F).

BULK FERMENT About 1 hour 30 minutes, then at 3°C (35°F) for 12 hours.

FOLD TO DEGAS After 1 hour 30 minutes.

CUT TO SIZE Place the dough on a floured baking mat. Gently roll out the dough by hand, keeping the shape rectangular. Using a knife, cut six long rectangles of the same size. Place them on baking sheets lined with parchment paper.

FINAL PROOF About 1 hour 15 minutes.

FINISH Sprinkles pumpkin seeds on top of the dough pieces.

BAKE In a deck oven at 250°C (480°F) for about 14 minutes.

COOL On a wire rack.

HEALTHY
FLAXSEED AND SUNFLOWER SEED BREAD

MADE WITH A VARIETY OF WHOLE-WHEAT FLOURS, THIS FLAXSEED AND SUNFLOWER SEED BREAD IS HIGH IN FIBER, MINERALS, AND VITAMINS. THE LARGE QUANTITY OF FLAXSEEDS AND SUNFLOWER SEEDS PROVIDES A SIGNIFICANT SUPPLY OF ESSENTIAL FATTY ACIDS—LIPIDS THAT ARE INDISPENSABLE FOR US—AND THAT OUR BODIES CANNOT SYNTHESIZE ON THEIR OWN, AND WHICH HELP TO PREVENT HEART DISEASE.

MAKES 3 LOAVES

KNEADING INGREDIENTS

Bread flour (T65)	**400 G (14 OZ)**
White spelt flour	**200 G (7 OZ)**
Whole-wheat Khorasan flour	**200 G (7 OZ)**
Rye flour (T170)	**100 G (3 ¼ OZ)**
Whole-wheat flour (T150)	**100 G (3 ½ OZ)**
Water	**800 G (1 ¾ LB)**
Salt	**30 G (1 OZ)**
Yeast	**5 G (3/16 OZ)**
Stiff levain	**600 G (1 LB 6 ⅛ OZ)**

FINAL KNEADING

Brown flaxseeds	**200 G (7 OZ)**
Sunflower seeds	**200 G (7 OZ)**
Bassinage water	**200 G (7 OZ)**

TO FINISH

Old-fashioned oats	**AS NEEDED**

METHOD

BASE TEMPERATURE	50 to 52°C (120 to 125°F).
INCORPORATE	In a spiral mixer, mix all the kneading ingredients in the bowl.
INITIAL MIX	On speed 1 for about 3 minutes.
KNEAD	On speed 2 for about 8 minutes.
INCORPORATE	Add the seeds and water in a trickle.
CONSISTENCY	Medium-firm dough.
DOUGH TEMPERATURE	23°C (75°F).
BULK FERMENT	About 2 hours.
FOLD TO DEGAS	After 1 hour.
SHAPE	Roll out the dough on a baking sheet to a thickness of about 4 centimeters (1 ½ inches). Moisten the surface of the dough and cover with old-fashioned oats.
FINAL PROOF	At room temperature for about 2 hours, then at 3°C (35°F) for 12 hours.
CUT	Using a serrated knife, cut into dough pieces weighing about 1 kilogram (2 lb 3 ¼ oz).
BAKE	In a deck oven at 250°C (480°F) for about 45 minutes, gradually lowering the temperature.
COOL	On a wire rack.

WHOLE-GRAIN BREAD

MAKES 4 LOAVES

KNEADING INGREDIENTS

Bread flour (T65)	800 G (1 ¾ LB)
Spelt flour (T150)	100 G (3 ½ OZ)
Rye flour (T170)	100 G (3 ½ OZ)
Water	650 G (1 LB 7 OZ)
Salt	20 G (¾ OZ)
Yeast	5 G (3/16 OZ)
Fermented dough	150 G (5 ¼ OZ)
Liquid levain	150 G (5 ¼ OZ)

FINAL KNEADING

Seed mix	150 G (5 ¼ OZ)
Sunflower seeds	35 G (1 ¼ OZ)
Bassinage water	AS NEEDED

SEED MIX

Sesame seeds	17 G (⅝ OZ)
Brown flaxseeds	17 G (⅝ OZ)
Golden flaxseeds	17 G (⅝ OZ)
Millet seeds	17 G (⅝ OZ)
Poppy seeds	8 G (¼ OZ)
Water	75 G (2 ⅝ OZ)

TO FINISH

Sesame seeds	AS NEEDED

FOR THE SEEDS

In a convection oven at 200°C (390°F), lightly toast the seeds for 15 minutes. Submerge the seeds in the water. Set aside at 3°C (35°F).

METHOD

BASE TEMPERATURE 56 to 60°C (135 to 140°F).
INCORPORATE In a stand mixer, mix all the kneading ingredients in the bowl.
INITIAL MIX On speed 1 for about 3 minutes.
KNEAD On speed 2 for about 5 minutes.
INCORPORATE Add the toasted seed mixture and sunflower seeds, then trickle in the bassinage water, if necessary.
CONSISTENCY Medium-firm dough.
DOUGH TEMPERATURE 23°C (75°F).
BULK FERMENT About 1 hour 30 minutes.
WEIGHT Four 500-gram (1 lb 1 ⅝-oz) dough pieces.
PRESHAPE Shape into balls.
REST About 20 minutes.
SHAPE Bâtard.
FINISH Moisten the surface of the bâtards, then roll them in the sesame seeds. Place the dough pieces in bannetons, seam side up.
FINAL PROOF At 5°C (40°F) for about 12 hours.
SCORE One slash.
BAKE In a deck oven at 250°C (480°F) for about 35 minutes, gradually lowering the temperature.
COOL On a wire rack.

GLUTEN-FREE
WHOLE-GRAIN BREAD

THIS BREAD HAS BEEN CREATED FOR PEOPLE WITH CELIAC DISEASE, ALSO KNOWN AS GLUTEN INTOLERANCE. ALL PRODUCTS BEARING THE WORDS "GLUTEN-FREE" MUST BE TESTED. THE RESIDUAL GLUTEN CONTENT MUST NOT EXCEED 20 MILLIGRAMS PER KILOGRAM IN THE END PRODUCT. AS A RESULT, AND DUE TO THE HIGH RISK OF WHEAT FLOUR CONTAMINATION, TRADITIONAL BAKERIES ARE NOT THE MOST APPROPRIATE PLACES FOR MANUFACTURING THESE SPECIFIC PRODUCTS.

MAKES 4 LOAVES

KNEADING INGREDIENTS

Cornstarch	**600 G (1 LB 6 1/8 OZ)**
Cream of rice	**300 G (10 1/2 OZ)**
Chestnut flour	**100 G (3 1/2 OZ)**
Xanthan gum	**15 G (1/2 OZ)**
Water at 35°C (95°F)	**930 G (2 LB 3/4 OZ)**
Salt	**18 G (5/8 OZ)**
Yeast	**20 G (3/4 OZ)**
Gluten-free fermented dough	**250 G (8 3/4 OZ)**
Seed mix	**200 G (8 3/4 OZ)**

SEED MIX

Sesame seeds	**22 G (3/4 OZ)**
Brown flaxseeds	**22 G (3/4 OZ)**
Golden flaxseeds	**22 G (3/4 OZ)**
Millet seeds	**22 G (3/4 OZ)**
Poppy seeds	**12 G (3/8 OZ)**
Water	**100 G (3 1/2 OZ)**

FOR THE SEED MIX

In a convection oven at 200°C (390°F), lightly toast the seeds for 15 minutes. Submerge the seeds in the water. Set aside at 3°C (35°F).

FOR THE PREP

Sift together cornstarch, cream of rice, chestnut flour, and xanthan gum.

METHOD

BASE TEMPERATURE 76°C to 80°C (170 to 175°F).

INCORPORATE In a stand mixer fitted with the paddle attachment, mix all the kneading ingredients in the bowl.

INITIAL MIX On the lowest speed for about 3 minutes.

KNEAD On speed 2 or about 1 minute on speed 2.

CONSISTENCY Soft dough, gelatinized.

DOUGH TEMPERATURE 30°C (85°F).

BULK FERMENT About 1 hour.

DEGAS Mix the dough with a whisk to deflate it.

WEIGHT Using a bowl scraper, place 550 grams (1 lb 3 3/8 oz) of dough into four greased 18 × 8 × 8-centimeter (7 × 3 1/4 × 3 1/4-inch) loaf pans.

FINISH Smooth the surface of the dough with a dampened hand.

FINAL PROOF About 45 minutes.

BAKE In a deck oven at 250°C (480°F) for about 45 minutes, gradually lowering the temperature.

COOL On a wire rack.

DUTCH CRUNCH TIGER BREAD

MAKES 6 LOAVES

KNEADING INGREDIENTS

Bread flour (T65)	**(900 G 1 LB 15 ¾ OZ)**
Rye flour (T170)	**100 G (3 ½ OZ)**
Walnut soaking water	**630 G (1 LB 6 ¼ OZ)**
Salt	**20 G (¾ OZ)**
Yeast	**5 G (3/16 OZ)**
Fermented dough	**150 G (5 ¼ OZ)**
Liquid levain	**150 G (5 ¼ OZ)**

FINAL KNEADING

Walnut soaking water (*bassinage*)	**50 G (1 ¾ OZ)**
Soaked toasted walnuts	**500 G (1 LB 1 ⅝ OZ)**

SOAKED TOASTED WALNUTS

Walnuts	**400 G (14 OZ)**
Water	**850 G (1 LB 14 OZ)**

TIGER BREAD COATING

Rye flour (T170)	**100 G (3 ½ OZ)**
Water	**170 G (6 OZ)**
Superfine sugar	**10 G (⅜ OZ)**
Yeast	**5 G (3/16 OZ)**
Salt	**1 G (1/32 OZ)**

FOR THE WALNUTS

In a convection oven at 150°C (300°F), toast the walnuts for 15 minutes. Stir the toasted walnuts into the 850 grams (1 lb 14 oz) of cold water. Let soak for at least 4 hours. Drain the walnuts and reserve the soaking water to add to the kneading.

FOR THE TIGER BREAD COATING (MAKE THIS AFTER THE DOUGH HAS BEEN WEIGHED)

Whisk all the ingredients together. Cover with plastic wrap and set aside at room temperature.

METHOD

BASE TEMPERATURE 54 to 58°C (130 to 135°F).
INCORPORATE In a stand mixer, mix all the kneading ingredients in the bowl.
INITIAL MIX On speed 1 for about 3 minutes.
KNEAD On speed 2 for about 5 minutes.
INCORPORATE Add a trickle of bassinage water. Add the drained walnuts.
CONSISTENCY Soft dough.
DOUGH TEMPERATURE 23°C (75°F).
BULK FERMENT About 1 hour 30 minutes, then at 3°C (35°F) for 12 hours.
FOLD TO DEGAS After 1 hour 30 minutes.
WEIGHT Six 400-gram (14-oz) dough pieces.
PRESHAPE Shape into balls.
REST About 30 minutes.
SHAPE Teardrops.
FINAL PROOF About 1 hour 30 minutes.
FINISH On a baking mat, brush with the tiger bread coating, then sift flour over the dough.
BAKE In a deck oven at 250°C (480°F) for about 35 minutes, gradually lowering the temperature.
COOL On a wire rack.

RUSTIC PAVÉ

MAKES 4 LOAVES

KNEADING INGREDIENTS

Bread flour (T65)	**900 G (1 LB 15 ¾ OZ)**
Rye flour (T170)	**100 G (3 ½ OZ)**
Water	**700 G (1 LB 8 ¾ OZ)**
Salt	**30 G (1 OZ)**
Yeast	**5 G (3/16 OZ)**
Stiff levain	**600 G (1 LB 6 ⅛ OZ)**

FINAL KNEADING INGREDIENT

Bassinage water	**200 G (7 OZ)**

METHOD

BASE TEMPERATURE	50 to 54°C (120 to 130°F).
INCORPORATE	In a spiral mixer, mix all the kneading ingredients in the bowl.
INITIAL MIX	On speed 1 for about 3 minutes.
KNEAD	On speed 2 for about 8 minutes.
INCORPORATE	A trickle of bassinage water.
CONSISTENCY	Soft dough.
DOUGH TEMPERATURE	22°C (70°F).
BULK FERMENT	About 1 hour, then at 3°C (35°F) for 12 hours.
FOLD TO DEGAS	After 1 hour.
CUT TO SIZE	Four dough pieces of about 630 grams (1 lb 6 ¼ oz) each. Place the dough pieces on a floured linen proofing cloth, seam side up.
FINAL PROOF	About 45 minutes.
SCORE	Diamond pattern.
BAKE	In a deck oven at 250°C (480°F) for about 40 minutes.
COOL	On a wire rack.

CHOCOLATE AND CRANBERRY PAVÉ

MAKES 6 LOAVES

KNEADING INGREDIENTS

Bread flour (T65)	**1 KG (2 LB 3 ¼ OZ)**
Water	**650 G (1 LB 7 OZ)**
Salt	**20 G (¾ OZ)**
Yeast	**10 G (⅜ OZ)**
Liquid levain	**150 G (5 ¼ OZ)**

FINAL KNEADING INGREDIENT

Bassinage water	**50 G (1 ¾ OZ)**

FILLING

Water	**70 G (2 ½ OZ)**
Unsweetened cocoa powder	**50 G (1 ¾ OZ)**
Sugar	**60 G (2 ⅛ OZ)**
Dried cranberries	**200 G (7 OZ)**
Dark couverture chocolate (55 percent cacao), chopped	**200 G (7 OZ)**

FOR THE FILLING

Stir the water, cocoa powder, and sugar together. Soak the dried cranberries in hot water for 10 minutes, then drain.

METHOD

BASE TEMPERATURE 62 to 66°C (145 to 150°F).

INCORPORATE In a spiral mixer, mix the flour and water in the bowl.

INITIAL MIX On speed 1 for about 3 minutes.

AUTOLYSIS About 1 hour.

INCORPORATE Add the salt, yeast, and liquid levain.

KNEAD On speed 1 for about 5 minutes, then on speed 2 for 2 minutes.

INCORPORATE On speed 2, add the bassinage water in a trickle, then add the cocoa mixture.

INCORPORATE Measure a 1.4-kilogram (3 lb 1 ⅜-oz) dough piece, then add the chopped dark chocolate and rehydrated cranberries to it.

CONSISTENCY Medium-firm dough.

DOUGH TEMPERATURE 23°C (75°F).

BULK FERMENT About 30 minutes, then 15 hours at 3°C (35°F).

FOLD TO DEGAS After 30 minutes of bulk fermentation.

WEIGHT Six 300-gram (10 ½-oz) dough pieces with the filling and six 110-gram (3 ⅞-oz) plain dough pieces.

PRESHAPE Shape into balls.

REST About 45 minutes.

SHAPE Using a rolling pin, roll out the four sides of the 300-gram (10 ½-oz) dough pieces, then fold over to form a cube. Roll out the 110-gram (3 ⅞-oz) dough pieces into 16-centimeter (6 ¼-inch)-diameter disks and moisten lightly. Place the pavés, seam side up, on the disks, then fold over the edges and encase the pavés inside. Place them on a linen proofing cloth, seam side down.

FINAL PROOF About 1 hour.

PREBAKE PREP Place the pavés on a sheet of parchment paper, then sift flour over them.

SCORE An "X" cut.

BAKE In a deck oven at 250°C (480°F) for about 20 minutes. After 12 minutes of baking, transfer to a wire rack.

COOL On a wire rack.

LEMON ROLLS

MAKES 50 ROLLS

KNEADING INGREDIENTS

Strong flour	1 KG (2 LB 3 ¼ OZ)
Milk	250 G (8 ¾ OZ)
Water	250 G (8 ¾ OZ)
Salt	20 G (¾ OZ)
Superfine sugar	60 G (2 ⅛ OZ)
Yeast	30 G (1 OZ)
Viennese fermented dough *(see page 28)*	250 G (8 ¾ OZ)
Unsalted butter	150 G (5 ¼ OZ)
Ground turmeric	6 G (3/16 OZ)
Candied citron, rinsed and processed	220 G (7 ¾ OZ)
Lemon zest	25 G (⅞ OZ)

LEMON DUTCH CRUNCH TIGER COATING

Rice flour	375 G (13 ¼ OZ)
Salt	7 G (¼ OZ)
Superfine sugar	35 G (1 ¼ OZ)
Yeast	35 G (1 ¼ OZ)
Ground turmeric	10 G (⅜ OZ)
Water	250 G (8 ¾ OZ)
Olive oil	75 G (2 ⅝ OZ)
Lemon juice	130 G (4 ½ OZ)

FOR THE LEMON TORTOISESHELL MIXTURE

Stir all the ingredients together. Set aside in a pastry bag.

METHOD

BASE TEMPERATURE 50 to 54°C (120 to 130°F).

INCORPORATE In a stand mixer, mix all the kneading ingredients in the bowl.

INITIAL MIX On speed 1 for about 3 minutes.

KNEAD On speed 2 for about 8 minutes.

CONSISTENCY Medium-firm dough.

DOUGH TEMPERATURE 23°C (75°F).

BULK FERMENT About 1 hour.

WEIGHT Fifty 45-gram (1 ½-oz) dough pieces.

SHAPE Shape into compact balls, then place them on baking sheets lined with parchment paper.

FINAL PROOF About 2 hours 15 minutes, then at 3°C (35°F) for 30 minutes.

FINISH Gently coat each roll with 18 grams (⅝ oz) of lemon Dutch crunch tiger mixture.

BAKE In a convection oven at 175°C (345°F) for about 17 minutes, on two stacked baking sheets to prevent the bottom of the rolls from browning too much.

COOL On a wire rack.

FANCY BREAD

MAKES 3 LOAVES

KNEADING INGREDIENTS

Bread flour (T65)	**900 G (1 LB 15 ¾ OZ)**
Whole-wheat flour (T150)	**100 G (3 ½ OZ)**
Water	**650 G (1 LB 7 OZ)**
Salt	**22 G (¾ OZ)**
Yeast	**6 G (3/16 OZ)**
Liquid levain	**250 G (8 ¾ OZ)**

METHOD

BASE TEMPERATURE	56 to 60°C (135 to 140°F).
INCORPORATE	In a spiral mixer, mix all the kneading ingredients in the bowl.
INITIAL MIX	On speed 1 for about 3 minutes.
AUTOLYSIS	1 hour.
INCORPORATE	Add the salt, yeast, and liquid levain.
KNEAD	On speed 1 for about 8 minutes, then on speed 2 for 2 minutes.
CONSISTENCY	Medium-firm dough.
DOUGH TEMPERATURE	23°C (75°F).
BULK FERMENT	About 1 hour 30 minutes.
WEIGHT	Three 450-gram (15 ⅞-oz) and three 100-gram (3 ½-oz) dough pieces, or three 450-gram (15 ⅞-oz) and six 50-gram (1 ¾-oz) dough pieces.
SHAPE	Shape the 450-gram (15 ⅞-oz) dough pieces into balls and shape rectangles with the 50-gram (1 ¾-oz) or 100-gram (3 ½-oz) dough pieces.
REST	About 20 minutes.
SHAPE	Bâtard for the 450-gram (15 ⅞-oz) dough pieces. Roll out the 50-gram (1 ¾-oz) dough pieces into 20-centimeter (8-inch) logs, flatten them gently with a rolling pin, and place them two by two on a linen couche cloth, twisting them together. Place the bâtards, seam side up, on the twists and fold the ends of the twists over the bâtards. Roll out the 100-gram (3 ½-oz) dough pieces into 7 × 24-centimeter (2 ¾ × 9 ½-inch) rectangles and use a fluted-edge pastry cutter to cut the two longest sides, then place them diagonally on the linen proofing cloth. Place the bâtards, seam side up, across the rectangles and fold the still visible ends of the rectangles over the bâtards.
FINAL PROOF	About 1 hour.
FINISH	On the baking mat, lightly sift flour over the dough pieces.
BAKE	In a deck oven at 250°C (480°F) for about 35 minutes.
COOL	On a wire rack.

REG ION AL

· B R
E A D
S · ·

SÜBROT

ORIGINALLY FROM ALSACE, THE WORD MEANS "PENNY BREAD," WHICH REFERS TO ITS PRICE DURING THE PERIOD BETWEEN WORLD WAR I AND WORLD WAR II, WHEN A LOAF COST A *SOU*, OR PENNY. THIS IS A FANCY BREAD. FIRST MADE DURING THE SECOND EMPIRE, IT BECAME POPULAR IN THE REGION AFTER ALSACE WAS ONCE AGAIN PART OF FRANCE.

MAKES 6 LOAVES

KNEADING INGREDIENTS

Bread flour (T65)	**1 KG (2 LB 3 1/4 OZ)**
Water	**600 G (1 LB 6 1/8 OZ)**
Salt	**21 G (3/4 OZ)**
Yeast	**7 G (1/4 OZ)**
Liquid levain	**250 G (8 3/4 OZ)**

TO FINISH

Unsalted butter, melted	**AS NEEDED**
Rye flour (T85)	**AS NEEDED**

METHOD

BASE TEMPERATURE	56 to 60°C (135 to 140°F).
INCORPORATE	In a spiral mixer, mix all the kneading ingredients in the bowl.
INITIAL MIX	On speed 1 for about 3 minutes.
KNEAD	On speed 2 for about 5 minutes.
CONSISTENCY	Medium-firm dough.
DOUGH TEMPERATURE	23°C (75°F).
WEIGHT	940-gram (2 lb 1-oz) dough pieces.
SHAPE	Compact ball.
BULK FERMENT	About 1 hour.
FOLD TO DEGAS	Square after 1 hour of bulk fermentation.
REST	About 30 minutes.
SHAPE	Degas the dough with a rolling pin, making it into a long rectangle. Fold the dough in a single turn and shape into two 28 × 20-centimeter (11 × 8-inch) dough pieces. Brush a thin layer of melted butter onto the first dough piece and remove the excess with paper towels. Dust lightly with rye flour. Place the second dough piece on top, then roll out to form a 33 × 25-centimeter (13 × 9 3/4-inch) rectangle. Cut out twelve 8-centimeter (3 1/4-inch) squares, then place them two by two, upright on a linen proofing cloth, with the opposite corner pointing up.
FINAL PROOF	About 45 minutes.
BAKE	In a deck oven at 250°C (480°F) for about 25 minutes.
COOL	On a wire rack.

BORDEAUX CROWN

ORIGINALLY FROM GIRONDE, THIS IS AN OLD SPECIALTY THAT CAN WEIGH UP TO 5 KILOGRAMS (11 POUNDS). THIS BREAD IS GREAT FOR SHARING, AND IT LOOKS WONDERFUL IN THE MIDDLE OF A ROUND TABLE. IT IS ONE OF FRANCE'S MOST BEAUTIFUL BREAD CROWNS.

MAKES 1 LOAF (1.65 KG/3 LB 10 OZ) OF DOUGH

KNEADING INGREDIENTS
COUNTRY-STYLE BREAD DOUGH

Bread flour (T65)	**800 G (1 ¾ LB)**
Whole-wheat flour (T150)	**100 G (3 ½ OZ)**
Rye flour (T170)	**100 G (3 ½ OZ)**
Water	**650 G (1 LB 7 OZ)**
Salt	**20 G (¾ OZ)**
Yeast	**5 G (3/16 OZ)**
Fermented dough	**150 G (5 ¼ OZ)**
Stiff levain	**150 G (5 ¼ OZ)**

FINAL KNEADING INGREDIENT

Bassinage water	**AS NEEDED**

METHOD

BASE TEMPERATURE	56 to 60°C (135 to 140°F).
INCORPORATE	In a spiral mixer, mix all the kneading ingredients in the bowl.
INITIAL MIX	On speed 1 for about 3 minutes.
KNEAD	On speed 1 for about 8 minutes, then speed 2 for 2 minutes.
INCORPORATE	A trickle of bassinage water, if necessary.
CONSISTENCY	Medium-firm dough.
DOUGH TEMPERATURE	23°C (75°F).
BULK FERMENT	About 1 hour 30 minutes.
WEIGHT	Seven 200-gram (7-oz) dough pieces and one 250-gram (8 ¾-oz) dough piece.
PRESHAPE	Shape into balls.
REST	About 20 minutes.
SHAPE	Roll out the 250-gram (8 ¾-oz) dough piece into a 30-centimeter (12-inch)-diameter disk. Reshape the 200-gram (7-oz) dough pieces. Place the 250-gram (8 ¾-oz) disk in the bottom of a 35-centimeter (14 ½-inch)-diameter ring banneton and dust lightly with rye flour, then add the remaining balls, seam side up. Make cuts in the center of the disk and fold the petals over the balls.
FINAL PROOF	At 5°C (40°F) for about 12 hours.
FINISH	On the baking mat, sift a dusting of flour over the crown.
BAKE	In a deck oven at 250°C (480°F) for about 50 minutes, gradually lowering the temperature.
COOL	On a wire rack.

COCOTTE

GASCON SOURDOUGH CORN BREAD

A RUSTIC BREAD ORIGINALLY FROM AQUITAINE, IT WAS USUALLY MADE BY COUNTRY FOLK. IN THE PAST, MILLET WAS MOSTLY USED, BUT IT WAS LATER REPLACED WITH CORN. CHARACTERIZED BY A MOIST YELLOW CRUMB, IT IS BAKED IN A PAN LINED WITH CABBAGE OR CHESTNUT LEAVES.

MAKES 7 LOAVES

KNEADING INGREDIENTS

Corn flour	**1 KG (2 LB 3 ¼ OZ)**
Water at 100°C (210°F)	**1.4 KG (3 LB 3 OZ)**
Salt	**30 G (1 OZ)**
Fermented dough	**850 G (1 LB 14 OZ)**
Stiff levain	**850 G (1 LB 14 OZ)**

TO FINISH

Cabbage leaves	**AS NEEDED**

FOR THE CABBAGE LEAVES

Blanch the cabbage leaves in boiling salted water for 5 minutes.

METHOD

BASE TEMPERATURE	144 to 148°C (290 to 300°F).
INCORPORATE	In a stand mixer, mix the corn flour, boiling water, and salt in the bowl.
INITIAL MIX	On speed 1 for about 3 minutes.
COOL	About 30 minutes, or until the dough reaches 60°C (140°F).
INCORPORATE	Add the stiff levain and the fermented dough.
KNEAD	On speed 1 for about 4 minutes, then speed 2 for 1 minute.
CONSISTENCY	Very soft dough, gelatinized.
DOUGH TEMPERATURE	40°C (105°F).
BULK FERMENT	About 1 hour 30 minutes.
WEIGHT	Using a bowl scraper, place 590 g (1 lb 4 ¾ oz) of dough into 14-centimeter (5 ½-inch)-diameter casseroles, greased and lined with cabbage leaves.
FINAL PROOF	About 15 minutes.
BAKE	In a deck oven at 240°C (465°F) for about 45 minutes, gradually lowering the temperature.
COOL	On a wire rack.

RYE TOURTE

ORIGINALLY FROM THE AUVERGNE REGION OF FRANCE, THIS RUSTIC BREAD HAS A THICK CRUST AND DEEP FURROWS RUNNING THROUGH THE WHITE FLOUR. ITS DENSE, MOIST BROWN CRUMB AND TANGY, SWEET TASTE GIVE IT AN ASTONISHING FLAVOR. THIS TOURTE WILL KEEP FOR SEVERAL DAYS. FINELY SLICED, IT IS THE PERFECT ACCOMPANIMENT FOR ALL LOCAL DISHES, CHEESES, AND SEAFOOD . . . A MUST-TRY!

MAKES 6 TOURTES

	REFRESHMENT
Rye flour (T85)	**500 G (1 LB 1 5/8 OZ)**
Rye flour (T170)	**500 G (1 LB 1 5/8 OZ)**
Water at 65°C (150°F)	**950 G (2 LB 1 1/2 OZ)**
Fermented dough	**425 G (15 OZ)**
Stiff levain	**425 G (15 OZ)**

KNEADING INGREDIENTS	
Rye flour (T85)	**500 G (1 LB 1 5/8 OZ)**
Rye flour (T170)	**500 G (1 LB 1 5/8 OZ)**
Water at 65°C (150°F)	**950 G (2 LB 1 1/2 OZ)**
Salt	**60 G (2 1/8 OZ)**
Fermented dough	**425 G (15 OZ)**
Stiff levain	**425 G (15 OZ)**
Refreshment	**2.8 KG (6 LB 3 OZ)**

FOR THE REFRESHMENT

In a stand mixer, mix all the ingredients for the refreshment on speed 1 for 6 minutes. The dough temperature should be 35°C (95°F).
Let ferment for 1 hour 30 minutes.

METHOD

BASE TEMPERATURE 110 to 114°C (230 to 240°F).
INCORPORATE In a stand mixer, mix all the kneading ingredients in the bowl.
INITIAL MIX On speed 1 for about 3 minutes.
KNEAD On speed 1 for about 3 minutes, then speed 2 for 1 minute.
CONSISTENCY Sticky dough, gelatinized.
DOUGH TEMPERATURE 35°C (95°F).
BULK FERMENT About 1 hour.
WEIGHT Six 940-gram (2 lb 1-oz) dough pieces.
SHAPE Gently form balls using the palm of your hands. Place them in floured bannetons, seam side up.
FINAL PROOF About 30 minutes.
BAKE In a deck oven at 250°C (480°F) for about 50 minutes, gradually lowering the temperature.
COOL On a wire rack.

RENNES BREAD

THIS BREAD, WHICH HAILS FROM BRITTANY, IS CHARACTERIZED BY ITS THINNESS, LARGE SIZE, AND "POLKA" SCORES CREATING A PATTERN OF DIAMONDS. TO MAKE IT, YOU WILL NEED ROUND, FLAT BANNETONS OR A LINEN PROOFING CLOTH. COMMONLY EATEN IN SOUPS, ITS THICK CRUST ALSO STANDS UP WELL TO THE DRIZZLY BRETON WEATHER.

MAKES 1 LOAF

KNEADING INGREDIENTS

Bread flour (T65)	**500 G (1 LB 1 5/8 OZ)**
Rye flour (T85)	**330 G (11 5/8 OZ)**
Whole-wheat flour (T150)	**170 G (6 OZ)**
Water	**700 G (1 LB 8 3/4 OZ)**
Salt	**26 G (7/8 OZ)**
Yeast	**5 G (3/16 OZ)**
Stiff levain	**500 G (1 LB 1 5/8 OZ)**

METHOD

BASE TEMPERATURE	60 to 62°C (140 to 145°F).
INCORPORATE	In a stand mixer with a C-shaped or spiral dough hook attachment, mix all the kneading ingredients in the bowl.
INITIAL MIX	On speed 1 for about 3 minutes.
KNEAD	On speed 1 for about 8 minutes.
CONSISTENCY	Firm dough.
DOUGH TEMPERATURE	23°C (75°F).
BULK FERMENT	About 2 hours.
WEIGHT	One 2.1-kilogram (2 lb 3 1/4-oz) dough piece.
SHAPE	Roll gently and flatten with a rolling pin to a diameter of about 32 centimeters (12 1/2 inches). Place the dough piece in a banneton or on a linen proofing cloth, seam side up.
FINAL PROOF	At 5°C (40°F) for about 12 hours.
FINISH	On the baking mat, sift flour over the dough piece.
SCORE	Diamond pattern.
BAKE	In a deck oven at 240°C (465°F) for about 1 hour, gradually lowering the temperature.
COOL	On a wire rack.

BRETON PLIÉ

ORIGINALLY FROM BRITTANY, THIS PLIÉ IS MADE WITH ONLY WHEAT FLOUR. IT HAS A CHARACTERISTIC SHAPE, WHICH INVOLVES FOLDING IT LIKE A WALLET WHEN BEING PLACED INTO THE OVEN. ITS SHAPE, ONCE USED IN FARM OVENS FOR BAKING LARGE LOAVES, SAVED SPACE IN THE OVEN, AMONG OTHER THINGS.

MAKES 4 LOAVES

KNEADING INGREDIENTS

Bread flour (T65)	**800 G (1 ³⁄₄ LB)**
Whole-wheat flour (T150)	**200 G (7 OZ)**
Water	**730 G (1 LB 9 ³⁄₄ OZ)**
Salt	**21 G (³⁄₄ OZ)**
Yeast	**2 G (¹⁄₁₆ OZ)**
Stiff levain	**250 G (8 ³⁄₄ OZ)**

FINAL KNEADING

Bassinage water	**AS NEEDED**

METHOD

BASE TEMPERATURE	56 to 60°C (135 to 140°F).
INCORPORATE	In a stand mixer, mix all the kneading ingredients in the bowl.
INITIAL MIX	On speed 1 for about 3 minutes.
KNEAD	On speed 2 for about 5 minutes.
INCORPORATE	A trickle of bassinage water, if necessary.
CONSISTENCY	Medium-firm dough.
DOUGH TEMPERATURE	23°C (75°F).
BULK FERMENT	About 2 hours.
WEIGHT	Four 500-gram (1 lb 1 ⁵⁄₈-oz) dough pieces.
PRESHAPE	Shape into balls.
REST	About 20 minutes.
SHAPE	Pear shapes about 30 centimeters (11 ³⁄₄ inches) long. Place them on a linen proofing cloth, seam side down, then fold the ends 5 centimeters (2 inches) back over the dough.
FINAL PROOF	At 5°C (40°F) for about 12 hours.
FINISH	Place them on the baking mat, then fold the dough pieces over themselves.
BAKE	In a deck oven at 250°C (480°F) for about 30 minutes, gradually lowering the temperature.
COOL	On a wire rack.

STANDARD BAGUETTE

ORIGINATING IN PARIS, THERE ARE VARIOUS ACCOUNTS OF HOW THE BAGUETTE CAME ABOUT. ONE STORY SAYS THAT AN ENGINEER CALLED FULGENCE BIENVENÜE, WHO WAS SUPERVISING THE CONSTRUCTION OF A MÉTRO TRANSIT SYSTEM, WAS WORRIED ABOUT THE KNIFE FIGHTS BETWEEN WORKERS OF DIFFERENT ORIGINS THAT OFTEN BROKE OUT IN THE TUNNELS. HE ASKED A BAKER TO CREATE AN ELONGATED LOAF (THAT COMPLIED WITH THE WEIGHT REGULATIONS FOR A BREAD LOAF) THAT WOULDN'T NEED TO BE SLICED OR CUT WITH A KNIFE, THUS PREVENTING THESE POTENTIAL WEAPONS FROM BEING TAKEN INTO THE TUNNELS.

MAKES 5 LOAVES

KNEADING INGREDIENTS

Strong flour	**1 KG (2 LB 3 ¼ OZ)**
Water	**620 G (1 LB 5 ⅞ OZ)**
Salt	**18 G (⅝ OZ)**
Yeast	**10 G (⅜ OZ)**
Fermented dough	**150 G (5 ¼ OZ)**

METHOD

BASE TEMPERATURE	50 to 54°C (120 to 130°F).
INCORPORATE	In a spiral mixer, mix the flour and water in the bowl.
INITIAL MIX	On speed 1 for about 3 minutes.
AUTOLYSIS	30 minutes.
INCORPORATE	The salt, yeast, and fermented dough.
KNEAD	Speed 2 for about 8 minutes.
CONSISTENCY	Medium-firm dough.
DOUGH TEMPERATURE	23°C (75°F).
BULK FERMENT	About 20 minutes.
WEIGHT	Five 335-grams (11 ¾-oz) dough pieces.
PRESHAPE	Oval.
REST	About 30 minutes.
SHAPE	Baguette. Place the baguettes on a linen proofing cloth, seam side down.
FINAL PROOF	At 8°C (45°F) for about 12 hours.
SCORE	Seven slashes.
BAKE	In a deck oven at 250°C (480°F) for about 20 minutes.
COOL	On a wire rack.

TRADITIONAL FRENCH BAGUETTE

THE ORIGIN OF THIS BAGUETTE IS RELATIVELY RECENT, ALTHOUGH IT HARKS BACK TO A PREWAR MANUFACTURING PROCESS (HENCE THE REFERENCE TO THE TRADITIONAL IRREGULARLY SHAPED AIR POCKETS IN THE CRUMB). IT WAS CREATED IN 1993 TO GIVE A NEW LEASE ON LIFE TO FRANCE'S ARTISANAL BAKING INDUSTRY, WHICH WAS FACING WHAT WAS CONSIDERED TO BE "UNFAIR" COMPETITION FROM SUPERMARKETS. IT IS OFTEN MADE WITH A LIQUID LEVAIN, WHICH GIVES IT A UNIQUE TASTE. THE PREPARATION PROCESS AND THE INGREDIENTS ARE SUBJECT TO STRICT RULES, WHICH ARE SET OUT IN A DECREE (DECREE NO. 93-1074 OF SEPTEMBER 13, 1993).

MAKES 5 LOAVES

KNEADING INGREDIENTS

Bread flour (T65)	**1 KG (2 LB 3 ¼ OZ)**
Water	**650 G (1 LB 7 OZ)**
Salt	**19 G (⅝ OZ)**
Yeast	**7 G (¼ OZ)**
Liquid levain	**100 G (3 ½ OZ)**

FINAL KNEADING

Bassinage water	**AS NEEDED**

METHOD

BASE TEMPERATURE	56 to 60°C (135 to 140°F).
INCORPORATE	In a spiral mixer, mix the flour and water in the bowl.
INITIAL MIX	On speed 1 for about 3 minutes.
AUTOLYSIS	1 hour minimum.
INCORPORATE	Add the salt, yeast, and liquid levain.
KNEAD	On speed 1 for about 8 minutes, then speed 2 for 1 minute.
INCORPORATE	A trickle of bassinage water, if necessary.
CONSISTENCY	Soft dough.
DOUGH TEMPERATURE	23°C (75°F).
BULK FERMENT	About 1 hour, then at 3°C (35°F) for 12 hours.
FOLD TO DEGAS	After 1 hour of bulk fermentation.
WEIGHT	Five 335-gram (11 ¾-oz) dough pieces.
PRESHAPE	Oval.
REST	About 45 minutes.
SHAPE	Baguette. Place the baguettes on a floured linen proofing cloth, seam side up.
FINAL PROOF	About 1 hour.
SCORE	Five slashes.
BAKE	In a deck oven at 250°C (480°F) for about 20 minutes.
COOL	On a wire rack.

BEAUCAIRE BREAD

HAILING FROM THE TOWN OF BEAUCAIRE IN FRANCE'S LANGUEDOC-ROUSSILLON REGION, WHERE IT IS SAID TO HAVE BEEN MADE BY THE "FOURNIERS," OR OVEN WORKERS, WHO WERE THE ANCESTORS OF THE TOWN'S BAKERS, THE ORIGINS OF THIS BREAD GO BACK TO THE FIFTEENTH CENTURY. SPLIT DOWN THE MIDDLE, THE CRUMB HAS A LOT OF AIR POCKETS AND A THIN CRUST.

MAKES 5 LOAVES

KNEADING INGREDIENTS

Bread flour (T65)	**900 G (1 LB 15 3/4 OZ)**
Rye flour (T170)	**100 G (3 1/2 OZ)**
Water	**570 G (1 1/4 LB)**
Salt	**25 G (7/8 OZ)**
Yeast	**5 G (3/16 OZ)**
Liquid levain	**600 G (1 LB 6 1/8 OZ)**

METHOD

BASE TEMPERATURE	56 to 60°C (135 to 140°F).
INCORPORATE	In a spiral mixer, mix all the kneading ingredients in the bowl.
INITIAL MIX	On speed 1 for about 3 minutes.
KNEAD	On speed 1 for about 7 minutes.
CONSISTENCY	Medium-firm dough.
DOUGH TEMPERATURE	23°C (75°F).
BULK FERMENT	About 1 hour 30 minutes, then at 3°C (35°F) for 12 hours.
FOLD TO DEGAS	After 1 hour 30 minutes.
SHAPE	Place the dough on a floured felt pad. Using a rolling pin, roll out to a 30 × 40-centimeter (11 3/4 inch × 15 1/2-inch) rectangle. Thinly roll out the bottom section of the rectangle. Using the rolling pin, apply light pressure to the middle of the remaining area. Moisten the center of the rectangle generously with water, then fold the top section over the damp area. Seal together using the moistened, thinly rolled area. Enclose the dough in the floured felt, making sure it is held in place well.
FINAL PROOF	About 30 minutes.
CUT TO SIZE	Using a chef's knife, cut into five strips about 6 centimeter (2 1/2 inches) wide. Place the dough pieces, turned on their sides, on the baking mat.
BAKE	In a deck oven at 250°C (480°F) for about 40 minutes, gradually lowering the temperature.
COOL	On a wire rack.

LODÈVE BREAD

FROM THE LANGUEDOC-ROUSSILLON REGION, THIS IS A SPECIALTY OF THE TOWN OF LODÈVE, FROM WHICH IT TAKES ITS NAME. TRADITIONALLY, THIS BREAD IS NEITHER WEIGHED NOR SHAPED AND IS MINIMALLY MANIPULATED. ITS HIGH MOISTURE CONTENT GIVES IT A SUPPLE CRUMB WITH A LOT OF AIR POCKETS. IN THE PAST, THE PRICE WAS WRITTEN IN CHALK RIGHT ON THE CRUST.

MAKES 5 LOAVES

KNEADING INGREDIENTS

Bread flour (T65)	**1 KG (2 LB 3 ¼ OZ)**
Water	**550 G (1 LB 3 ⅜ OZ)**
Salt	**25 G (⅞ OZ)**
Yeast	**5 G (3/16 OZ)**
Liquid levain	**600 G (1 LB 6 ⅛ OZ)**

FINAL KNEADING

Bassinage water	**100 G (3 ½ OZ)**

METHOD

BASE TEMPERATURE	52 to 56°C (125 to 135°F).
INCORPORATE	In a spiral mixer, mix all the kneading ingredients in the bowl.
INITIAL MIX	On speed 1 for about 3 minutes.
KNEAD	On speed 2 for about 5 minutes.
INCORPORATE	A trickle of bassinage water.
CONSISTENCY	Soft dough.
DOUGH TEMPERATURE	23°C (75°F).
BULK FERMENT	About 1 hour 30 minutes, then at 3°C (35°F) for 12 hours.
FOLD TO DEGAS	After 1 hour 30 minutes.
SHAPE	Place the dough on a felt pad, then fold it over twice to make a long dough piece. Place the dough on a floured linen couch cloth, making sure it is held in place well.
REST	About 1 hour.
CUT TO SIZE	Using a knife, cut five triangles of the same size, then place them on a diagonal edge on a floured linen proofing cloth, seam side up.
FINAL PROOF	About 30 minutes.
BAKE	In a deck oven at 250°C (480°F) for about 35 minutes.
COOL	On a wire rack.

BRIÉ BREAD

WITH A TIGHT WHITE CRUMB AND COMPACT TEXTURE, THIS BREAD FROM NORMANDY CAN BE TRACED BACK TO THE FOURTEENTH CENTURY. ALSO KNOWN AS "SAILOR'S BREAD," IT WILL KEEP FOR A LONG TIME, MAKING IT POPULAR WITH FISHERS AND SEAFARERS.

MAKES 8 LOAVES

KNEADING INGREDIENTS

Bread flour (T65)	**1 KG (2 LB 3 ¼ OZ)**
Water	**150 G (5 ¼ OZ)**
Salt	**18 G (⅝ OZ)**
Yeast	**15 G (½ OZ)**
Fermented dough	**2.75 KG (6 LB)**
Butter	**150 G (5 ¼ OZ)**

METHOD

BASE TEMPERATURE	70 to 74°C (160 to 165°F).
INCORPORATE	In a spiral mixer, mix all the kneading ingredients in the bowl.
INITIAL MIX	On speed 1 for about 6 minutes.
KNEAD	On speed 2 for about 6 minutes.
CONSISTENCY	Firm dough.
DOUGH TEMPERATURE	23°C (75°F).
BULK FERMENT	About 15 minutes.
WEIGHT	Eight 500-gram (1 lb 1 ⅝-oz) dough pieces.
PRESHAPE	Shape into balls.
REST	About 15 minutes.
SHAPE	Bâtard. Place them on a linen proofing cloth, seam side down.
FINAL PROOF	About 2 hours (cover the bâtards to prevent crusting).
SCORE	One slash down the center, then three parallel slashes on each side.
BAKE	In a deck oven, with plenty of steam, at 240°C (465°F) for about 25 minutes.
COOL	On a wire rack.

PRÉFOU

ORIGINALLY FROM THE PAYS DE LA LOIRE REGION, IT WAS ORIGINALLY JUST A PIECE OF DOUGH PUT INTO THE OVEN BY THE BAKER TO CHECK WHETHER THE RIGHT BAKING TEMPERATURE HAD BEEN REACHED. THE WORD MEANS "PREOVEN," HENCE THE NAME OF THIS BREAD. TO AVOID WASTING IT, AND TO TREAT THE EAGER EATERS WAITING BY THE OVEN, THIS BREAD WAS TRADITIONALLY EATEN HOT, SPREAD WITH BUTTER AND GARLIC.

MAKES 6 LOAVES

KNEADING INGREDIENTS TRADITIONAL FRENCH BREAD DOUGH

Bread flour (T65)	**1 KG (2 LB 3 ¼ OZ)**
Water	**600 G (1 LB 6 ⅛ OZ)**
Salt	**21 G (¾ OZ)**
Yeast	**7 G (¼ OZ)**
Liquid levain	**250 G (8 ¾ OZ)**

FINAL KNEADING

Bassinage water	**50 G (1 ¾ OZ)**

GARLIC BUTTER

Unsalted butter	**500 G (1 LB 1 ⅝ OZ)**
Garlic, degermed and chopped	**125 G (4 ⅜ OZ)**
Salt	**15 G (½ OZ)**
Parsley, chopped	**15 G (½ OZ)**

FOR THE GARLIC BUTTER

Using a mixer fitted with the paddle attachment, cream the butter, then add the garlic, salt, and parsley.

METHOD

BASE TEMPERATURE 56 to 60°C (135 to 140°F).
INCORPORATE In a spiral mixer, mix the flour and water in the bowl.
INITIAL MIX On speed 1 for about 3 minutes.
AUTOLYSIS About 1 hour.
INCORPORATE Add the salt, yeast, and liquid levain.
KNEAD On speed 1 for about 5 minutes, then speed 2 for 2 minutes.
INCORPORATE A trickle of bassinage water.
CONSISTENCY Medium-firm dough.
DOUGH TEMPERATURE 23°C (75°F).
BULK FERMENT About 1 hour 15 minutes.
WEIGHT Six 320-gram (11 ¼-oz) dough pieces.
PRESHAPE Round.
REST About 15 minutes.
SHAPE Short baguettes, placed on a linen proofing cloth, seam side down.
FINAL PROOF About 45 minutes.
BAKE In a deck oven at 250°C (480°F) for about 12 minutes.
COOL On a wire rack.
ASSEMBLY When cool, cut the baguettes in half.
Spread each side with 50 grams (1 ¾ oz) of garlic butter, then put the halves back together.
Before serving, wrap the préfous in parchment paper and heat at 200°C (390°F) for 10 minutes, turning them over after 5 minutes to let the butter soak into both sides.

COLLIER BREAD

ORIGINALLY FROM THE POITOU-CHARENTES REGION, THE SHAPE OF THIS BREAD IS REMINISCENT OF A HORSE'S COLLAR. IT CAN BE MADE IN TWO WAYS: EITHER BY SPLITTING THE DOUGH DOWN THE MIDDLE AND PROOFING IT IN A SPECIAL BANNETON (A PAIN COLLIER BANNETON), OR BY JOINING TWO BAGUETTES TOGETHER AT BOTH ENDS.

MAKES 4 LOAVES

KNEADING INGREDIENTS

Bread flour (T65)	**900 G (1 LB 15 3/4 OZ)**
Rye flour (T170)	**100 G (3 1/2 OZ)**
Water	**650 G (1 LB 7 OZ)**
Salt	**21 G (3/4 OZ)**
Yeast	**5 G (3/16 OZ)**
Liquid levain	**300 G (10 1/2 OZ)**

FINAL KNEADING

Bassinage water	**50 G (1 3/4 OZ)**

METHOD

BASE TEMPERATURE	56 to 60°C (135 to 140°F).
INCORPORATE	In a spiral mixer, mix all the kneading ingredients in the bowl.
INITIAL MIX	On speed 1 for about 3 minutes.
KNEAD	On speed 2 for about 5 minutes.
INCORPORATE	A trickle of bassinage water, if necessary.
CONSISTENCY	Soft dough.
DOUGH TEMPERATURE	23°C (75°F).
BULK FERMENT	About 1 hour 30 minutes, then at 3°C (35°F) for 12 hours.
FOLD TO DEGAS	After 1 hour 30 minutes.
WEIGHT	Four 250-gram (8 3/4-oz) dough pieces.
SHAPE	Oval, not too compact.
REST	About 1 hour.
SHAPE	Pointed, not too compact baguettes about 30 centimeters (11 3/4 inches) long. Join the ends of the two baguettes together. Place them on a floured linen proofing cloth, seam side down. Separate in the center to form the collar.
FINAL PROOF	About 1 hour 30 minutes.
SCORE	No scoring, because the seam will open on its own.
BAKE	In a deck oven at 250°C (480°F) for about 30 minutes.
COOL	On a wire rack.

MAIN DE NICE

FROM THE CITY OF NICE IN PROVENCE-ALPES-CÔTE D'AZUR, THIS BREAD OWES ITS NAME, WITH *MAIN* MEANING "HAND," TO ITS FOUR-FINGERED HAND SHAPE. ALSO KNOWN AS "MONTE-DESSUS," TWO LOAVES FAMOUSLY FEATURE IN A PHOTOGRAPH OF PICASSO TAKEN BY ROBERT DOISNEAU. IN ITALY, A SIMILAR BREAD IS KNOWN AS "MANINA FERRARESE."

MAKES 4 LOAVES

KNEADING INGREDIENTS

Bread flour (T65)	**1 KG (2 LB 3 1/4 OZ)**
Water	**560 G (1 LB 3/4 OZ)**
Salt	**20 G (3/4 OZ)**
Yeast	**10 G (3/8 OZ)**
Liquid levain	**150 G (5 1/4 OZ)**
Olive oil	**80 G (2 7/8 OZ)**

METHOD

BASE TEMPERATURE	54 to 58°C (130 to 135°F).
INCORPORATE	In a stand mixer, mix all the kneading ingredients in the bowl.
INITIAL MIX	On speed 1 for about 3 minutes.
KNEAD	On speed 2 for about 5 minutes.
CONSISTENCY	Medium-firm dough.
DOUGH TEMPERATURE	23°C (75°F).
BULK FERMENT	About 1 hour 30 minutes, then at 3°C (35°F) for 12 hours.
FOLD TO DEGAS	After 1 hour 30 minutes.
WEIGHT	Four 450-gram (15 7/8-oz) dough pieces.
PRESHAPE	Long oval.
REST	About 1 hour.
SHAPE	Using a dough sheeter, roll out the dough into a 1 meter × 15-centimeter (39 × 6-inch) strip. Make a lengthwise cut at each end, then roll them toward the center like a croissant. Fold the two fingers on the left over the other two, spreading them to form a hand. Place it on a linen proofing cloth, seam side down.
FINAL PROOF	About 1 hour.
BAKE	In a deck oven, with plenty of steam, at 250°C (480°F) for about 25 minutes.
COOL	On a wire rack.

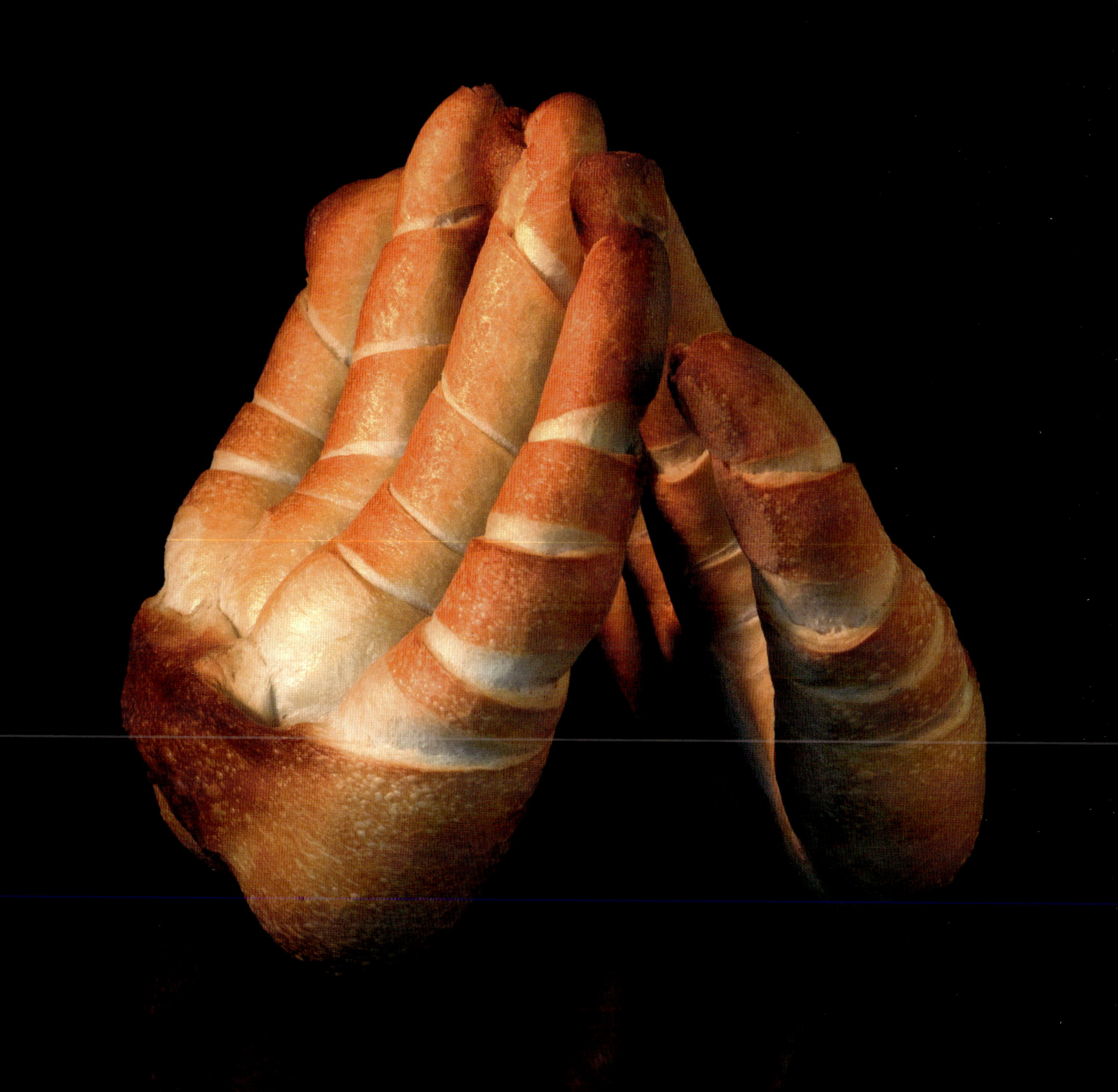

FOUGASSE

ORIGINATING IN PROVENCE-ALPES-CÔTE D'AZUR, AND ALSO COMMON IN ITALY, THIS LEAF-SHAPED FLATBREAD IS FULL OF AIR POCKETS. IN THE PAST, IT WAS USED TO TEST THE TEMPERATURE OF THE WOOD-FIRED OVENS. A BREAD THAT IS EASY TO BREAK AND SHARE, IT IS IDEAL FOR AN APERITIF WITH FRIENDS.

MAKES 4 LOAVES

KNEADING INGREDIENTS

Bread flour (T65)	**1 KG (2 LB 3 1/4 OZ)**
Water	**600 G (1 LB 6 1/8 OZ)**
Salt	**21 G (3/4 OZ)**
Yeast	**7 G (1/4 OZ)**
Liquid levain	**250 G (8 3/4 OZ)**

FINAL KNEADING

Bassinage water	**60 G (2 1/8 OZ)**
Olive oil	**70 G (2 1/2 OZ)**

METHOD

BASE TEMPERATURE	54 to 58°C (130 to 135°F).
INCORPORATE	In a stand mixer, mix all the kneading ingredients in the bowl.
INITIAL MIX	On speed 1 for about 3 minutes.
KNEAD	On speed 2 for about 5 minutes.
INCORPORATE	A trickle of bassinage water, if necessary, followed by the olive oil.
CONSISTENCY	Soft dough.
DOUGH TEMPERATURE	23°C (75°F).
BULK FERMENT	About 1 hour 30 minutes, then at 3°C (35°F) for 12 hours.
FOLD TO DEGAS	After 1 hour 30 minutes.
WEIGHT	Four 500-gram (1 lb 1 5/8-oz) dough pieces.
SHAPE	Drop shape.
REST	About 2 hours.
SHAPE	Slide a board under the baking mat. Gently flatten the dough pieces on the mat, then make seven cuts with a pastry cutter. Stretch the cuts to form the fougasse.
BAKE	In a deck oven at 260°C (500°F) for about 14 minutes.
COOL	On a wire rack.

LYON CROWN

THIS CROWN FROM THE CITY OF LYON (RHÔNE-ALPES) IS MADE WITH WHEAT FLOUR. WHAT MAKES IT SPECIAL IS THAT IT IS BAKED SEAM SIDE UP, SO THE SEAM OPENS ON ITS OWN WHILE IN THE OVEN.

MAKES 1 LOAF (1.65 KG/3 LB 10 OZ OF DOUGH)

KNEADING INGREDIENTS
COUNTRY-STYLE BREAD DOUGH

Bread flour (T65)	**800 G (1 3/4 LB)**
Whole-wheat flour (T150)	**200 G (7 OZ)**
Water	**650 G (1 LB 7 OZ)**
Salt	**20 G (3/4 OZ)**
Yeast	**5 G (3/16 OZ)**
Fermented dough	**150 G (5 1/4 OZ)**
Stiff levain	**150 G (5 1/4 OZ)**

FINAL KNEADING

Bassinage water	**AS NEEDED**
Rye Flour	**AS NEEDED**

METHOD

BASE TEMPERATURE	56 to 60°C (135 to 140°F).
INCORPORATE	In a spiral mixer, mix all the kneading ingredients in the bowl.
INITIAL MIX	On speed 1 for about 3 minutes.
KNEAD	On speed 1 for about 8 minutes, then speed 2 for 2 minutes.
INCORPORATE	A trickle of bassinage water, if necessary.
CONSISTENCY	Medium-firm dough.
DOUGH TEMPERATURE	23°C (75°F).
BULK FERMENT	About 1 hour 30 minutes.
WEIGHT	One 1.65-kilogram (3 lb 10-oz) dough piece.
PRESHAPE	Shape into a ball.
REST	About 40 minutes.
SHAPE	A 32-centimeter (12 1/2-inch)-diameter ring. Lightly flour the surface of the ring with rye flour. Using your fingertips, press the surface of the ring to make folds. Place it in a floured 37-centimeter (14 1/2-inch)-diameter ring banneton, seam side up.
FINAL PROOF	At 5°C (40°F) for about 12 hours.
SCORE	No scoring needed, because the folds will open on their own.
FINISH	On the baking mat, sift a dusting of whole-wheat flour over the crown.
BAKE	In a deck oven at 250°C (480°F) for about 50 minutes, gradually lowering the temperature.
COOL	On a wire rack.

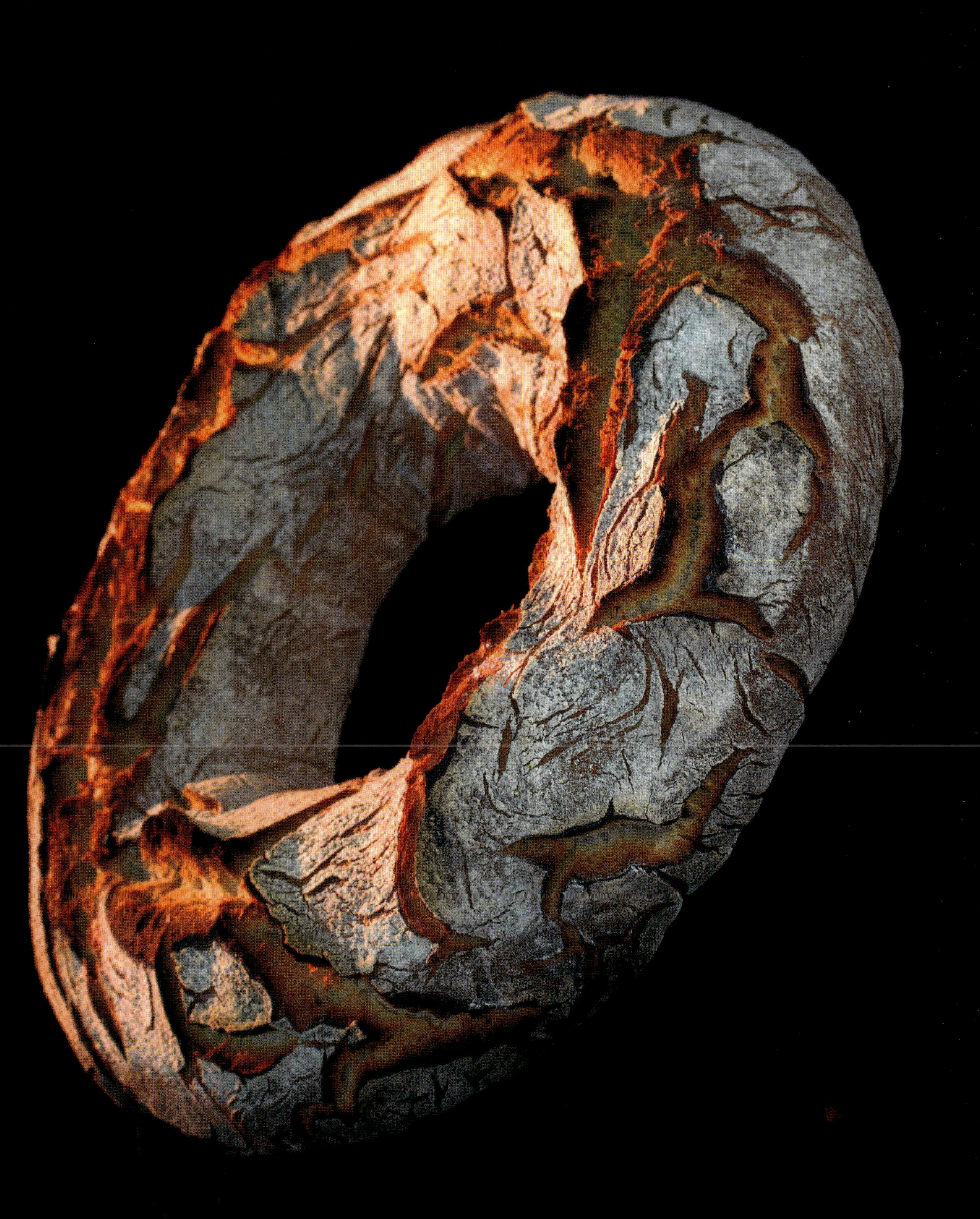

B
REA
DS
OF

THE
·WO
RLD
• • •

PRETZELS

ORIGINALLY FROM GERMANY, THESE CAN BE RECOGNIZED BY THEIR CHARACTERISTIC KNOTTED SHAPE. A TRADITIONAL PRODUCT FOUND AT GERMAN CHRISTMAS MARKETS, HOMEMADE PRETZELS ARE OFTEN SPRINKLED WITH COARSE SALT. THEY ARE ALSO A POPULAR SNACK AT BEER FESTIVALS. PRETZEL SOLUTION, ALSO KNOWN AS "LYE SOLUTION," REFERS TO A SOLUTION OF SODIUM HYDROXIDE (LYE). IT IS SOLD EITHER READY TO USE OR CONCENTRATED, TO BE DILUTED TO A 5% SOLUTION IN WATER.

MAKES 18

KNEADING INGREDIENTS

Strong flour	**1 KG (2 LB 3 1/4 OZ)**
Milk	**500 G (1 LB 1 5/8 OZ)**
Salt	**20 G (3/4 OZ)**
Superfine sugar	**20 G (3/4 OZ)**
Yeast	**35 G (1 1/4 OZ)**
Liquid levain	**250 G (8 3/4 OZ)**
Unsalted butter	**150 G (5 1/4 OZ)**
Sunflower oil	**50 G (1 3/4 OZ)**

TO FINISH

Pretzel solution	**AS NEEDED**
Sesame seeds	**80 G (2 7/8 OZ)**
Salt flakes	**20 G (3/4 OZ)**

METHOD

BASE TEMPERATURE	46 to 50°C (115 to 120°F).
INCORPORATE	In a stand mixer, mix all the kneading ingredients in the bowl.
INITIAL MIX	On speed 1 for about 3 minutes.
KNEAD	On speed 2 for about 8 minutes.
CONSISTENCY	Medium-firm dough.
DOUGH TEMPERATURE	23°C (75°F).
BULK FERMENT	About 5 minutes.
WEIGHT	Eighteen 110-gram (3 7/8-oz) dough pieces.
PRESHAPE	Oval.
REST	About 10 minutes.
SHAPE	Pretzel knots.
FINAL PROOF	About 15 minutes, then at 3°C (35°F) for 1 hour.
FINISH	Dip the pretzels in the solution, drain, and place them on greased baking sheets.
SCORE	Using a baker's lame, score the top of the pretzels.
FINISH	Sprinkle with the sesame seeds and salt flakes.
BAKE	In a deck oven at 220°C (430°F) for about 15 minutes.
COOL	On a wire rack.

POTATO BREAD

THE ANCESTOR OF THIS *KARTOFFELBROT*, OR POTATO BREAD, WAS DEVELOPED IN THE EIGHTEENTH CENTURY BY ANTOINE AUGUSTIN PARMENTIER, WHO WAS SEEKING WAYS TO COMBAT FAMINE. DURING WORLD WAR I, *KRIEGSKARTOFFELBROT* (POTATO WAR BREAD, OR "K.K. BREAD") WAS GIVEN TO PRISONERS OF WAR IN GERMAN CAMPS. TODAY, THIS LIGHT, FLAVORSOME BREAD, WHICH HAS A LONG SHELF LIFE, IS A POPULAR CHOICE IN GERMANY.

MAKES 4

KNEADING INGREDIENTS

Bread flour (T65)	**775 G (1 LB 11 3/8 OZ)**
Potato flakes	**125 G (4 3/8 OZ)**
Whole-wheat flour (T150)	**100 G (3 1/2 OZ)**
Water	**900 G (1 LB 15 3/4 OZ)**
Salt	**23 G (7/8 OZ)**
Yeast	**8 G (1/4 OZ)**
Stiff levain	**300 G (10 1/2 OZ)**

FINAL KNEADING

Bassinage water	**100 G (3 1/2 OZ)**

METHOD

BASE TEMPERATURE	60 to 65°C (140 to 144°F).
INCORPORATE	In a spiral mixer, mix all the ingredients in the bowl.
INITIAL MIX	On speed 1 for about 3 minutes.
KNEAD	On speed 2 for about 8 minutes.
INCORPORATE	A trickle of bassinage water.
CONSISTENCY	Soft dough.
DOUGH TEMPERATURE	23°C (75°F).
BULK FERMENT	About 1 hour 30 minutes.
WEIGHT	Four 580-grams (1 lb 4 1/2-oz) dough pieces.
PRESHAPE	Shape into balls.
REST	About 30 minutes.
SHAPE	Long bâtards. Place them on a floured linen proofing cloth, seam side up.
FINAL PROOF	At 5°C (40°F) for about 12 hours.
SCORE	Four slashes.
BAKE	In a deck oven at 250°C (480°F) for about 35 minutes, gradually lowering the temperature.
COOL	On a wire rack.

KOREAN WHOLE-GRAIN SANDWICH BREAD

MAKES 5 LOAVES

KNEADING INGREDIENTS

Strong flour	**1 KG (2 LB 3 1/4 OZ)**
Milk	**700 G (1 LB 8 3/4 OZ)**
Salt	**18 G (5/8 OZ)**
Superfine sugar	**50 G (1 3/4 OZ)**
Honey	**50 G (1 3/4 OZ)**
Yeast	**30 G (1 OZ)**
Unsalted butter	**80 G (2 7/8 OZ)**

SEED MIXTURE

Sesame seeds	**25 G (7/8 OZ)**
Poppy seeds	**25 G (7/8 OZ)**
Golden flaxseed	**25 G (7/8 OZ)**
Millet seeds	**25 G (7/8 OZ)**
Pumpkin seeds	**25 G (7/8 OZ)**
Water	**125 G (4 3/8 OZ)**

FOR THE SEED MIXTURE

Lightly toast the seed mixture in a convection oven at 175°C (345°F) for 20 minutes. Submerge the seeds in water. Set aside at 3°C (35°F).

METHOD

BASE TEMPERATURE 50 to 54°C (120 to 130°F).
INCORPORATE In a stand mixer, mix all the kneading ingredients in the bowl.
INITIAL MIX On speed 1 for about 3 minutes.
KNEAD On speed 2 for about 8 minutes.
INCORPORATE On speed 1, add the seed mixture.
CONSISTENCY Soft dough.
DOUGH TEMPERATURE 26°C (80°F).
BULK FERMENT About 1 hour.
WEIGHT Five 150-g (5 1/4-oz) dough pieces.
PRESHAPE Oval.
REST About 20 minutes.
SHAPE Degas the dough pieces. Using a rolling pin, roll out and make a single turn. Stretch again in the opposite direction, then roll up loosely and place them in greased 18 × 8 × 8-centimeter (7 × 3 1/4 × 3 1/4-inch sandwich loaf pans.
FINAL PROOF About 1 hour 15 minutes.
BAKE In a deck oven at 190°C (375°F) for about 20 minutes.
COOL On a wire rack.

KAISERBROT

ORIGINALLY FROM AUSTRIA, AND KNOWN AS *PAIN EMPEREUR* IN FRANCE, THIS LOAF HAS AN UNUSUAL AND COMPLEX SHAPE. ACCORDING TO LEGEND, IT REPRESENTS THE FIVE POINTS OF THE IMPERIAL CROWN OF AUSTRIA. THESE DAYS, IT IS OFTEN SHAPED WITH A PASTRY CUTTER AND BAKED AFTER ONLY A SHORT PROOF.

MAKES 4 LOAVES

KNEADING INGREDIENTS

Bread flour (T65)	**850 G (1 LB 14 OZ)**
Whole-wheat flour (T150)	**150 G (5 1/4 OZ)**
Water	**650 G (1 LB 7 OZ)**
Salt	**22 G (3/4 OZ)**
Yeast	**5 G (3/16 OZ)**
Liquid levain	**300 G (10 1/2 OZ)**

FINAL KNEADING

Bassinage water	**50 G (1 3/4 OZ)**

METHOD

BASE TEMPERATURE 56 to 60°C (135 to 140°F).

INCORPORATE In a spiral mixer, mix all the ingredients in the bowl.

INITIAL MIX On speed 1 for about 3 minutes.

KNEAD On speed 2 for about 5 minutes.

INCORPORATE A trickle of bassinage water.

CONSISTENCY Soft dough.

DOUGH TEMPERATURE 23°C (75°F).

BULK FERMENT About 1 hour 30 minutes, then at 3°C (35°F) for 12 hours.

FOLD TO DEGAS After 1 hour 30 minutes.

WEIGHT Four 500-gram (1 lb 1 5/8-oz) dough pieces.

PRESHAPE Shape into balls, not too compact.

REST About 1 hour 15 minutes.

SHAPE Degas the dough pieces into 18-centimeter (7-inch)-diameter disks.
Using a rolling pin, roll out one-quarter of each dough piece on the left-hand side.
Fold the lower section into the center of the dough and place your left thumb (for right-handers) in the center.
Keeping your left thumb in the center, fold the edge of the dough over your thumb with the right hand and seal.
Turning the dough clockwise and repeat the process four times. The last fold allows for the dough to take the place of your left thumb.
Place them in floured proofing baskets, seam side up.

FINAL PROOF About 1 hour 30 minutes.

BAKE In a deck oven at 250°C (480°F) for about 40 minutes, gradually lowering the temperature.

COOL On a wire rack.

VIENNA BREAD

THIS AUSTRIAN BREAD DIFFERS FROM A TRADITIONAL FRENCH BAGUETTE, BECAUSE MILK AND FAT ARE INCLUDED IN THE INGREDIENTS, AS WELL AS SUGAR BEING ADDED LATER ON. AN AUSTRIAN OFFICER CALLED AUGUST ZANG IS THOUGHT TO HAVE INTRODUCED IT TO PARIS IN THE 1840S, ALTHOUGH BACK THEN IT WAS MADE WITH A WHITE OAT FLOUR.

MAKES 21 LOAVES

KNEADING INGREDIENTS

Strong flour	**1 KG (2 LB 3 1/4 OZ)**
Water	**275 G (9 3/4 OZ)**
Milk	**275 G (9 3/4 OZ)**
Salt	**18 G (5/8 OZ)**
Superfine sugar	**100 G (3 1/2 OZ)**
Yeast	**30 G (1 OZ)**
Viennese fermented dough *(see page 28)*	**250 G (8 3/4 OZ)**
Unsalted butter	**150 G (5 1/4 OZ)**

METHOD

BASE TEMPERATURE	48 to 52°C (120 to 125°F).
INCORPORATE	In a stand mixer, mix all the kneading ingredients in the bowl.
INITIAL MIX	On speed 1 for about 3 minutes.
KNEAD	On speed 2 for about 8 minutes.
CONSISTENCY	Medium-firm dough.
DOUGH TEMPERATURE	23°C (75°F).
BULK FERMENT	About 45 minutes.
WEIGHT	Twenty-one 100-gram (3 1/2-oz) dough pieces.
PRESHAPE	Shape into balls.
REST	At 3°C (35°F) for 1 hour.
SHAPE	Short, fat baguettes.
GLAZE	Egg.
SCORE	Sausage cut.
FINAL PROOF	At 3°C (35°F) for about 12 hours, then at 27°C (80°F) for about 3 hours.
GLAZE	Whisked egg.
BAKE	In a deck oven at 200°C (390°F) for about 15 minutes.
COOL	On a wire rack.

BAGELS

ORIGINALLY FROM EASTERN EUROPE, BAGELS WERE BROUGHT TO NORTH AMERICA BY JEWISH IMMIGRANTS. TWO CHARACTERISTICS DEFINE THEM: ONE IS THEIR RING SHAPE, AND THE OTHER IS THAT THEY ARE COOKED TWICE. FIRST, THEY ARE QUICKLY BOILED, THEN THEY ARE BAKED IN THE OVEN. THEY ARE ALSO RECOGNIZABLE BY THEIR SHINY CRUST.

MAKES 17 BAGELS

KNEADING INGREDIENTS

Oat flour	**1 KG (2 LB 3 1/4 OZ)**
Water	**300 G (10 1/2 OZ)**
Milk	**300 G (10 1/2 OZ)**
Salt	**20 G (3/4 OZ)**
Honey	**15 G (1/2 OZ)**
Yeast	**10 G (3/8 OZ)**
Stiff levain	**200 G (7 OZ)**
Unsalted butter	**70 G (2 1/2 OZ)**

TO FINISH

Egg whites	**AS NEEDED**
Sesame seeds	**AS NEEDED**

METHOD

BASE TEMPERATURE	50 to 54°C (120 to 130°F).
INCORPORATE	In a stand mixer, mix all the kneading ingredients in the bowl.
INITIAL MIX	On speed 1 for about 3 minutes.
KNEAD	On speed 2 for about 8 minutes.
CONSISTENCY	Medium-firm dough.
DOUGH TEMPERATURE	23°C (75°F).
BULK FERMENT	About 10 minutes.
WEIGHT	Seventeen 10-gram (3 7/8-oz) dough pieces.
PRESHAPE	Oval.
REST	About 10 minutes.
SHAPE	Stretch out the dough into logs, join the two ends, and press them together to make rings about 10 centimeter (4 inches) in diameter. Place them on guitar sheets.
FINAL PROOF	About 45 minutes.
SCALDING	Cook the bagels in boiling water for about 45 seconds on each side.
FINISH	Brush the bagels with egg white. Place them on baking sheets lined with parchment paper. Sprinkle with sesame seeds.
BAKE	In a deck oven at 220°C (430°F) for about 16 minutes.
COOL	On a wire rack.

MANTOU BUNS

THESE CHINESE ROLLS OWE THEIR CRUSTLESSNESS AND WHITE COLOR TO THE FACT THEY ARE MADE WITH WHEAT FLOUR AND THEN STEAMED. TRADITIONALLY SERVED WITH MEAT AND VEGETABLE DISHES, THEY CAN BE STUFFED WITH A VARIETY OF FILLINGS.

MAKES 31 BUNS

KNEADING INGREDIENTS

Bread flour (T65)	**1 KG (2 LB 3 1/4 OZ)**
Water	**550 G (1 LB 3 3/8 OZ)**
Salt	**18 G (5/8 OZ)**
Superfine sugar	**50 G (1 3/4 OZ)**
Yeast	**25 G (7/8 OZ)**
Baking powder	**15 G (1/2 OZ)**
Fermented dough	**1 KG (2 LB 3 1/4 OZ)**
Soybean oil	**25 G (7/8 OZ)**

METHOD

BASE TEMPERATURE	60 to 64°C (140 to 145°F).
INCORPORATE	In a stand mixer, mix all the kneading ingredients in the bowl.
INITIAL MIX	On speed 1 for about 3 minutes.
KNEAD	On speed 2 for about 5 minutes.
CONSISTENCY	Firm dough.
DOUGH TEMPERATURE	23°C (75°F).
BULK FERMENT	About 10 minutes.
WEIGHT	Thirty-one 85-gram (3-oz) dough pieces.
PRESHAPE	Shape into balls.
REST	About 15 minutes.
SHAPE	Shape into balls, then place them on baking sheets lined with parchment paper.
FINAL PROOF	At 27°C (80°F) for about 30 minutes.
BAKE	In a steamer at 100°C (212°F) for about 12 minutes.
COOL	On a wire rack.

RUGBRØD

A DARK RYE LOAF ENRICHED WITH OATS AND SEEDS, THIS IS THE ULTIMATE DANISH BREAD. IT FORMS THE BASE FOR THE DANES' NATIONAL DISH, THE FAMOUS *SMØRREBRØD*—SLICES OF BREAD WITH A VARIETY OF TOPPINGS, RESULTING IN COLORFUL OPEN SANDWICHES. ANOTHER BENEFIT OF THIS BREAD IS THAT IT HAS A LONG SHELF LIFE, AND IT CAN ALSO BE RECYCLED INTO CRISPY CHIPS WITH AN AROMA OF TOASTED SEEDS.

MAKES 9 LOAVES

REFRESHMENT

Rye flour (T170)	**500 G (1 LB 1 5/8 OZ)**
Water at 12°C (55°F)	**500 G (1 LB 1 5/8 OZ)**
Black malt	**20 G (3/4 OZ)**
Stiff levain	**10 G (3/8 OZ)**

SEED MIX

Old-fashioned oats	**500 G (1 LB 1 5/8 OZ)**
Sunflower seeds	**500 G (1 LB 1 5/8 OZ)**
Golden flaxseed	**300 G (10 1/2 OZ)**
Water at 60°C (140°F)	**1.2 KG (2 LB 10 3/8 OZ)**

KNEADING INGREDIENTS

Whole-wheat flour (T150)	**400 G (14 OZ)**
Bread flour (T65)	**300 G (10 1/2 OZ)**
Rye flour (T170)	**150 G (5 1/4 OZ)**
Water	**750 G (1 LB 10 1/2 OZ)**
Salt	**50 G (1 3/4 OZ)**
Yeast	**10 G (3/8 OZ)**
Fermented dough	**400 G (14 OZ)**
Refreshment	**1 KG (2 1/4 LB)**

FINAL KNEADING

Seed mix	**2.5 KG (5 1/2 LB)**

TO FINISH

Old-fashioned oats	**AS NEEDED**

FOR THE REFRESHMENT

In a stand mixer, mix all the refreshment ingredients on speed 1 for 6 minutes.

Let ferment at room temperature for 15 hours.

FOR THE SEED MIX

Combine all the ingredients and let stand for 1 hour.

METHOD

BASE TEMPERATURE 72 to 76°C (160 to 170°F).

INCORPORATE In a stand mixer, mix all the kneading ingredients in the mixing bowl.

INITIAL MIX On speed 1 for about 3 minutes.

KNEAD On speed 2 for about 6 minutes.

INCORPORATE Add the seed mixture.

CONSISTENCY Soft, sticky dough.

DOUGH TEMPERATURE 35°C (95°F).

BULK FERMENT About 1 hour 30 minutes.

WEIGHT Using a bowl scraper, place 600-gram (1 lb 5 1/8-oz) portions of dough into nine greased 18 × 8 × 8-centimeter (7 × 3 1/4 × 7 3 1/4-inch) loaf pans.

FINISH Smooth the surface of the dough with a dampened hand, and sprinkle with oats.

FINAL PROOF About 1 hour 15 minutes.

BAKE In a deck oven at 240°C (465°F) for about 50 minutes, gradually lowering the temperature.

COOL On a wire rack.

POLAR BREAD

MAKES 16 LOAVES

KNEADING INGREDIENTS

Bread flour (T65)	**900 G (1 LB 15 ¾ OZ)**
Rye flour (T85)	**50 G (1 ¾ OZ)**
Potato flakes	**50 G (1 ¾ OZ)**
Water	**500 G (1 LB 1 ⅝ OZ)**
Salt	**18 G (⅝ OZ)**
Invert sugar	**50 G (1 ¾ OZ)**
Baking powder	**10 G (⅜ OZ)**
Yeast	**20 G (¾ OZ)**
Liquid levain	**100 G (3 ½ OZ)**
Sunflower oil	**70 G (2 ½ OZ)**

METHOD

BASE TEMPERATURE	54 to 56°C (130 to 135°F).
INCORPORATE	In a stand mixer, mix all the kneading ingredients in the bowl.
INITIAL MIX	On speed 1 for about 3 minutes.
KNEAD	On speed 2 for about 6 minutes.
CONSISTENCY	Medium-firm dough.
DOUGH TEMPERATURE	23°C (75°F).
BULK FERMENT	About 30 minutes.
WEIGHT	Sixteen 900-gram (1 lb 15 ¾-oz) dough pieces.
PRESHAPE	Oval.
REST	About 30 minutes.
PREP THE DOUGH PIECES	Roll out the dough pieces into 40 × 60-centimeter (15 ½ × 23 ½-inch) rectangles. Place them on silicone mats.
REST	About 30 minutes.
CUT TO SIZE	Using a 16-centimeter (6 ¼-inch)-diameter round pastry cutter, cut 16 disks from the dough pieces. Remove the scraps.
FINAL PROOF	About 1 hour.
FINISH	Prick with a roller docker or fork.
BAKE	In a deck oven at 260°C (500°F), or in a convection oven with steam at 200°C (390°F), for about 6 minutes.
COOL	Between two kitchen towels.

BURGER BUNS

ORIGINATING IN HAMBURG, GERMANY, BURGER BUNS ARE TYPICALLY ASSOCIATED WITH HAMBURGERS. THESE ROUND, SOFT BREAD ROLLS, OFTEN SPRINKLED WITH WHITE SESAME SEEDS, ARE WHAT MAKE THIS SANDWICH FAMOUS. TODAY, THEY ARE EMBLEMATIC OF AMERICAN CULTURE AND HAVE BECOME IMMENSELY POPULAR ALL AROUND THE WORLD.

MAKES 20 BUNS

KNEADING INGREDIENTS

Strong flour	**1 KG (2 LB 3 1/4 OZ)**
Water	**250 G (8 3/4 OZ)**
Milk	**270 G (9 1/2 OZ)**
Salt	**18 G (5/8 OZ)**
Superfine sugar	**80 G (2 7/8 OZ)**
Yeast	**30 G (1 OZ)**
Viennese fermented dough *(see page 28)*	**375 G (13 1/4 OZ)**
Unsalted butter	**200 G (7 OZ)**

TO FINISH

Sesame seeds	**AS NEEDED**

METHOD

BASE TEMPERATURE	48 to 52°C (120 to 125°F).
INCORPORATE	In a stand mixer, mix all the kneading ingredients in the bowl.
INITIAL MIX	On speed 1 for about 3 minutes.
KNEAD	On speed 2 for about 8 minutes.
CONSISTENCY	Medium-firm dough.
DOUGH TEMPERATURE	23°C (75°F).
BULK FERMENT	About 5 minutes.
WEIGHT	Twenty 110-gram (3 7/8-oz) dough pieces.
SHAPE	Shape into balls.
FINISH	Moisten the surface of the balls, then roll them in sesame seeds. Place the buns on baking sheets lined with parchment paper.
FINAL PROOF	At 27°C (80°F) for about 2 hours.
BAKE	In a deck oven at 200°C (390°F) for about 15 minutes.
COOL	On a wire rack.

INJERA

ORIGINALLY FROM ETHIOPIA, INJERA IS A THIN PANCAKE, 35 TO 50 CENTIMETERS (14 TO 19 ½ INCHES) IN DIAMETER, MADE WITH TEFF FLOUR AND WITHOUT SALT. YOU WILL NEED A LARGE SKILLET OR AN INJERA OVEN TO MAKE THEM. SERVING AS BOTH PLATE AND CUTLERY, THIS ATYPICAL YET TASTY BREAD IS A STAPLE OF MANY ETHIOPIAN MEALS.

MAKES 20 BREADS

REFRESHMENT

Teff flour	**1 KG (2 LB 3 ¼ OZ)**
Water at 25°C (75°F)	**1 KG (2 LB 3 ¼ OZ)**
Liquid levain	**100 G (3 ½ OZ)**

KNEADING INGREDIENTS

Water at 35°C (95°F)	**1 KG (2 LB 3 ¼ OZ)**
Yeast	**20 G (¾ OZ)**
Refreshment	**2.1 KG (2 LB 3 ¼ OZ)**

FOR THE REFRESHMENT

In a mixer fitted with the paddle attachment, beat all the ingredients on speed 1 for 3 minutes.
Leave to ferment for 12 hours.

METHOD

BASE TEMPERATURE 76 to 80°C (170 to 175°F).

INCORPORATE In a stand mixer fitted with a whisk attachment, whip all the kneading ingredients in the bowl.

INITIAL MIX On speed 1 for about 3 minutes.

KNEAD On speed 1 for about 2 minutes, then on speed 2 for 1 minute.

CONSISTENCY Batter.

DOUGH TEMPERATURE 28°C (80°F).

FINAL PROOF About 3 hours.

BAKE In a greased, hot skillet, pour in 150 grams (5 ¼ oz) of the batter.
When firm, cover for about 1 minute to prevent it from drying out.
Repeat to create 20 breads in all.

COOL Between two kitchen towels.

CIABATTA

THIS ITALIAN BREAD, WHICH IS NOW POPULAR IN MANY COUNTRIES, IS CHARACTERIZED BY ITS HIGHLY HYDRATED DOUGH, TO WHICH OLIVE OIL IS OFTEN ADDED. BAKING IN A VERY HOT OVEN GIVES IT A FINE, CRISPY CRUST AND A CRUMB WITH A LOT OF AIR POCKETS. THIS BASIC BREAD IS USED WIDELY TO MAKE SANDWICHES.

MAKES 6 LOAVES

KNEADING INGREDIENTS

Bread flour (T65)	**1 KG (2 LB 3 1/4 OZ)**
Water	**600 G (1 LB 6 1/8 OZ)**
Salt	**22 G (3/4 OZ)**
Yeast	**7 G (1/4 OZ)**
Liquid levain	**300 G (10 1/2 OZ)**

FINAL KNEADING

Bassinage water	**120 G (4 1/4 OZ)**
Bassinage olive oil	**70 G (2 1/2 OZ)**

METHOD

BASE TEMPERATURE	54 to 58°C (130 to 135°F).
INCORPORATE	In a stand mixer, mix all the kneading ingredients in the bowl.
INITIAL MIX	On speed 1 for about 3 minutes.
KNEAD	On speed 1 for about 5 minutes, then on speed 3 for 1 minute.
INCORPORATE	Add the bassinage water, then drizzle in the bassinage olive oil.
CONSISTENCY	Soft dough.
DOUGH TEMPERATURE	23°C (75°F).
BULK FERMENT	About 1 hour 30 minutes, then at 3°C (35°F) for 12 hours.
FOLD TO DEGAS	After 1 hour 30 minutes.
SHAPE	Place the dough on a floured felt pad. Gently roll out the dough by hand, keeping the shape rectangular. Using a knife, cut out six rectangles of the same size. Place them on a lightly floured linen proofing cloth, seam side up.
FINAL PROOF	About 30 minutes.
BAKE	In a deck oven at 260°C (500°F) for about 14 minutes.
COOL	On a wire rack.

FOCACCIA

THE CHARACTERISTIC SOFT TEXTURE OF THIS FLAT BREAD FROM ITALY IS MAINLY DUE TO THE OLIVE OIL THAT IS ADDED DURING KNEADING. FOCACCIA COMES IN DIFFERENT VERSIONS IN ITS COUNTRY OF ORIGIN: SOMETIMES WITH SALT, FRESH TOMATOES, AND AROMATIC HERBS, AND IT CAN ALSO BE TOPPED WITH ONIONS, CHEESE, MEAT, OR VEGETABLES. SOME REGIONS EVEN HAVE SWEET VERSIONS.

MAKES 4 LOAVES

KNEADING INGREDIENTS

Bread flour (T65)	**875 G (1 LB 14 7/8 OZ)**
Potato flakes	**125 G (4 3/8 OZ)**
Water	**700 G (1 LB 8 3/4 OZ)**
Salt	**20 G (3/4 OZ)**
Yeast	**7 G (1/4 OZ)**
Liquid levain	**150 G (5 1/4 OZ)**

FINAL KNEADING

Bassinage water	**50 G (1 3/4 OZ)**
Bassinage olive oil	**75 G (2 5/8 OZ)**

TO FINISH

Olive oil	**AS NEEDED**
Salt flakes	**AS NEEDED**

METHOD

BASE TEMPERATURE	54 to 56°C (130 to 135°F).
INCORPORATE	In a stand mixer, mix all the kneading ingredients in the bowl.
INITIAL MIX	On speed 1 for about 3 minutes.
KNEAD	On speed 2 for about 6 minutes.
INCORPORATE	Add the bassinage water and olive oil in a thin stream.
CONSISTENCY	Soft dough.
DOUGH TEMPERATURE	23°C (75°F).
BULK FERMENT	About 2 hours, then at 3°C (35°F) for 12 hours.
FOLD TO DEGAS	After 1 hour of bulk fermentation.
WEIGHT	Four 500-grams (1 lb 1 5/8-oz) dough pieces.
SHAPE	Roll out the dough into 10 × 34-centimeter (4 × 13 1/2-inch) rectangles. Place the dough pieces on baking sheets lined with oiled parchment paper.
FINAL PROOF	About 1 hour 30 minutes.
FINISH	Make holes in the dough with oiled fingers, then sprinkle lightly with salt flakes.
BAKE	In a deck oven at 250°C (480°F) about 14 minutes.
COOL	On a wire rack.

MANAKISH

ORIGINALLY FROM LEBANON, THIS FLATBREAD IS MADE WITH A LEAVENED DOUGH, ROLLED OUT AND THEN TOPPED WITH OLIVE OIL AND A MIXTURE OF SPICES CALLED ZA'ATAR. THEY ARE SERVED FOLDED, FILLED WITH ONIONS, TOMATOES, AND CUCUMBERS. INEXPENSIVE TO MAKE AND EASY TO PREPARE, THESE STUFFED FLATBREADS ARE POPULAR IN LEBANON AND THROUGHOUT THE MIDDLE EAST, WHERE THEY ARE ENJOYED AT ALL TIMES OF THE DAY.

MAKES 14 FLATBREADS

KNEADING INGREDIENTS

Bread flour (T65)	**1 KG (2 LB 3 ¼ OZ)**
Water	**550 G (1 LB 3 ⅜ OZ)**
Salt	**20 G**
Honey	**10 G (⅜ OZ)**
Yeast	**10 G (⅜ OZ)**
Liquid levain	**100 G (3 ½ OZ)**
Olive oil	**50 G (1 ¾ OZ)**

TO FINISH

Za'atar	**140 G (5 OZ)**

ZA'ATAR

Thyme	**12 G (⅜ OZ)**
Sumac	**4 G (⅛ OZ)**
Toasted sesame seeds	**12 G (⅜ OZ)**
Olive oil	**120 G (4 ¼ OZ)**
Salt	**2 G (1/16 OZ)**
Lemon, zest only	¼

FOR THE ZA'ATAR

Mix all the ingredients together.

METHOD

BASE TEMPERATURE	56 to 60°C (135 to 140°F).
INCORPORATE	In a stand mixer, mix all the kneading ingredients in the bowl.
INITIAL MIX	On speed 1 for about 3 minutes.
KNEAD	On speed 2 for about 3 minutes.
CONSISTENCY	Firm dough.
DOUGH TEMPERATURE	24°C (75°F).
BULK FERMENT	About 1 hour.
WEIGHT	Fourteen 120-gram (4 ¼-oz) dough pieces.
PRESHAPE	Shape into balls.
REST	About 30 minutes, then at 3°C (35°F) for 1 hour.
SHAPE	Roll the dough pieces into 24-centimeter (9 ½-inch) disks.
FINISH	On the baking mat, brush the disks with the za'atar.
BAKE	In a deck oven at 280°C (535°F) for about 3 minutes.
COOL	Between two kitchen towels.

TORTILLA WRAPS

ORIGINALLY FROM MEXICO, THE TRADITIONAL RECIPE CALLS FOR CORN FLOUR, BUT MORE RECENTLY THEY ARE ALSO BEING MADE WITH WHEAT FLOUR. A UBIQUITOUS INGREDIENT IN THE MEXICAN DIET, THE TORTILLA DATES BACK THOUSANDS OF YEARS. TORTILLAS CAN BE USED TO ENWRAP MULTIPLE FILLINGS.

MAKES 13 TORTILLAS

KNEADING INGREDIENTS

Bread flour (T65)	**1 KG (2 LB 3 1/4 OZ)**
Water	**335 G (11 3/4 OZ)**
Salt	**18 G (5/8 OZ)**
Honey	**95 G (3 3/8 OZ)**
Baking powder	**5 G (3/16 OZ)**
Liquid levain	**200 G (7 OZ)**
Sunflower oil	**130 G (4 1/2 OZ)**

METHOD

BASE TEMPERATURE	54 to 58°C (130 to 135°F).
INCORPORATE	In a stand mixer, mix all the kneading ingredients in the bowl.
INITIAL MIX	On speed 1 for about 3 minutes.
KNEAD	On speed 2 for about 6 minutes.
CONSISTENCY	Firm dough.
DOUGH TEMPERATURE	24°C (75°F).
BULK FERMENT	No fermentation.
WEIGHT	Thirteen 130-gram (4 1/2-oz) dough pieces.
PRESHAPE	Shape into balls.
SHAPE	Using a dough sheeter, roll out the dough pieces into disks 1 millimeter (1/32 inch) thick and about 35 centimeters (14 inches) in diameter.
COOK	In a hot, dry pan for about 10 seconds per side.
COOL	Between two kitchen towels.

PITA BREADS

ORIGINATING IN THE MIDDLE EAST, PITA (OR PITTA) BREAD IS A ROUND, HOLLOW FLATBREAD THAT CAN BE FILLED WITH MEAT AND VEGETABLES. IT IS ALSO KNOWN AS LEBANESE, TURKISH, SYRIAN, OR ARABIC BREAD, AS WELL AS *KHUBZ* OR *BALADI*. IT IS SOMETIMES CALLED "GREEK BREAD," BECAUSE GREEK RESTAURANTS SERVE IT AS A BASE FOR SANDWICHES.

MAKES 19 FLATBREADS

KNEADING INGREDIENTS

Bread flour (T65)	**1 KG (2 LB 3 1/4 OZ)**
Water	**600 G (1 LB 6 1/8 OZ)**
Salt	**20 G (3/4 OZ)**
Yeast	**7 G (1/4 OZ)**
Liquid levain	**150 G (5 1/4 OZ)**

FINAL KNEADING

Bassinage water	**120 G (4 1/4 OZ)**
Bassinage olive oil	**50 G (1 3/4 OZ)**

METHOD

BASE TEMPERATURE	54 to 58°C (130 to 135°F).
INCORPORATE	In a stand mixer, mix all the kneading ingredients in the bowl.
INITIAL MIX	On speed 1 for about 3 minutes.
KNEAD	On speed 2 for about 6 minutes.
INCORPORATE	Add the bassinage water and olive oil in a thin stream.
CONSISTENCY	Soft dough.
DOUGH TEMPERATURE	23°C (75°F).
BULK FERMENT	About 1 hour, then at 3°C (35°F) for 12 hours.
FOLD TO DEGAS	After 1 hour.
WEIGHT	Nineteen 100-gram (3 1/2-oz) dough pieces.
PRESHAPE	Shape into balls.
REST	About 2 hours.
SHAPE	Gently degas the dough pieces while rolling them out into disks about 16 centimeters (6 1/4 inches) in diameter.
BAKE	In a deck oven at 280°C (535°F) for about 4 minutes.
COOL	Between two dish towels.

BLINIS

THE SINGULAR WORD FOR “BLINI” IS ACTUALLY THE RUSSIAN PLURAL FORM БЛИНЫ (TRANSCRIBED AS *BLINY* OR *BLINI*). IN ENGLISH, THE PLURAL IS “BLINIS.” BECAUSE OF THEIR SHAPE AND COLOR, BLINIS WERE A SYMBOL OF THE SUN IN PRE-CHRISTIAN TIMES AND WERE GIVEN RITUAL SIGNIFICANCE FOR SLAV PEOPLES. TRADITIONALLY BAKED AT THE END OF WINTER, THEY MARK THE RETURN OF THE SUN AND WARMER DAYS. THIS CUSTOM HAS BEEN ADOPTED BY THE ORTHODOX CHURCH AND IS STILL PRACTICED TODAY. BLINIS ARE ALSO SERVED AT FUNERAL WAKES TO HONOR THE DEAD.

MAKES 32 BLINIS

INGREDIENTS

Bread flour (T65)	**500 G (1 LB 1 5/8 OZ)**
Buckwheat flour	**500 G (1 LB 1 5/8 OZ)**
Milk	**1.56 KG (3 LB 7 OZ)**
Salt	**18 G (5/8 OZ)**
Yeast	**40 G (1 3/8 OZ)**
Egg yolks	**240 G (8 1/2 OZ)**
Egg whites	**360 G (12 5/8 OZ)**

METHOD

In a mixer fitted with the paddle attachment, beat all the ingredients except the egg yolks and whites.
Let ferment for 1 hour.
Add the egg yolks to the ferment mixture.
Beat the egg whites until stiff, then fold gently into the mixture.
Preheat a lightly greased 12-centimeter (5-inch)-diameter blini pan.
Pour 100 grams (3 1/2 oz) of the batter into the pan.
Cook the blini for about 3 minutes, then turn over.
Continue cooking for about 2 minutes.
Cool on a wire rack.
Repeat with the remaining batter to create 32 blinis in all.

CLA
· SS
· IC
· · ·

VIE
NNO
ISE
RIE

BOSTOCKS

MAKES 10 PASTRIES

INGREDIENTS

Day-old brioches mousseline	**2**
Almond cream *(see page 30)*	**300 G (10 ½ OZ)**

FOR THE RUM SYRUP

Water	**50 G (1 ¾ OZ)**
Superfine sugar	**50 G (1 ¾ OZ)**
Rum	**5 G (³⁄₁₆ OZ)**

TO FINISH

Sliced almonds	**AS NEEDED**
Confectioners' sugar	**AS NEEDED**

FOR THE RUM SYRUP

In a saucepan, combine the water, sugar, and rum. Bring to a boil, then set aside at 3°C (35°F).

METHOD

CUT TO SIZE From the brioche mousseline, cut ten 2.5-centimeter (1-inch)-wide slices.

FILL Lightly brush one side with the rum syrup. Using a pastry bag fitted with a number 8 round tip, cover the brioche slices with 30 grams (1 oz) of almond cream. Generously cover the tops of the bostocks with sliced almonds. Place them on baking sheets lined with parchment paper.

BAKE In a convection oven at 160°C (320°F), or in a deck oven at 190°C (375°F), for about 12 minutes.

COOL On a wire rack.

FINISH Sprinkle the bostocks with confectioners' sugar.

BRIOCHES À TÊTE

MAKES 45 BRIOCHES

KNEADING INGREDIENTS BRIOCHE DOUGH

Strong flour	**1 KG (2 LB 3 1/4 OZ)**
Eggs	**630 G (1 LB 6 1/4 OZ)**
Salt	**18 G (5/8 OZ)**
Superfine sugar	**150 G (5 1/4 OZ)**
Yeast	**30 G (1 OZ)**
Viennese fermented dough *(see page 28)*	**200 G (7 OZ)**

FINAL KNEADING INGREDIENTS

Unsalted butter	**500 G (1 LB 1 5/8 OZ)**

METHOD

BASE TEMPERATURE 48 to 52°C (120 to 125°F).

INCORPORATE In a stand mixer, mix all the kneading ingredients in the bowl.

INITIAL MIX On speed 1 for about 5 minutes.

KNEAD On speed 2 for about 5 minutes.

INCORPORATE Add the butter on speed 1 and mix until the dough is smooth.

CONSISTENCY Medium-firm dough.

DOUGH TEMPERATURE 23°C (75°F).

BULK FERMENT About 30 minutes, then at 3°C (35°F) for about 12 hours.

FOLD TO DEGAS Gently, after 30 minutes of bulk fermentation.

WEIGHT Forty-five 55-gram (2-oz) dough pieces.

PRESHAPE Shape into balls.

REST At 3°C (35°F) for about 2 hours.

SHAPE Shape the balls into cylinders. Divide each cylinder into two parts to make the body and head of each brioche. Place the bodies in greased brioche à tête molds and make a deep indentation in them. Shape the heads and place them in the center of the bodies.

FINAL PROOF At 27°C (80°F) for about 2 hours.

GLAZE Whisked egg.

BAKE In a convection oven at 145°C (295°F), or in a deck oven at 180°C (355°F), for about 14 minutes.

COOL On a wire rack.

CROISSANT

MAKES 30 CROISSANTS

KNEADING INGREDIENTS LEAVENED LAMINATED DOUGH

Strong flour	1 KG (2 LB 3 1/4 OZ)
Water	420 G (14 3/4 OZ)
Egg	50 G (1 3/4 OZ)
Salt	18 G (5/8 OZ)
Superfine sugar	130 G (4 1/2 OZ)
Yeast	40 G (1 3/8 OZ)
Viennese fermented dough *(see page 28)*	200 G (7 OZ)
Unsalted butter	100 G (3 1/2 OZ)

TURNING (TOURAGE)

Dry butter *(see page 10)*	500 G (1 LB 1 5/8 OZ)

METHOD

BASE TEMPERATURE	46 to 50°C (115 to 120°F).
INCORPORATE	In a stand mixer, mix all the kneading ingredients in the bowl.
INITIAL MIX	On speed 1 for about 3 minutes.
KNEAD	On speed 1 for about 8 minutes, then on speed 2 for 2 minutes.
CONSISTENCY	Medium-firm dough.
DOUGH TEMPERATURE	23°C (75°F).
WEIGHT	One 1.9-kilogram (4 ¼-lb) dough piece.
PRESHAPE	Shape into a ball.
BULK FERMENT	About 40 minutes.
FOLD TO DEGAS	After 20 minutes of bulk fermentation.
SHAPE	Oval.
BULK FERMENT	In the freezer for about 30 minutes, then at 1°C (35°F) for 12 hours.
TURNING (*TOURAGE*)	Degas the dough. Encase the butter in the dough, then make one single and one double turn *(see page 14)*.
REST	At 1°C (35°F) for about 45 minutes.
CUT TO SIZE	Using a dough sheeter, roll the dough to a thickness of 3.5 millimeters (3/16 inch), then cut into thirty 9 × 25-centimeter (3 ½ × 9 ¾-inch) triangles **(1)**. Make a cut in the center of the base of each triangle **(2)**.
SHAPE	Roll up the croissants **(3 to 7)**. Place them on baking sheets lined with parchment paper.
GLAZE	Whisked egg **(8)**.
FINAL PROOF	At 27°C (80°F) for about 2 hours.
GLAZE	Whisked egg.
BAKE	In a convection oven at 170°C (340°F), or in a deck oven at 200°C (390°F), for about 16 minutes.
COOL	On a wire rack.

1

2

3

4

5

6

7

8

HAM CROISSANTS

MAKES 30 CROISSANTS

KNEADING INGREDIENTS CROISSANT DOUGH

Strong flour	**1 KG (2 LB 3 1/4 OZ)**
Water	**250 G (8 3/4 OZ)**
Milk	**250 G (8 3/4 OZ)**
Salt	**18 G (5/8 OZ)**
Superfine sugar	**80 G (2 7/8 OZ)**
Yeast	**40 G (1 3/8 OZ)**
Unsalted butter	**70 G (2 1/2 OZ)**
Viennese fermented dough *(see page 28)*	**200 G (7 OZ)**

TURNING (TOURAGE)

Dry butter *(see page 10)*	**500 G (1 LB 1 5/8 OZ)**

FILLING

Ham, in 18-g (5/8-OZ) strips	**30**
Whole-grain mustard	**270 G (9 1/2 OZ)**

TO FINISH

Gruyère cheese, grated	**240 G (8 1/2 OZ)**

METHOD

BASE TEMPERATURE	46 to 50°C (115 to 120°F).
INCORPORATE	In a stand mixer, mix all the kneading ingredients in the bowl.
INITIAL MIX	On speed 1 for about 3 minutes.
KNEAD	On speed 1 for about 8 minutes, then on speed 2 for 2 minutes.
CONSISTENCY	Medium-firm dough.
DOUGH TEMPERATURE	23°C (75°F).
WEIGHT	One 1.91-kilogram (2 lb 3 1/4-oz) dough piece.
PRESHAPE	Shape into a ball.
BULK FERMENT	About 30 minutes.
FOLD TO DEGAS	After 15 minutes.
SHAPE	Oval.
BULK FERMENT	In the freezer for about 30 minutes, then at 1°C (35°F) for 12 hours.
TURNING (TOURAGE)	Degas the dough. Encase the dry butter in the dough. Make one single turn and one double turn *(see page 14)*.
REST	At 1°C (35°F) for about 45 minutes.
CUT TO SIZE	Using a dough sheeter, roll the dough to a thickness of 3.5 millimeters (3/16 inch), then cut into thirty 9 × 25-centimeter (3 1/2 × 9 3/4-inch) triangles. Spread a dash of whole-grain mustard and place one strip of ham on each one.
SHAPE	Roll up the croissants *(see page 189)*. Place them on baking sheets lined with parchment paper.
GLAZE	Whisked egg.
FINAL PROOF	At 27°C (80°F) for about 2 hours.
GLAZE	Whisked egg.
FINISH	Lightly sprinkle with grated Gruyère.
BAKE	In a convection oven at 180°C (355°F), or in a deck oven at 210°C (410°F), for about 20 minutes.
COOL	On a wire rack.

ALMOND CROISSANTS

MAKES 15 CROISSANTS

INGREDIENTS

Day-old croissants *(see page 186)*	**15**
Almond cream *(see page 30)*	**1.05 KG (2 LB 5 OZ)**

RUM SYRUP

Water	**50 G (1 ¾ OZ)**
Superfine sugar	**50 G (1 ¾ OZ)**
Rum	**5 G (3/16 OZ)**

TO FINISH

Sliced almonds	**AS NEEDED**
Confectioners' sugar	**AS NEEDED**

FOR THE RUM SYRUP

In a saucepan, combine the water, sugar, and rum. Bring to a boil. Set aside at 3°C (35°F).

METHOD

CUT Make a cut along the base of each croissant.

FILL Generously brush both sides with the rum syrup. Using a pastry bag fitted with a basketweave tip, pipe 40 grams (1 ⅜ oz) of almond cream on the lower area of the croissants, then close up with the upper part. Cover the top of the croissants with 30 grams (1 oz) of almond cream. Sprinkle the surface of the croissants with the sliced almonds to cover completely. Place them on baking sheets lined with parchment paper.

BAKE In a convection oven at 160°C (320°F), or in a deck oven at 190°C (375°F), for about 25 minutes.

COOL On a wire rack.

FINISH Sprinkle the croissants with confectioners' sugar.

DAVID BEDU'S STRIPED CROISSANTS

DAVID BEDU, A FRENCH BAKER FROM SANCERRE WHO NOW LIVES IN FLORENCE, ITALY, CREATED THIS STRIPED CROISSANT IN 2010. IT IS NOW A CLASSIC FRENCH VIENNOISERIE PRODUCT. INITIALLY, IT WAS PREPARED EITHER WITHOUT A FILLING OR WITH A GIANDUJA CREAM. A TRUE NOVELTY TEN YEARS AGO, THIS STRIPED CROISSANT HAS SINCE INSPIRED A HOST OF BAKERS AND IS A POPULAR PRODUCT IN MANY BAKERIES AROUND THE WORLD.

MAKES 30 CROISSANTS

PLAIN LEAVENED LAMINATED DOUGH

Croissant dough *(see page 186)*	**1.7 KG (3 ¾ LB)**
Dry butter *(see page 10)*	**500 G (1 LB 1 ⅝ OZ)**

FOR THE COCOA CROISSANT DOUGH

Croissant dough *(see page 186)*	**240 G (8 ½ OZ)**
Unsweetened cocoa powder	**24 G (⅞ OZ)**
Milk	**24 G (⅞ OZ)**
Unsalted butter	**12 G (⅜ OZ)**

FILLING (OPTIONAL)

Chocolate sticks 6 × 1.5 cm (2 ½ × ⅝ inches) *(see page 31)*	**30**

TO FINISH

Neutral syrup *(see page 31)*	**AS NEEDED**

FOR THE COCOA CROISSANT DOUGH

In a mixer fitted with the paddle attachment, mix the ingredients for the cocoa croissant dough on speed 1 until smooth. Bulk ferment for about 40 minutes, then rest at 1°C (35°F) for 12 hours.

METHOD

TURNING (TOURAGE) Degas the dough. Encase the butter in the 1.7 kilogram (3 ¾ lb) of dough. Make one single and one double turn *(see page 14)*. Moisten the surface of the dough, then roll out the cocoa croissant dough to the size of the turning (*tourage*) dough.

REST At 1°C (35°F) for about 45 minutes.

CUT TO SIZE Using a dough sheeter, roll out the dough to a thickness of 3.5 millimeters (3/16 inch).
Cut into thirty 9 × 25-centimeter (3 ½ × 9 ¾-inch) triangles.

SHAPE Roll the croissants *(see page 186)* with a chocolate stick (optional). Place them on baking sheets lined with parchment paper.

GLAZE Whisked egg.

FINAL PROOF At 27°C (80°F) for about 2 hours.

GLAZE Whisked egg.

BAKE In a convection oven at 170°C (340°F), or in a deck oven at 200°C (390°F), for about 16 minutes.

FINISH Brush with neutral syrup.

COOL On a wire rack.

DANISH PASTRIES

MAKES 32 PASTRIES

LEAVENED LAMINATED DOUGH

Croissant dough *(see page 186)*	**1.95 KG (4 1/4 LB)**
Dry butter *(see page 10)*	**500 G (1 LB 1 5/8 OZ)**

FILLING

Plain pastry cream *(see page 30)*	**640 G (1 LB 6 1/2 OZ)**
Apricot halves in syrup	**64**

TO FINISH

Neutral glaze	**AS NEEDED**
Confectioners' sugar	**AS NEEDED**

FOR THE APRICOT HALVES

Drain the apricot halves and place them on a wire rack. Dry in a convection oven, with the vent open, at 100°C (210°F) for about 15 minutes.

TURNING (TOURAGE) Degas the dough. Encase the dry butter in the dough. Make one single turn and one double turn *(see page 14)*.

REST At 1°C (35°F) for about 45 minutes.

CUT TO SIZE Using a dough sheeter, roll out the dough to a thickness of 3.5 millimeters (3/16 inch), then into a 44 × 88-centimeter (17 1/2 × 34 1/2-inch) rectangle. Cut into thirty-two 11-centimeter (4 1/4-inch) squares.

SHAPE Using a rolling pin, lightly roll down one of the tips of the squares, then moisten. This will make it easier to seal. Place a 20-gram (3/4 oz) strip of pastry cream diagonally, then place one apricot half on each side of the pastry cream. Fold over the two free corners, ending with the flatter, moistened corner. Place them on baking sheets lined with parchment paper.

GLAZE Whisked egg.

FINAL PROOF At 27°C (80°F) for about 2 hours.

GLAZE Whisked egg.

BAKE In a convection oven at 170°C (340°F), or in a deck oven at 200°C (390°F), for about 18 minutes.

COOL On a wire rack.

FINISH Dust the pastries with confectioners' sugar, then glaze the apricot halves.

PAIN AU CHOCOLAT

MAKES 30 PASTRIES

KNEADING INGREDIENTS
LEAVENED LAMINATED DOUGH

Strong flour	1 KG (2 LB 3 ¼ OZ)
Water	420 G (14 ¾ OZ)
Egg	50 G (1 ¾ OZ)
Salt	18 G (⅝ OZ)
Superfine sugar	130 G (4 ½ OZ)
Yeast	40 G (1 ⅜ OZ)
Viennese fermented dough *(see page 28)*	200 G (7 OZ)
Unsalted butter	100 G (3 ½ OZ)

TURNING (*TOURAGE*)

Dry butter *(see page 10)*	500 G (1 LB 1 ⅝ OZ)

FILLING

Chocolate sticks (5 g/ 3/16 OZ)	60

METHOD

BASE TEMPERATURE	46 to 50°C (115 to 120°F).
INCORPORATE	In a stand mixer, mix all the kneading ingredients in the bowl.
INITIAL MIX	On speed 1 for about 3 minutes.
KNEAD	On speed 1 for about 8 minutes, then on speed 2 for 2 minutes.
CONSISTENCY	Medium-firm dough.
DOUGH TEMPERATURE	23°C (75°F).
WEIGHT	One 1.95-kilograms (4 ¼-lb) dough piece.
PRESHAPE	Shape into a ball.
BULK FERMENT	About 40 minutes.
FOLD TO DEGAS	After 20 minutes of bulk fermentation.
SHAPE	Oval.
BULK FERMENT	In the freezer for about 30 minutes, then at 1°C (35°F) for 12 hours.
TURNING (TOURAGE)	Degas the dough pieces. Encase the dry butter in the dough. Make two double turns *(see page 14)*.
REST	At 1°C (35°F) for about 45 minutes.
CUT TO SIZE	Using a dough sheeter, roll out the dough to a thickness of 3.5 millimeters (3/16 inch). Cut into thirty 8.5 × 15-centimeters (3 3/8 × 6-inch) rectangles **(1)**.
SHAPE	Roll up the rectangles, incorporating two sticks of chocolate as you roll **(2, 3, 4, 5)**. Place them on baking sheets lined with parchment paper.
GLAZE	Whisked egg **(6)**.
FINAL PROOF	At 27°C (80°F) for about 2 hours.
GLAZE	Whisked egg.
BAKE	In a convection oven at 170°C (340°F), or in a deck oven at 200°C (390°F), for about 16 minutes.
COOL	On a wire rack.

1

2

3

4

5

6

MILK BREAD

MAKES 30 LOAVES

KNEADING INGREDIENTS
MILK BREAD DOUGH

Strong flour	**1 KG (2 LB 3 1/4 OZ)**
Milk	**660 G (1 LB 7 1/4 OZ)**
Salt	**18 G (5/8 OZ)**
Superfine sugar	**120 G (4 1/4 OZ)**
Yeast	**30 G (1 OZ)**
Viennese fermented dough *(see page 28)*	**200 G (7 OZ)**
Unsalted butter	**125 G (4 3/8 OZ)**

METHOD

BASE TEMPERATURE	46 to 50°C (115 to 120°F).
INCORPORATE	In a stand mixer, mix all the kneading ingredients in the bowl.
INITIAL MIX	On speed 1 for about 5 minutes.
KNEAD	On speed 2 for about 8 minutes.
CONSISTENCY	Medium-firm dough.
DOUGH TEMPERATURE	23°C (75°F).
BULK FERMENT	About 30 minutes.
WEIGHT	70-gram (2 1/2-oz) dough pieces.
PRESHAPE	Shape into balls.
REST	At 3°C (35°F) for about 12 hours.
SHAPED	Short, fat baguettes. Place them on baking sheets lined with parchment paper.
GLAZE	Whisked egg.
FINAL PROOF	At 27°C (80°F) for about 1 hour 15 minutes.
GLAZE	Whisked egg.
SCORE	With a pair of scissors.
BAKE	In a convection oven at 160°C (320°F), or in a deck oven at 190°C (375°F), for about 15 minutes.
COOL	On a wire rack.

RAISIN BREAD

MAKES 32 PASTRIES

LEAVENED LAMINATED DOUGH

Croissant dough *(see page 186)*	**1.95 KG (4 ¼ LB)**
Dry butter *(see page 10)*	**500 G (1 LB 1 ⅝ OZ)**

FILLING

Plain pastry cream *(see page 30)*	**500 G (1 LB 1 ⅝ OZ)**
Raisins	**280 G (9 ⅞ OZ)**
Water	**110 G (3 ⅞ OZ)**

TO FINISH

Neutral syrup *(see page 31)*	**AS NEEDED**

TOPPING

The day before, place the raisins in the water to soak. Cover with plastic wrap and set aside.

METHOD

TURNING (*TOURAGE*) Degas the dough. Encase the butter in the dough, then make one single and one double fold *(see page 14)*.

REST At 1°C (35°F) for about 45 minutes.

PRESHAPE Using a dough sheeter, roll out the dough to a thickness of 3.5 millimeters (³⁄₁₆ inch), then into a 40 × 128-centimeter (15 ½ × 50-inch) rectangle.

SHAPE Using a rolling pin, roll out the lower section of the dough to obtain a 4-centimeter (1 ½-inch) band, then moisten. Using a spatula, spread the pastry cream over the remaining dough, then sprinkle with the raisins. Roll up the dough to form a spiral, then seal with the thin band of moistened dough.

CUT TO SIZE Cut into 4-centimeter (1 ½-inch)-wide slices. Place them on baking sheets lined with parchment paper.

GLAZE Whisked egg.

FINAL PROOF At 27°C (80°F) for about 2 hours.

GLAZE Whisked egg.

BAKE In a convection oven at 170°C (340°F), or in a deck oven at 200°C (390°F). for about 18 minutes.

FINISH Brush the raisin breads with neutral syrup.

COOL On a wire rack.

BRIOCHE BREAD

MAKES 9 LOAVES

KNEADING INGREDIENTS

BRIOCHE DOUGH

Strong flour	**1 KG (2 LB 3 1/4 OZ)**
Eggs	**325 G (11 1/2 OZ)**
Milk	**325 G (11 1/2 OZ)**
Salt	**18 G (5/8 OZ)**
Superfine sugar	**150 G (5 1/4 OZ)**
Yeast	**30 G (1 OZ)**
Viennese fermented dough *(see page 28)*	**250 G (8 3/4 OZ)**

FINAL KNEADING

Unsalted butter	**250 G (8 3/4 OZ)**

METHOD

BASE TEMPERATURE	48 to 52°C (120 to 125°F).
INCORPORATE	In a stand mixer, mix all the kneading ingredients in the bowl.
INITIAL MIX	On speed 1 for about 5 minutes.
KNEAD	On speed 2 for about 5 minutes.
INCORPORATE	On speed 1, add the butter until the dough is smooth.
CONSISTENCY	Medium-firm dough.
DOUGH TEMPERATURE	23°C (75°F).
BULK FERMENT	About 30 minutes, then at 3°C (35°F) for 12 hours.
FOLD TO DEGAS	Lightly, after 30 minutes of bulk fermentation.
WEIGHT	Thirty-six 35-gram (1 1/4-oz) dough pieces and thirty-six 30-gram (1-oz) dough pieces.
PRESHAPE	Shape into balls.
REST	At 3°C (35°F) for about 1 hour.
SHAPE	Shape into balls. Place four 30-gram (1-oz) balls in the corners of greased 18 × 8 × 8 centimeter (7 × 3 1/4 × 3 1/4-inch) loaf pans, and four 35-gram (1 1/4-oz) balls in the center.
GLAZE	Whisked egg.
FINAL PROOF	At 27°C (80°F) for about 2 hours.
GLAZE	Whisked egg.
BAKE	In a convection oven at 145°C (295°F), or in a deck oven at 180°C (355°F), for about 20 minutes.
COOL	On a wire rack.

BEAR PAWS

MAKES 32 PASTRIES

LEAVENED LAMINATED DOUGH		FILLING	
Croissant dough *(see page 186)*	**1.95 KG (4 ¼ LB)**	Almond cream *(see page 30)*	**640 G (1 LB 6 ½ OZ)**
Dry butter *(see page 10)*	**500 G (1 LB 1 ⅝ OZ)**		

METHOD

TURNING (TOURAGE) Degas the dough. Encase the dry butter in the dough. Make one single turn and one double turn *(see page 14)*.

REST At 1°C (35°F) for about 45 minutes.

CUT TO SIZE Using a dough sheeter, roll out the dough to a thickness of 3 millimeters (⅛ inch), then into a 32 × 144-centimeter (12 ½ × 57-inch) rectangle. Cut into 9 × 16-centimeter (3 ½ × 6 ¼-inch) rectangles.

SHAPE Place 20 grams (¾ oz) of almond cream in the center of the rectangles. Moisten the edges of the rectangles as well as the lower section. Fold in half to form pockets, then seal. Using a knife, make three incisions about 2 centimeters (¾ inch) apart on the sealed side. Enlarge the incisions slightly. Turn the bear paws over and place them on baking sheets lined with parchment paper.

GLAZE Beaten egg.

FINAL PROOF At 27°C (80°F) for about 2 hours.

GLAZE Beaten egg.

BAKE In a convection oven at 170°C (340°F), or in a deck oven at 200°C (390°F), for about 16 minutes.

COOL On a wire rack.

CREAM-FILLED PLIÉS

MAKES 32 PASTRIES

LEAVENED LAMINATED DOUGH

Croissant dough *(see page 186)*	**1.95 KG (4 1/4 LB)**
Dry butter *(see page 10)*	**500 G (1 LB 1 5/8 OZ)**

FILLING

Pastry cream *(see page 30)*	**640 G (1 LB 6 1/2 OZ)**

TO FINISH

Confectioners' sugar	**AS NEEDED**

METHOD

TURNING (TOURAGE) Degas the dough. Encase the dry butter in the dough. Make one single turn and one double turn *(see page 14)*.

REST At 1°C (35°F) for about 45 minutes.

CUT TO SIZE Using a dough sheeter, roll out the dough to a thickness of 3 millimeters (1/8 inch), then into a 30 × 160-centimeter (11 3/4 × 63-inch) rectangle. Cut into 30 × 5-centimeter (11 3/4 × 2-inch) rectangles.

SHAPE Place 20 grams (3/4 oz) of pastry cream on the bottom half of the rectangles. Lightly moisten the edges around the cream. Fold the top half over and seal firmly. Turn the pliés over and place them on baking sheets lined with parchment paper.

GLAZE Whisked egg.

FINAL PROOF At 27°C (80°F) for about 2 hours.

GLAZE Whisked egg.

BAKE In a convection oven at 170°C (340°F), or in a deck oven at 200°C (390°F), for about 16 minutes.

COOL On a wire rack.

FINISH Dust the pastries with confectioners' sugar.

CHOCOLATE TWISTS

MAKES 32 PASTRIES

LEAVENED LAMINATED DOUGH		FILLING	
Croissant dough *(see page 186)*	**1.95 KG (4 1/4 LB)**	Pastry cream *(see page 30)*	**400 G (14 OZ)**
Dry butter *(see page 10)*	**500 G (1 LB 1 5/8 OZ)**	Chocolate chips	**260 G (9 1/8 OZ)**

METHOD

TURNING (TOURAGE) Degas the dough. Encase the dry butter in the dough. Make one single turn and one double turn *(see page 14)*.

REST At 1°C (35°F) for about 45 minutes.

PRESHAPE Using a dough sheeter, roll out the dough to a thickness of 3.5 millimeters (3/16 inch), then into a 46 × 96-centimeter (18 × 38-inch) rectangle.

SHAPE Using a spatula, spread the pastry cream over the entire dough and sprinkle with the chocolate chips.
Fold the dough in two to obtain a 23 × 96-centimeter (9 × 38-inch) rectangle.

CUT TO SIZE Cut into 3-centimeter (1 1/4-inch)-wide strips, twist the strips, and place them on Viennese baguette baking sheets lined with parchment paper.

GLAZE Whisked egg.

FINAL PROOF At 27°C (86°F) for about 2 hours.

GLAZE Whisked egg.

BAKE In a convection oven at 170°C (340°F), or in a deck oven at 200°C (390°F), for about 16 minutes.

COOL On a wire rack.

FLAKY
LEMON BRIOCHE

MAKES 6 PASTRIES

KNEADING INGREDIENTS

Strong flour	**1 KG (2 LB 3 ¼ OZ)**
Eggs	**420 G (14 ¾ OZ)**
Milk	**100 G (3 ½ OZ)**
Salt	**18 G (⅝ OZ)**
Superfine sugar	**40 G (1 ⅜ OZ)**
Yeast	**30 G (1 OZ)**
Butter	**250 G (8 ¾ OZ)**

FINAL KNEADING

Superfine sugar	**80 G (2 ⅞ OZ)**
Viennese fermented dough *(see page 28)*	**300 G (10 ½ OZ)**

TURNING (TOURAGE)

Dry butter *(see page 14)*	**460 G (1 LB ¼ OZ)**

LEMON SYRUP

Superfine sugar	**300 G (10 ½ OZ)**
Water	**200 G (7 OZ)**
Lemons	**2**
Limes	**2**

FOR THE LEMON SYRUP

Wash, zest, and squeeze the juice from the lemons and limes. Bring the water and sugar to a boil.
Add the zests, cover with plastic wrap, and set aside in the refrigerator. Add the lemon and lime juices to the cold syrup.

METHOD

BASE TEMPERATURE 50 to 54°C (120 to 130°F).
INCORPORATE In a stand mixer, mix all the kneading ingredients in the bowl.
INITIAL MIX On speed 1 for about 7 minutes.
INCORPORATE Add the 80 grams (2 ⅞ oz) of sugar and the fermented dough.
KNEAD On speed 1 for about 7 minutes, then on speed 2 for 1 minute.
CONSISTENCY Firm dough.
DOUGH TEMPERATURE 23°C (75°F).
BULK FERMENT About 20 minutes.
WEIGHT One 2.2-kilogram (4 lb 13 ½-oz) dough ball.
PRESHAPE Rectangle.
REST About 30 minutes, then at 3°C (35°F) for 12 hours.
TURNING (TOURAGE) Degas the dough. Encase 460 g (1 lb ¼ oz) of the dry butter in the dough. Make one single turn, then one double turn *(see page 14)*.
REST At 3°C (35°F) for about 45 minutes.
CUT TO SIZE Cut the dough in half lengthwise and place one half on top of the other. Roll out the dough into a roughly 100 × 28 centimeter (39 × 11 inch) rectangle. Cut into six strips lengthwise.
SHAPE Fold up the pastry strips accordion style, then place them resting on one side in greased 30 × 8 × 8-centimeter (11 ¾ × 3 ¼ × 3 ¼-inch) loaf pans.
FINAL PROOF About 2 hours 30 minutes.
BAKE In a convection oven at 155°C (310°F) for about 30 minutes.
FINISH Soak the pastries generously with the lemon and lime syrup.
COOL On a wire rack.

BEIGNETS

IN CHRISTIAN COUNTRIES, BEFORE LENT AND ITS DAYS OF ABSTINENCE, IT WAS TRADITIONAL TO CELEBRATE AND EAT "FATS" (HENCE THE FAMOUS *MARDI GRAS*, OR "FAT TUESDAY"). WITH SO MANY PEOPLE CELEBRATING, PASTRIES HAD TO BE MADE QUICKLY AND CHEAPLY. IT WAS ALSO A QUESTION OF USING UP STOCKS OF BUTTER, OIL, AND EGGS BEFORE THE 40 DAYS OF FASTING THAT WERE TO FOLLOW, WHICH IS HOW THE BEIGNET CAME ABOUT. DEPENDING ON THE REGION, BEIGNETS HAVE DIFFERENT NAMES AND SHAPES; AMONG THEM, THEY ARE CALLED BUGNES IN LYON, MERVEILLES IN BORDEAUX, BOTTEREAUX IN NANTES, ROUSSETTES IN PROVENCE, TOURTISSEAUX IN POITOU.

MAKES 120 BEIGNETS

KNEADING INGREDIENTS

Strong flour	**1 KG (2 LB 3 ¼ OZ)**
Eggs	**200 G (7 OZ)**
Milk	**250 G (8 ¾ OZ)**
Orange blossom water	**50 G (1 ¾ OZ)**
Salt	**22 G (¾ OZ)**
Superfine sugar	**200 G (7 OZ)**
Yeast	**25 G (⅞ OZ)**
Liquid levain	**300 G (10 ½ OZ)**

FINAL KNEADING

Unsalted butter	**400 G (14 OZ)**
Lemons, zest only	**2**
Oranges, zest only	**2**

TO FINISH

Oil	**AS NEEDED**
Confectioners' sugar	**AS NEEDED**

METHOD

BASE TEMPERATURE	48 to 52°C (120 to 125°F).
INCORPORATE	In a stand mixer, mix all the kneading ingredients in the bowl.
INITIAL MIX	On speed 1 for about 3 minutes.
KNEAD	On speed 2 for about 6 minutes.
INCORPORATE	On speed 1, add the butter and mix until the dough is smooth. Add the zests.
CONSISTENCY	Medium-firm dough.
DOUGH TEMPERATURE	23°C (75°F).
BULK FERMENT	About 1 hour, then at 3°C (35°F) for 12 hours.
CUT TO SIZE	Using a dough sheeter, roll out the dough to a thickness of 4 millimeters (⅛ inch). Cut into 5-centimeter (2-inch) diamond shapes.
SHAPE	Make an incision through the middle of the diamond and pass one end through the cut.
FINAL PROOF	At 24°C (75°F) on lightly greased guitar sheets for about 2 hours.
COOK	In oil heated to 180°C (355°F), fry for about 1 minute on each side.
COOL	On a wire rack.
FINISH	Sprinkle with confectioners' sugar.

BRIOCHE ROYALE

MAKES 10 LOAVES

KNEADING INGREDIENTS

Strong flour	**1 KG (2 LB 3 ¼ OZ)**
Eggs	**650 G (1 LB 7 OZ)**
Salt	**18 G (⅝ OZ)**
Superfine sugar	**150 G (5 ¼ OZ)**
Yeast	**25 G (⅞ OZ)**
Viennese fermented dough *(see page 28)*	**250 G (8 ¾ OZ)**

FINAL KNEADING

Unsalted butter	**500 G (1 LB 1 ⅝ OZ)**
Chocolate wafers (pistoles) 64%	**350 G (12 ⅜ OZ)**
Candied orange, diced	**350 G (12 ⅜ OZ)**
Roasted, skinned hazelnuts	**250 G (8 ¾ OZ)**

MACARONADE

Almond flour	**330 G (11 ⅝ OZ)**
Superfine sugar	**230 G (8 ⅛ OZ)**
Egg whites	**230 G (8 ⅛ OZ)**

TO FINISH

Sliced almonds	**AS NEEDED**
Confectioners' sugar	**AS NEEDED**

FOR THE MACARONADE

Mix the sugar and almond flour. Stir all the ingredients together.

METHOD

BASE TEMPERATURE 48 to 52°C (120 to 125°F).

INCORPORATE In a stand mixer, mix all the kneading ingredients in the bowl.

INITIAL MIX On speed 1 for about 5 minutes.

KNEAD On speed 2 for about 5 minutes.

INCORPORATE On speed 1, add the butter and mix until the dough is smooth. Add the chocolate wafers, diced candied orange, and hazelnuts.

CONSISTENCY Medium-firm dough.

DOUGH TEMPERATURE 23°C (75°F).

BULK FERMENT About 1 hour 30 minutes.

WEIGHT Ten 350-gram (12 ⅜-oz) dough pieces.

PRESHAPE Shape into balls.

REST About 30 minutes.

SHAPE Bâtard. Place them in greased 18 × 8 × 8-centimeter (7 × 3 ¼ × 3 ¼-inch) loaf pans.

FINAL PROOF At 3°C (35°F) for about 12 hours, then at 27°C (80°F) for 3 hours.

FINISH Coat the brioches with the macaronade, then sprinkle with the sliced almonds and confectioners' sugar.

BAKE In a deck oven at 180°C (355°F) for about 20 minutes.

COOL On a wire rack.

BRIOCHE CROWN

THE ORIGIN OF THE BRIOCHE GOES BACK TO MEDIEVAL TIMES, WITH RECIPES FROM THE PERIOD BASED ON FLOUR, YEAST, BUTTER, MILK, AND EGGS. AT THE TIME, BRIOCHES WERE ONE OF THE FESTIVE CAKES SERVED ON SPECIAL OCCASIONS, SUCH AS CHRISTENINGS, WEDDINGS, AND COMMUNIONS. TODAY, THE BRIOCHE IS ONE OF FRANCE'S MOST EMBLEMATIC PRODUCTS.

MAKES 10 LOAVES

KNEADING INGREDIENTS

Strong flour	**1 KG (2 LB 3 ¼ OZ)**
Eggs	**650 G (1 LB 7 OZ)**
Salt	**18 G (⅝ OZ)**
Superfine sugar	**150 G (5 ¼ OZ)**
Yeast	**25 G (⅞ OZ)**
Viennese fermented dough *(see page 28)*	**250 G (8 ¾ OZ)**

FINAL KNEADING

Unsalted butter	**500 G (1 LB 1 ⅝ OZ)**

METHOD

BASE TEMPERATURE	48 to 52°C (110 to 125°F).
INCORPORATE	In a stand mixer, mix all the kneading ingredients in the bowl.
INITIAL MIX	On speed 1 for about 5 minutes.
KNEAD	On speed 2 for about 5 minutes.
INCORPORATE	On speed 1, add the butter and mix until the dough is smooth.
CONSISTENCY	Medium-firm dough.
DOUGH TEMPERATURE	23°C (75°F).
BULK FERMENT	About 1 hour, then at 3°C (35°F) for 2 hours.
WEIGHT	Ten 250-gram (8 ¾-oz) dough pieces.
PRESHAPE	Shape into balls.
REST	At 3°C (35°F) for about 1 hour.
SHAPE	Rings. Place them on baking sheets lined with parchment paper.
FINAL PROOF	At 3°C (35°F) for about 12 hours, then at 27°C (80°F) for 3 hours.
GLAZE	Whisked egg.
SCORE	With a pair of scissors.
BAKE	In a deck oven at 180°C (355°F) for about 20 minutes.
COOL	On a wire rack.

KUGELHOPF

THERE ARE SO MANY STORIES ON HOW THIS DELICIOUS ALSATIAN SPECIALTY CAME ABOUT THAT IT IS DIFFICULT TO SAY WHICH MIGHT BE TRUE. THE OLDEST VERSION ATTRIBUTES ITS ORIGINS TO THE MAGI, OR THREE WISE MEN, WHOSE *KUGELHOPF* (MEANING "TURBANS") ARE SAID TO HAVE INSPIRED ITS SHAPE.

MAKES 8 CAKES

KNEADING INGREDIENTS

Strong flour	1 KG (2 LB 3 1/4 OZ)
Eggs	275 G (9 3/4 OZ)
Milk	275 G (9 3/4 OZ)
Salt	22 G (3/4 OZ)
Superfine sugar	180 G (6 3/8 OZ)
Yeast	20 G (3/4 OZ)
Liquid levain	300 G (10 1/2 OZ)

FINAL KNEADING

Unsalted butter	350 G (12 3/8 OZ)
Macerated raisins	500 G (1 LB 1 5/8 OZ)

MACERATED RAISINS

Water	140 G (5 OZ)
Raisins	400 G (14 OZ)
Vanilla bean	1

TO FINISH

Raw almonds	90 G (3 1/8 OZ)
Unsalted butter	300 G (10 1/2 OZ)
Granulated sugar	AS NEEDED

FOR THE MACERATED RAISINS

Bring the water to a boil. Pour the hot water over the raisins and the halved and scraped out vanilla bean, then set aside.

TO FINISH

Arrange the almonds in the bottom of the greased pans. Heat the butter to obtain a brown butter.

METHOD

BASE TEMPERATURE	48 to 52°C (120 to 125°F).
INCORPORATE	In a stand mixer, mix all the kneading ingredients in the bowl.
INITIAL MIX	On speed 1 for about 5 minutes.
KNEAD	On speed 2 for about 5 minutes.
INCORPORATE	On speed 1, add the butter and mix until the dough is smooth. Add the macerated raisins.
CONSISTENCY	Soft dough.
DOUGH TEMPERATURE	23°C (75°F).
BULK FERMENT	About 3 hours.
WEIGHT	Eight 360-gram (12 5/8-oz) dough pieces.
PRESHAPE	Shape into balls.
REST	At 3°C (35°F) for 30 minutes.
SHAPE	Pierce a hole through the center of the balls, shape into small rings, and place them in the pans.
FINAL PROOF	At 3°C (35°F) for about 12 hours, then at 27°C (80°F) for about 2 hours.
BAKE	In a convection oven at 145°C (295°F), or in a deck oven at 180°C (355°F), for about 25 minutes.
COOL	On a wire rack.
FINISH	Dip the kugelhopfs in the melted butter and let the butter soak in for 5 minutes. Roll in the granulated sugar.

ROI DE BORDEAUX

IN BORDEAUX, WHERE THIS CROWN IS CALLED A "PARISIAN GALETTE," THE RECIPE DOES *NOT* INCLUDE FRANGIPANE PASTE. IN THIS RECIPE, THE CROWNS ARE ROUND, GOLDEN, AND BRIOCHE LIKE, TOPPED WITH CANDIED FRUIT AND GRANULATED SUGAR. OF COURSE, THE PERSON WHO FINDS THE CHARM (OR, TRADITIONALLY, THE BEAN) BECOMES KING OR QUEEN OF THE DAY.

MAKES 8 CAKES

KNEADING INGREDIENTS

Strong flour	**1 KG (2 LB 3 ¼ OZ)**
Eggs	**450 G (15 ⅞ OZ)**
Salt	**18 G (⅝ OZ)**
Syrup	**450 G (15 ⅞ OZ)**
Yeast	**10 G (⅜ OZ)**
Viennese fermented dough *(see page 28)*	**400 G (14 OZ)**

FINAL KNEADING

Syrup	**280 G (9 ⅞ OZ)**

SYRUP

Unsalted butter	**300 G (10 ½ OZ)**
Orange juice	**50 G (1 ¾ OZ)**
Superfine sugar	**250 G (8 ¾ OZ)**
Orange blossom water	**100 G (3 ½ OZ)**
Rum	**30 G (1 OZ)**
Oranges, zest only	**2**
Lemon, zest only	**1**
Vanilla bean	**1**

TO FINISH

Green candied melon	**AS NEEDED**
Red candied melon	**AS NEEDED**
Granulated sugar	**AS NEEDED**

FOR THE SYRUP

Heat the ingredients. Cover with plastic wrap and set aside at 3°C (35°F).

METHOD

BASE TEMPERATURE 48 to 52°C (120 to 125°F).
INCORPORATE In a stand mixer, mix all the kneading ingredients in the bowl.
INITIAL MIX On speed 1 for about 3 minutes.
KNEAD On speed 1 for about 25 minutes.
INCORPORATE On speed 1, add the reserved syrup in a thin stream.
CONSISTENCY Soft dough.
DOUGH TEMPERATURE 23°C (75°F).
BULK FERMENT About 2 hours.
WEIGHT Eight 325-gram (11 ½-oz) dough pieces.
PRESHAPE Shape into balls.
REST About 30 minutes.
SHAPE Rings. Place them on baking sheets lined with parchment paper.
FINAL PROOF About 1 hour 30 minutes, then at 3°C (35°F) for 12 hours.
GLAZE Whisked egg.
FINISH Place the slices of candied melon in an attractive arrangement, then sprinkle the perimeter of the crown with granulated sugar.
BAKE In a deck oven at 180°C (355°F) for about 25 minutes.
COOL On a wire rack.

KOUIGN-AMANN

ORIGINALLY FROM THE TOWN OF DOUARNENEZ IN BRITTANY, THESE WERE ACCIDENTALLY INVENTED BY THE BAKER YVES-RENÉ SCORDIA IN ABOUT 1860. THIS IS A RICH DOUGH, THANKS TO THE BUTTER AND SUGAR IN IT. IN THE BRETON LANGUAGE, *KOUIGN* MEANS "CAKE" OR "BRIOCHE" AND *AMANN* MEANS "BUTTER."

MAKES 5 CAKES

KNEADING INGREDIENTS

Strong flour	**1 KG (2 LB 3 ¼ OZ)**
Milk	**700 G**
Salt	**25 G (⅞ OZ)**
Yeast	**20 G (¾ OZ)**
Unsalted butter	**100 G (3 ½ OZ)**

FINAL KNEADING

Bassinage milk	**150 G (5 ¼ OZ)**

TURNING (*TOURAGE*) INGREDIENTS

Dry butter	**800 G (1 ¾ LB)**
Superfine sugar	**800 G (1 ¾ LB)**
Vanilla bean	**1**

FOR THE TURNING (*TOURAGE*) INGREDIENTS

Scrape out the vanilla bean and stir the seeds into the sugar. Mix well and set aside.

METHOD

BASE TEMPERATURE 48 to 52°C (120 to 125°F).

INCORPORATE In a stand mixer, mix all the kneading ingredients in the bowl.

INITIAL MIX On speed 1 for about 3 minutes.

KNEAD On speed 2 for about 6 minutes.

INCORPORATE Add the bassinage milk in a thin stream.

CONSISTENCY Soft dough.

DOUGH TEMPERATURE 23°C (75°F).

BULK FERMENT About 1 hour.

WEIGHT One 2-kilogram (4 lb 6-oz) dough piece.

PRESHAPE Shape into a compact ball.

REST At 3°C (35°F) for about 12 hours.

TURNING (TOURAGE) After shaping the dry butter into a 30-centimeter (11 ¾-inch) square, encase the vanilla sugar in the butter using an envelope fold. Encase the butter in the rolled-out dough. Make one single turn, then one double turn *(see page 14)*.

CUT TO SIZE Using a dough sheeter, roll out the dough to a thickness of 6 millimeters (¼ inch), then to a 26 × 130-centimeter (10 ¼ × 51-inch) rectangle. Cut into five 25-centimeter (9 ¾-inch) squares.

SHAPE Fold the corners of each square into the center and invert it into a 22-centimeter (8 ¾-inch)-diameter silicone mold.

FINAL PROOF About 1 hour.

BAKE In a convection oven at 165°C (330°F), or in a deck oven at 180°C (355°F), for about 45 minutes.

COOL In the mold. After cooling, turn the kouign-amanns out onto a wire rack.

BUCKWHEAT OR SESAME KOUIGN-AMANNS

MAKES 40 CAKES

KNEADING INGREDIENTS

Strong flour	900 G
Toasted buckwheat flour	100 G (3 ½ OZ)
OR	
Strong flour	1 KG (2 LB 3 ¼ OZ)
Black sesame seeds, toasted and ground	70 G (2 ½ OZ)
Milk	700 G (1 LB 8 ¾ OZ)
Salt	25 G (⅞ OZ)
Yeast	20 G (¾ OZ)
Unsalted butter	100 G (3 ½ OZ)

FINAL KNEADING

Bassinage milk	150 G (5 ¼ OZ)

TURNING (*TOURAGE*)

Dry butter *(see page 10)*	800 G (1 ¾ LB)
Superfine sugar	800 G (1 ¾ LB)
Oranges, zest only	2
OR	
Black sesame seeds, toasted and ground	80 G (2 ⅞ OZ)

TO FINISH

Toasted buckwheat grains	AS NEEDED

FOR THE TOASTED INGREDIENTS

For the buckwheat recipe, toast the flour and buckwheat grains in a convection oven at 170°C (340°F) for about 20 minutes.
For the sesame seed recipe, toast the two quantities of black sesame seeds in a convection oven at 150°C (300°F) for about 25 minutes. Cool, then process in a food processor.

METHOD

BASE TEMPERATURE 48 to 52°C (120 to 125°F).
INCORPORATE In a stand mixer, mix all the kneading ingredients in the bowl.
INITIAL MIX On speed 1 for about 3 minutes.
KNEAD On speed 2 for about 6 minutes.
INCORPORATE Add the bassinage milk in a thin stream.
CONSISTENCY Soft dough.
DOUGH TEMPERATURE 23°C (75°F).
PRESHAPE Shape into a ball.
BULK FERMENT About 1 hour.
PRESHAPE Oval.
BULK FERMENT About 1 hour.
DEGAS Degas with a dough sheeter and make one single turn *(see page 14)*, then degas again.
REST At 1°C (35°F) for about 12 hours.
TURNING (*TOURAGE*) After making a 40-centimeter (15 ½-inch) square with the dry butter, encase the orange sugar or sesame sugar in the butter, using an envelope fold.
Encase the butter in the rolled-out dough. Make two double turns *(see page 14)*.
CUT TO SIZE Using a dough sheeter, roll out the dough to a thickness of 6 millimeters (¼ inch), then into a 38 × 92-centimeter (15 × 36-inch) rectangle.
Cut out forty 9-centimeter (3 ½-inch) squares.
SHAPE Fold the corners of each square into the center and invert into an 8-centimeter (3 ¼-inch)-diameter silicone mold.
FINAL PROOF At room temperature for about 1 hour.
BAKE In a convection oven at 165°C (330°F), or in a deck oven at 180°C (355°F), for about 35 minutes.
COOL In the molds. When cool, turn the kouign-amanns out onto a wire rack.

GALETTE COMTOISE

MAKES 8 GALETTES

BRIOCHE DOUGH

(see page 184)	**1 KG (2 LB 3 ¼ OZ)**

GOUMEAU MIXTURE

Orange blossom choux dough	**2.1 KG (2 LB 3 ¼ OZ)**
Pastry cream *(see page 30)*	**1.5 KG**

ORANGE BLOSSOM CHOUX DOUGH

Water	**700 G (1 LB 8 ¾ OZ)**
Unsalted butter	**280 G (9 ⅞ OZ)**
Superfine sugar	**280 G (9 ⅞ OZ)**
Salt	**20 G (¾ OZ)**
Strong flour	**420 G (14 ¾ OZ)**
Eggs	**560 G (1 LB ¾ OZ)**
Orange blossom water	**110 G (3 ⅞ OZ)**

FOR THE GOUMEAU MIXTURE

While the brioche dough is resting, make the choux dough *(see page 29)*, adding the orange blossom water after the eggs, then make the pastry cream *(see page 30)*. In a mixer fitted with the paddle attachment, stir the choux dough with the still-warm pastry cream until smooth.

METHOD

WEIGHT Eight 120-gram (4 ¼-oz) brioche dough pieces.
PRESHAPE Shape into balls.
REST At 3°C (35°F) for about 30 minutes.
SHAPE Using a rolling pin, roll out the brioche dough into 26-centimeter (10 ¼-inch)-diameter disks and place them on baking sheets lined with parchment paper
REST At 3°C (35°F) for about 30 minutes.
TOP Place 450 grams (15 ⅞ oz) of the warm goumeau mixture on each galette.
Using a spatula, spread the mixture to the edge of each brioche disk.
FINAL PROOF At 27°C (80°F) for about 30 minutes.
GLAZE Whisked egg. Brush over the entire surface of the disks.
FINISH Using a fork, make a square lattice pattern.
BAKE In a deck oven at 200°C (390°F), or in a convection oven at 180°C (355°F), for about 16 minutes.
COOL On a wire rack.

GÂCHE

ORIGINALLY FROM THE VENDÉE REGION, THIS IS A REGIONAL BREAD THAT WAS TRADITIONALLY MADE AT HOME FOR EASTER. IT WAS ALSO MADE FOR WEDDINGS, WHEN THE GODFATHER AND GODMOTHER WOULD OFFER IT TO THE BRIDE. THIS POPULAR PASTRY, WHICH CAN BE RECOGNIZED BY ITS OVAL SHAPE AND LENGTHWISE SLASH, IS USUALLY FLAVORED WITH RUM AND IS UNCTUOUS, THANKS TO THE CREAM USED IN ITS PREPARATION.

MAKES 7 LOAVES

KNEADING INGREDIENTS

Oat flour	**600 G (1 LB 6 1/8 OZ)**
Eggs	**200 G (7 OZ)**
Crème fraîche	**200 G (7 OZ)**
Salt	**18 G (5/8 OZ)**
Superfine sugar	**150 G (5 1/4 OZ)**
Yeast	**10 G (3/8 OZ)**
Sponge levain	**660 G (1 LB 7 1/4 OZ)**

FINAL KNEADING

Superfine sugar	**150 G (5 1/4 OZ)**
Unsalted butter	**250 G (8 3/4 OZ)**
Rum	**50 G (1 3/4 OZ)**

SPONGE LEVAIN

Oat flour	**400 G (14 OZ)**
Milk	**250 G (8 3/4 OZ)**
Yeast	**10 G (3/8 OZ)**

FOR THE SPONGE LEVAIN

Three hours before kneading, in a stand mixer, mix the flour, cold milk, and yeast in the bowl. Let ferment at room temperature for 3 hours.

METHOD

BASE TEMPERATURE 48 to 52°C (120 to 125°F).
INCORPORATE In a stand mixer, mix all the kneading ingredients in the bowl.
INITIAL MIX On speed 1 for about 3 minutes.
KNEAD On speed 2 for about 5 minutes.
INCORPORATE On speed 1, gradually add the sugar, butter, and rum until the dough is smooth.
CONSISTENCY Medium-firm dough.
DOUGH TEMPERATURE 23°C (75°F).
BULK FERMENT About 2 hours 30 minutes.
WEIGHT Seven 325-gram (11 1/2-oz) dough pieces.
PRESHAPE Shape into balls.
REST About 30 minutes.
SHAPED Short bâtards. Place the dough pieces on baking sheets lined with parchment paper.
FINAL PROOF At 3°C (35°F) for about 12 hours, then at 27°C (80°F) for 4 hours.
TO FINISH Let the dough pieces rest at 3°C (35°C) for a few minutes. This will make it easier to roll the dough.
GLAZE Whisked egg.
SCORE One slash.
BAKE In a deck oven at 160°C (320°F) for about 25 minutes.
COOL On a wire rack.

TARTE AU SUCRE

ORIGINALLY FROM THE NORTH OF FRANCE, THIS *TARTE* IS USUALLY MADE WITH A BRIOCHE DOUGH AND TOPPED WITH BUTTER AND SUGAR. THE LARGE AMOUNT OF BUTTER USED CAUSES HOLLOWS TO FORM IN THE DOUGH, WHICH IN FRENCH ARE CALLED *GOFFES* OR *GLAUS*. WHEN SUGAR WAS NOT SUCH A COMMON INGREDIENT, HONEY WAS USED AS A SWEETENER.

MAKES 10 TARTES

KNEADING INGREDIENTS

BRIOCHE DOUGH

Strong flour	1 KG (2 LB 3 1/4 OZ)
Eggs	650 G (1 LB 7 OZ)
Salt	18 G (5/8 OZ)
Superfine sugar	150 G (5 1/4 OZ)
Yeast	25 G (7/8 OZ)
Viennese fermented dough *(see page 28)*	250 G (8 3/4 OZ)

FINAL KNEADING

Unsalted butter	500 G (1 LB 1 5/8 OZ)

FILLING

Unsalted butter	350 G (12 3/8 OZ)
Superfine sugar	450 G (15 7/8 OZ)

METHOD

BASE TEMPERATURE	48 to 52°C (130 to 125°F).
INCORPORATE	In a stand mixer, mix all the kneading ingredients in the bowl.
INITIAL MIX	On speed 1 for about 5 minutes.
KNEAD	About on speed 2 for 5 minutes.
INCORPORATE	On speed 1, add the butter and mix until the dough is smooth.
CONSISTENCY	Medium-firm dough.
DOUGH TEMPERATURE	23°C (75°F).
BULK FERMENT	About 1 hour, then at 3°C (37.4°F) for 12 hours.
WEIGHT	Ten 250-gram (8 3/4-oz) dough pieces.
PRESHAPE	Shape into balls.
REST	At 3°C (35°F) for about 1 hour.
SHAPE	Roll out the dough into 24-centimeter (9 1/2-inch)-diameter disks and place them on baking sheets lined with parchment paper
FINAL PROOF	At 27°C (80°F) for about 3 hours.
TOP	Insert small cubes of butter into the dough and sprinkle with sugar. No glaze.
BAKE	In a deck oven at 200°C (390°F) for about 15 minutes.
COOL	On a wire rack.

BATTU PICARD

ORIGINALLY FROM PICARDY, IN 1900 THIS CAKE WAS OFFICIALLY RECOGNIZED AS A REGIONAL SPECIALTY. ITS LIGHT TEXTURE IS ACHIEVED BY BEATING THE DOUGH FOR A LONG TIME, HENCE ITS NAME (*BATTU* MEANS "BEATEN"). BATTU PICARD IS OFTEN SERVED AT VILLAGE FESTIVALS AS WELL AS AT LARGE FAMILY CELEBRATIONS, SUCH AS CHRISTENINGS AND COMMUNIONS. BAKED IN A FLUTED, CYLINDRICAL MOLD, IT LOOKS LIKE A CHEF'S HAT.

MAKES 8 CAKES

KNEADING INGREDIENTS

Strong flour	**1 KG (2 LB 3 ¼ OZ)**
Eggs	**750 G**
Egg yolks	**250 G (8 ¾ OZ)**
Salt	**18 G (⅝ OZ)**
Yeast	**100 G (3 ½ OZ)**

FINAL KNEADING

Superfine sugar	**430 G**
Unsalted butter	**650 G (1 LB 7 OZ)**

METHOD

BASE TEMPERATURE	48 to 52°C (120 to 125°F).
INCORPORATE	In a mixer fitted with the paddle attachment, mix all the kneading ingredients in the bowl.
INITIAL MIX	On speed 1 for about 3 minutes.
KNEAD	On speed 3 for about 10 minutes.
INCORPORATE	On speed 1, gradually add the sugar, then the softened butter. On speed 2, beat until smooth.
CONSISTENCY	Very soft dough.
DOUGH TEMPERATURE	23°C (75°F).
BULK FERMENT	About 40 minutes.
WEIGHT	Using a bowl scraper, place 400 grams (14 oz) of dough into greased 16-centimeter (6 ¼-inch)-diameter picard molds.
FINAL PROOF	About 3 hours.
BAKE	In a convection oven at 145°C (295°F) for about 35 minutes, or in a deck oven at 165°C (325°F) for about 45 minutes.
COOL	On a wire rack.

OLIVE OIL BREAD

ORIGINALLY FROM PROVENCE-ALPES-CÔTE D'AZUR, THIS IS A SWEET FLATBREAD FLAVORED WITH OLIVE OIL AND CITRUS FRUIT. ONE OF THIRTEEN CHRISTMAS DESSERTS MADE IN PROVENCE, IT IS TRADITIONALLY BROKEN INTO PIECES IN THE WAY THAT CHRIST IS SAID TO HAVE BROKEN BREAD.

MAKES 7 LOAVES

KNEADING INGREDIENTS

Strong flour	1 KG (2 LB 3 1/4 OZ)
Water	400 G (14 OZ)
Eggs	150 G (5 1/4 OZ)
Orange juice	70 G (2 1/2 OZ)
Lemon juice	30 G (1 OZ)
Salt	18 G (5/8 OZ)
Superfine sugar	200 G (7 OZ)
Yeast	40 G (1 3/8 OZ)
Olive oil	100 G (3 1/2 OZ)

FINAL KNEADING

Lemon, zest only	1
Orange, zest only	1
Green anise seeds	5 G (3/16 OZ)
Olive oil	100 G (3 1/2 OZ)

TO FINISH

Olive oil	100 G (3 1/2 OZ)

METHOD

BASE TEMPERATURE 46 to 50°C (115 to 120°F).

INCORPORATE In a stand mixer, mix all the kneading ingredients in the bowl.

INITIAL MIX On speed 1 for about 3 minutes.

KNEAD On speed 2 for about 10 minutes.

INCORPORATE On speed 1, add the zests and green anise seeds, then the olive oil and mix until the dough is smooth.

CONSISTENCY Soft dough.

DOUGH TEMPERATURE 23°C (75°F).

BULK FERMENT About 2 hours.

WEIGHT Seven 300-gram (10 1/2-oz) dough pieces.

PRESHAPE Shape into balls.

REST About 1 hour.

SHAPE Roll out into 22-centimeter (8 3/4-inch)-diameter disks. Use a bowl scraper to make six cuts, then place them on baking sheets lined with parchment paper.

FINAL PROOF At 27°C (80°F) for about 2 hours.

BAKE In a deck oven at 200°C (390°F) for about 20 minutes.

FINISH Brush the loaves with olive oil.

COOL On a wire rack.

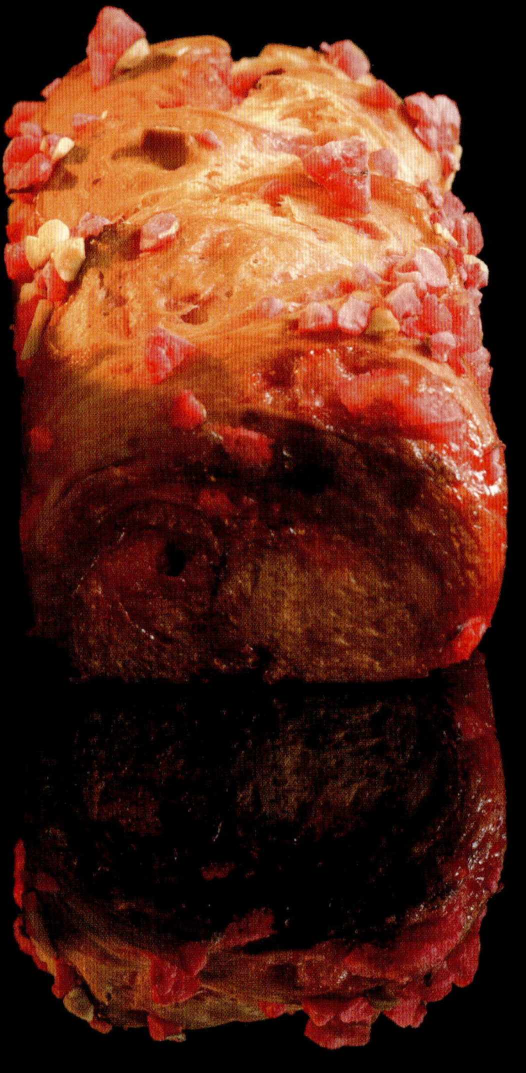

SAINT-GENIX

THIS BRIOCHE, STUDDED WITH PINK PRALINES, IS ORIGINALLY FROM SAINT-GENIX-SUR-GUIERS IN THE RHÔNE-ALPES REGION. DURING BAKING, THE PRALINES MELT A LITTLE, ADDING FLAVOR AND CREAMINESS TO THE BRIOCHE. INVENTED IN ABOUT 1880 BY PIERRE LABULLY, HIS ORIGINAL STORE STILL STANDS ON THE CHURCH SQUARE IN THE VILLAGE.

MAKES 6 LOAVES

KNEADING INGREDIENTS

Strong flour	1 KG (2 LB 3 ¼ OZ)
Eggs	300 G (10 ½ OZ)
Milk	250 G (8 ¾ OZ)
Salt	22 G (¾ OZ)
Superfine sugar	200 G (7 OZ)
Yeast	20 G (¾ OZ)
Liquid levain	300 G (10 ½ OZ)

FINAL KNEADING

Unsalted butter	400 G (14 OZ)
Crushed pink pralines	400 G (14 OZ)
Lemons, zest only	2

TO FINISH

Crushed pink pralines	AS NEEDED

METHOD

BASE TEMPERATURE 48 to 52°C (120 to 125°F).

INCORPORATE In a stand mixer, mix all the kneading ingredients in the bowl.

INITIAL MIX On speed 1 for about 5 minutes.

KNEAD On speed 2 for about 5 minutes.

INCORPORATE On speed 1, add the butter and mix until the dough is smooth. Mix in the zests, then the pink pralines.

CONSISTENCY Medium-firm dough.

DOUGH TEMPERATURE 23°C (75°F).

BULK FERMENT About 3 hours.

WEIGHT Six 480-gram (1-lb 1-oz) dough pieces.

SHAPE Oval.

REST 30 minutes.

SHAPE 30-centimeter (11 ¾-inch)-long logs. Place them in greased 30 × 8 × 8-centimeter (11 ¾ × 3 ¼ × 3 ¼-inch) loaf pans lined with parchment paper.

FINAL PROOF At 3°C (35°F) for about 12 hours, then at 27°C (80°F) for about 3 hours.

GLAZE Whisked egg.

FINISH Using a pair of scissors, make zigzag cuts on the surface of the brioche, then sprinkle with the crushed pink pralines.

BAKE In a convection oven at 145°C (295°F), or in a deck oven at 180°C (355°F) for about 25 minutes.

COOL On a wire rack.

PRALINE GALETTE

FROM THE RHÔNE-ALPES REGION, THIS BRIOCHE TART IS FILLED WITH CRUSHED PINK PRALINES AND CRÈME FRAÎCHE.

MAKES 8 GALETTES

KNEADING INGREDIENTS
BRIOCHE DOUGH

Strong flour	1 KG (2 LB 3 1/4 OZ)
Eggs	650 G (1 LB 7 OZ)
Salt	18 G (5/8 OZ)
Superfine sugar	150 G (5 1/4 OZ)
Yeast	25 G (7/8 OZ)
Viennese fermented dough *(see page 28)*	250 G (8 3/4 OZ)

FINAL KNEADING

Unsalted butter	500 G (1 LB 1 5/8 OZ)

FILLING

Créme fraîche	800 G (1 3/4 LB)
Crushed pink pralines	1.12 KG (2 LB 7 1/2 OZ)

METHOD

BASE TEMPERATURE 48 to 52°C (120 to 125°F).
INCORPORATE In a stand mixer, mix all the kneading ingredients in the bowl.
INITIAL MIX On speed 1 for about 5 minutes.
KNEAD On speed 2 for about 5 minutes.
INCORPORATE On speed 1, add the butter and mix until the dough is smooth.
CONSISTENCY Medium-firm dough.
DOUGH TEMPERATURE 23°C (75°F).
BULK FERMENT About 1 hour, then at 3°C (35°F) for 12 hours.
WEIGHT Eight 320-gram (11 1/4-oz) dough pieces.
PRESHAPE Shape into balls.
REST At 3°C (35°F) for about 1 hour.
SHAPE Roll out the dough into 28-centimeter (11-inch)-diameter disks and place them on baking sheets lined with parchment paper.
FINAL PROOF At 27°C (80°F) for about 2 hours 30 minutes.
FILL Using your fingertips, gently degas the edges of the galettes, then run a roller docker over the center or prick with a fork. Top each galette with 100 G (3 1/2 oz) of crème fraîche, then sprinkle with 140 grams (5 oz) of crushed pralines.
GLAZE Whisked egg. Brush the glaze around the perimeter of the galettes.
BAKE In a convection oven at 180°C (355°F) for about 18 minutes.
COOL On a wire rack.

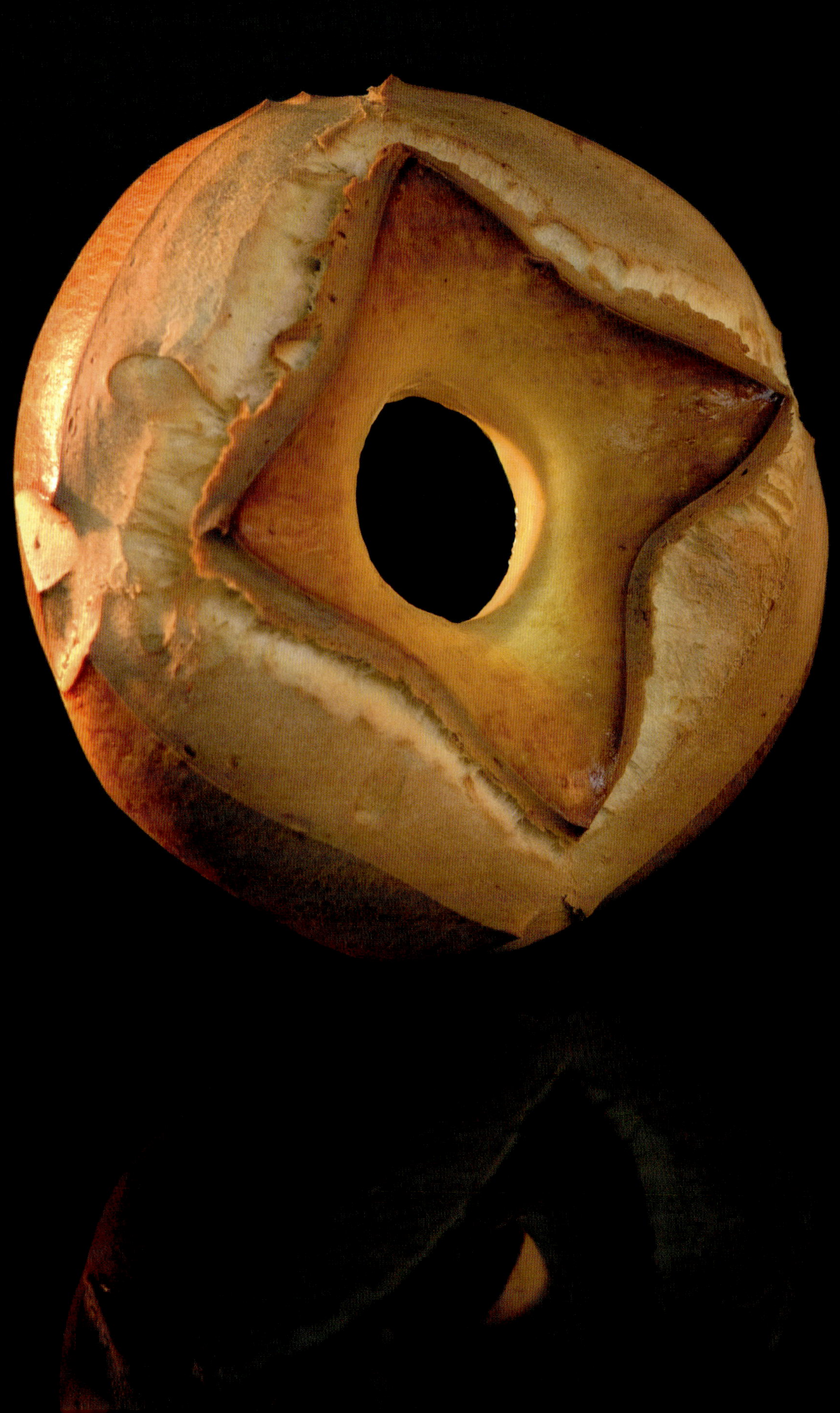

POGNE DE ROMANS

FROM THE TOWN OF ROMANS-SUR-ISÈRE IN THE DRÔME REGION, ITS DISTINCTIVE CHARACTER IS DUE TO A LEVAIN-BASED FERMENTATION PROCESS. TRADITIONALLY BAKED AT EASTER, ITS ORIGINS DATE BACK TO MEDIEVAL TIMES. ITS NAME REFERS TO A HANDFUL (*POGNE* MEANS "HAND" IN THE LOCAL DIALECT) OF DOUGH TAKEN FROM A BATCH OF BREAD DOUGH, WHICH IS THEN ENRICHED BY ADDING EGGS, BUTTER, ETC.

MAKES 3 LOAVES

KNEADING INGREDIENTS

Strong flour	**500 G (1 LB 1 $\frac{5}{8}$ OZ)**
Oat flour	**500 G (1 LB 1 $\frac{5}{8}$ OZ)**
Eggs	**350 G (12 $\frac{3}{8}$ OZ)**
Orange blossom water	**70 G (2 $\frac{1}{2}$ OZ)**
Rum	**40 G (1 $\frac{3}{8}$ OZ)**
Orange juice	**70 G (2 $\frac{1}{2}$ OZ)**
Salt	**24 G ($\frac{7}{8}$ OZ)**
Yeast	**2 G**
Stiff levain	**450 G (15 $\frac{7}{8}$ OZ)**
Unsalted butter	**250 G (8 $\frac{3}{4}$ OZ)**
Lemons, zest only	**2**
Oranges, zest only	**2**

FINAL KNEADING

Superfine sugar	**300 G (10 $\frac{1}{2}$ OZ)**

METHOD

BASE TEMPERATURE	54 to 58°C (130 to 135°F)
INCORPORATE	In a stand mixer, mix all the kneading ingredients in the bowl
INITIAL MIX	On speed 1 for about 3 minutes.
KNEAD	On speed 1 for about 25 minutes.
INCORPORATE	On speed 1, add the sugar until the dough is smooth.
CONSISTENCY	Firm dough.
DOUGH TEMPERATURE	25°C (75°F).
BULK FERMENT	About 4 hours.
WEIGHT	Three 850-gram (1 lb 14-oz) dough pieces.
SHAPE	Shape into not too compact balls.
REST	About 45 minutes.
SHAPE	Rings.
FINAL PROOF	At 24°C (75°F) for 12 to 24 hours, then at 3°C (35°F) for 24 to 48 hours.
GLAZE	Whisked egg.
SCORE	Square.
BAKE	In a deck oven at 180°C (355°F) for about 40 minutes.
COOL	On a wire rack.

MO

DE

RN

VIE
NNO
ISE
RIE

MARRON AND BLACK CURRANT BOSTOCKS

MAKES 10 PASTRIES

INGREDIENTS

Day-old Nanterre brioches *(see page 206)*	2

MARRON ALMOND CREAM

Almond flour	50 G (1 ¾ OZ)
Chestnut paste (*pâte de marron*)	30 G (1 OZ)
Superfine sugar	30 G (1 OZ)
Unsalted butter, softened	40 G (1 ⅜ OZ)
Eggs	50 G (1 ¾ OZ)

BLACK CURRANT CREAM

Black currant puree	80 G (2 ⅞ OZ)
Superfine sugar	20 G (¾ OZ)
Cornstarch	6 G (3/16 OZ)

FILLING

Marron cream	100 G (3 ½ OZ)
Neutral syrup *(see page 31)*	70 G (2 ½ OZ)

TO FINISH

Chopped toasted almonds	AS NEEDED
Confectioners' sugar	AS NEEDED

FOR THE MARRON ALMOND CREAM

In a stand mixer fitted with the paddle attachment, beat the marron paste and superfine sugar to loosen. Add the softened butter and almond flour and beat until smooth. Gradually add the eggs and beat the mixture for about 30 seconds. Set aside at 3°C (35°F).

FOR THE BLACK CURRANT CREAM

Combine the sugar and starch. In a saucepan, stir the black currant puree together with the starch-sugar mixture, then bring to a boil. Set aside in a pastry bag at 3°C (35°F).

METHOD

CUT TO SIZE Cut ten slices 2.5 centimeter (1 inch) wide from the Nanterre brioches.

FILL Lightly brush one side with the neutral syrup.
Pipe 10 grams (⅜ oz) of marron cream and 10 grams (⅜ oz) of black currant cream in fine lines on each slice, alternating the two creams. Using a pastry bag fitted with a basketweave tip, top with 20 grams (¾ oz) of marron almond cream. Generously top the surface of the bostocks with chopped toasted almonds. Place them on baking sheets lined with parchment paper.

BAKE In a convection oven at 160°C (320°F), or in a deck oven at 190°C, for about 14 minutes.

COOL On a wire rack.

FINISH Sprinkle with confectioners' sugar.

ORANGE BRIOCHES

MAKES 10 BRIOCHES

ORANGE BRIOCHE DOUGH

Brioche dough *(see page 184)*	**1 KG (2 LB 3 ¼ OZ)**
Candied orange, diced	**200 G (7 OZ)**
Orange blossom water	**25 G (⅞ OZ)**

ORANGE ALMOND PASTE

Almond paste 50%	**520 G (1 LB 2 ⅝ OZ)**
Orange juice	**26 G (⅞ OZ)**
Orange, zest only	**1**
Candied orange, diced	**260 G (9 ⅛ OZ)**

CRUNCHY ALMONDS

Chopped almonds	**100 G (3 ½ OZ)**
Superfine sugar	**100 G (3 ½ OZ)**
Water	**25 G (⅞ OZ)**

TO FINISH

Confectioners' sugar	**AS NEEDED**

FOR THE ORANGE BRIOCHE DOUGH

In a stand mixer, beat the orange brioche dough ingredients on speed 1 until smooth. Bulk ferment for about 45 minutes. Lightly fold to degas the dough, then proof at 3°C (35°F) for 12 hours.

FOR THE ORANGE ALMOND PASTE

In a stand mixer fitted with the paddle attachment, loosen the almond paste with the orange juice and zest, then add the diced candied orange. Set aside at 3°C (35°F) for 30 minutes. Divide the orange almond paste into 80-gram (2 ⅞-oz) pieces, then shape into ten 23-centimeter (9-inch)-long ropes. Cover with plastic wrap and set aside at 3°C (35°F).

FOR THE CRUNCHY ALMONDS

Bring the water and sugar to a boil to make a syrup. Boil for 1 minute, then add the almonds. Over a very low heat, stir constantly with a spatula until the sugar crystallizes. Spread the crunchy almonds on a baking sheet and set aside.

METHOD

PRESHAPE Using a dough sheeter, roll out the dough to a thickness of 4 millimeters (⅛ inch), then into a 46 × 40-centimeter (18 × 15 ½-inch) rectangle.

REST In the freezer for about 15 minutes.

CUT TO SIZE Cut out ten 23 × 8-centimeter (9 × 3 ¼-inch) strips.

SHAPE Lightly moisten the dough strips, then place a rope of orange almond paste down the center of each strip. Fold the two sides of the strips over the orange almond paste and seal. Pinch together the two ends of each dough piece and place them in greased 24 × 5 × 5 centimeter (9 ½ × 2 × 2-inch) loaf pan.

FINAL PROOF At 27°C (80°F) for about 2 hours 30 minutes.

GLAZE Beaten egg.

FINISH Top with a sprinkling of crunchy almonds.

BAKE In a deck oven at 160°C (320°F) for about 20 minutes.

COOL On a wire rack.

FINISH Sprinkle with confectioners' sugar.

SPICED BRIOCHES

MAKES 12 BRIOCHES

KNEADING INGREDIENTS

BRIOCHE DOUGH

Strong flour	1 KG (2 LB 3 ¼ OZ)
Eggs	650 G (1 LB 7 OZ)
Salt	18 G (⅝ OZ)
Invert sugar	60 G (2 ⅛ OZ)
Yeast	30 G (1 OZ)

FINAL KNEADING

Unsalted butter	500 G (1 LB 1 ⅝ OZ)
Spiced syrup	300 G (10 ½ OZ)
Candied melon, diced	400 G (14 OZ)
Candied orange, diced	100 G (3 ½ OZ)

SPICED SYRUP

Superfine sugar	300 G (10 ½ OZ)
Water	400 G (14 OZ)
Cloves	6
Star anise	5
Cinnamon sticks	4
Vanilla bean	½
Orange, zest only	1

ORANGE GLAZE

Orange juice	140 G (5 OZ)
Grand Marnier®	20 G (¾ OZ)
Confectioners' sugar	640 G (1 LB 6 ½ OZ)

FOR THE SPICE SYRUP

Bring the water and sugar to a boil. Add the remaining ingredients. Cover with plastic wrap and set aside. Strain before using.

FOR THE ORANGE GLAZE

Combine all the ingredients.

METHOD

BASE TEMPERATURE	48 to 52°C (120 125°F).
INCORPORATE	In a stand mixer, mix all the kneading ingredients in the mixing bowl.
INITIAL MIX	On speed 1 for about 3 minutes.
KNEAD	On speed 2 for about 8 minutes.
INCORPORATE	On speed 1, gradually add the butter, kneading until the dough is smooth, then add the spiced syrup and candied fruit.
CONSISTENCY	Soft dough.
DOUGH TEMPERATURE	23°C (75°F).
BULK FERMENT	About 2 hours.
WEIGHT	Twelve 250-gram (8 ¾-oz) dough pieces.
PRESHAPE	Shape into a ball.
REST	At room temperature for about 30 minutes.
SHAPE	Ring. Place the rings in greased 16-centimeter (6 ¼-inch) diameter Kugelhopf molds.
FINAL PROOF	At 27°C (80°F) for about 1 hour 15 minutes.
BAKE	In a convection oven at 150°C (300°F), or in a deck oven at 180°C (355°F), for about 30 minutes.
FINISH	Brush the brioches with the remaining spiced syrup.
COOL	On a wire rack.
TO FINISH	Glaze the brioches with the orange glaze. Dry in a convection oven, with the vent open, at 90°C (195°F) for about 3 minutes.

VANILLA AND CARAMEL BRIOCHES

MAKES 10 BRIOCHES

PLAIN BRIOCHE DOUGH

(see page 184)	**500 G (1 LB 1 5/8 OZ)**

VANILLA CARAMEL

Superfine sugar	**210 G (7 3/8 OZ)**
Whipping cream 35% fat	**140 G (5 OZ)**
Unsalted butter, softened	**140 G (5 OZ)**
Salt	**4 G (1/8 OZ)**
Vanilla bean	**1**

MACARONADE

Almond flour	**40 G (1 3/8 OZ)**
Confectioners' sugar	**40 G (1 3/8 OZ)**
Egg whites	**36 G (1 1/4 OZ)**

TO FINISH

Confectioners' sugar	**AS NEEDED**
Gold leaf	**AS NEEDED**

FOR THE VANILLA CARAMEL

In a saucepan, melt the sugar gradually over low heat to obtain a very light caramel. Over low heat, gently whisk in the cooled cream and cook until it reaches 110°C (230°F). Pour into a bowl and cool to 35°C (95°C). Add the softened butter, salt, and vanilla and stir until smooth. Set aside at 3°C (35°F) and use at room temperature.

FOR THE MACARONADE

Combine all the ingredients. Set aside at 3°C (35°F).

WEIGHT	Ten 50-gram (1 3/4-oz) dough pieces.
PRESHAPE	Shape into balls.
REST	At 3°C (35°F) for about 30 minutes.
SHAPE	Shape into balls, then flatten slightly. Place the dough pieces in greased 8-centimeter (3 1/4-inch) diameter, 6-centimeter (2 1/2-inch)-deep molds.
FINAL PROOF	At 27°C (80°F) for about 2 hours 30 minutes.
PREBAKE PREP	Using a pastry bag, pipe a thin layer of macaronade over each one, then sprinkle generously with confectioners' sugar.
BAKE	In a convection oven at 150°C (300°F), or in a deck oven at 180°C (355°F), for about 13 minutes.
COOL	On a wire rack.
TO FINISH	When cool, pierce the top of each brioche. Using a pastry bag, fill each brioche with 45 grams (1 1/2 oz) of vanilla caramel. Top each brioche with a drop of caramel and decorate with gold leaf.

LEMON AND BLACK CURRANT BRIOCHES

MAKES 40 BRIOCHES

KNEADING INGREDIENTS
LEMON BRIOCHE DOUGH

Strong flour	**1 KG (2 LB 3 1/4 OZ)**
Eggs	**650 G (1 LB 7 OZ)**
Salt	**18 G (5/8 OZ)**
Invert sugar	**60 G (2 1/8 OZ)**
Yeast	**30 G (1 OZ)**

FINAL KNEADING

Unsalted butter	**500 G (1 LB 1 5/8 OZ)**
Lemon and lime syrup	**300 G (10 1/2 OZ)**
Candied lemon and lime, diced and chopped	**250 G (8 3/4 OZ)**

LEMON AND LIME SYRUP

Superfine sugar	**150 G (5 1/4 OZ)**
Water	**200 G (7 OZ)**
Lemons, zest only	**2**
Limes, zest only	**2**

BLACK CURRANT CREAM

Black currant puree	**500 G (1 LB 1 5/8 OZ)**
Superfine sugar	**240 G (8 1/2 OZ)**
Custard powder	**30 G (1 OZ)**

BLACK CURRANT GLAZE

Black currant puree	**200 G (7 OZ)**
Confectioners' sugar	**700 G (1 LB 8 3/4 OZ)**

FOR THE LEMON AND LIME SYRUP

Bring the water and sugar to a boil. Add the zests and set aside at 3°C (35°F).

FOR THE BLACK CURRANT CREAM

Combine the sugar and custard powder. Bring the black currant puree to a boil. Add the sugar- and-custard mixture and bring to a boil. Set aside at 3°C (35°F).

FOR THE BLACK CURRANT GLAZE

Combine all the ingredients.

METHOD

BASE TEMPERATURE 48 to 52°C (120 to 125°F).

INCORPORATE In a stand mixer, mix all the kneading ingredients in the mixing bowl.

INITIAL MIX On speed 1 for about 3 minutes.

KNEAD On speed 2 for about 8 minutes.

INCORPORATE On speed 1, gradually add the butter and mix until the dough is smooth, then add the lemon and lime syrup and chopped candied lemon and lime.

CONSISTENCY Soft dough.

DOUGH TEMPERATURE 23°C (75°F).

BULK FERMENT About 2 hours.

WEIGHT Forty 70-gram (2 1/2-oz) dough pieces.

PRESHAPE Oval.

REST At room temperature for about 45 minutes.

SHAPE Degas the dough pieces lengthwise. Spread 16 grams (1/2 oz) of black currant cream over the length of the dough. Roll up the dough, making sure to keep the cream in the middle. Bring the two ends edge to edge to form a small ring. Place the rings in greased 10-centimeter (4-inch)-diameter Kugelhopf molds.

FINAL PROOF At 27°C (80°F) for about 1 hour 30 minutes.

BAKE In a convection oven (295°F) at 145°C, or in a deck oven at 180°C (355°F), for about 17 minutes.

COOL On a wire rack.

FINISH Glaze the brioches with the black currant glaze, then dry in a convection oven at 90°C (195°F) for 3 minutes.

FLAKY CAPPUCCINO BRIOCHES

MAKES 6 BRIOCHES

PLAIN DOUGH

Flaky brioche dough *(see page 29)*	**1.15 KG (2 ½ LB)**

COFFEE AND COCOA DOUGH

Flaky brioche dough *(see page 29)*	**1.07 KG (2 LB 5 ½ OZ)**
Coffee paste	**40 G (1 ⅜ OZ)**
Unsweetened cocoa powder	**20 G (¾ OZ)**
Water	**20 G (¾ OZ)**

TURNING (TOURAGE)

Dry butter *(see page 10)*	**460 G (1 LB ¼ OZ)**

FILLING

Chocolate sticks 3.5 × 1.5 centimeter (1 ⅜ × ⅝ inch) *(see page 31)*	**72**

COFFEE SYRUP

Superfine sugar	**100 G (3 ½ OZ)**
Espresso coffee	**125 G (4 ⅜ OZ)**

FOR THE COFFEE AND COCOA DOUGH

In a stand mixer fitted with the paddle attachment, beat the coffee and cocoa dough ingredients on speed 1 until smooth.
Bulk ferment about 40 minutes, then rest at 1°C (35°F) for 12 hours.

FOR THE COFFEE SYRUP

Stir the hot coffee and sugar together. Set aside at 3°C (35°F).

METHOD

TURNING (*TOURAGE*) Degas the dough pieces. Encase the butter between the plain and coffee-cocoa dough pieces. Make two single turns *(see page 14)*.

REST At 1°C (35°F) for about 45 minutes.

PRESHAPE Using a dough sheeter, roll out the dough into a 60 × 30-centimeter (23 ½ × 11 ¾-inch) rectangle.

CUT TO SIZE Cut the dough in half lengthwise and place one half on top of the other.

PRESHAPE Using a dough sheeter, roll out the dough into a 100 × 30-centimeter (39 × 11 ¾-inch) rectangle.

CUT TO SIZE Cut six 100 × 5-centimeter (39 × 2-inch) strips.

SHAPE Fold the dough strips accordion style, then place them on their side in greased 30 × 8 × 8-centimeter (11 ¾ × 3 ¼ × 3 ¼-inch) loaf pans. Insert a chocolate stick into the hollow of each fold

FINAL PROOF At 27°C (80°F) for about 2 hours 30 minutes.

BAKE In a convection oven at 155°C (310°F), or in a deck oven 180°C (355°F), for about 30 minutes.

FINISH Generously brush the brioches with the coffee syrup.

COOL On a wire rack.

FLAKY CHOCOLATE BRIOCHES

MAKES 6 BRIOCHES

PLAIN DOUGH

Flaky brioche dough *(see page 29)*	**1.95 KG (4 LB 4 1/2 OZ)**
Dry butter	**460 G (1 LB 1/4 OZ)**

COCOA DOUGH

Flaky brioche dough *(see page 29)*	**250 G (8 3/4 OZ)**
Cocoa powder	**25 G (7/8 OZ)**
Water	**25 G (7/8 OZ)**

FILLING

Chocolate sticks 3.5 × 1.5 cm (1 3/8 × 5/8 inch) *(see page 31)*

TO FINISH

Neutral syrup *(see page 31)*

FOR THE COCOA DOUGH

In a stand mixer fitted with the paddle attachment, beat the cocoa dough ingredients on speed 1 until smooth. Bulk ferment about 40 minutes, then rest at 1°C (35°F) for 12 hours.

METHOD

TURNING (TOURAGE) Degas the dough. Encase the dry butter in the plain dough. Make two single turns *(see page 14)*. Moisten the surface of the dough, then roll out the cocoa dough to the size of the kneaded dough.

REST At 1°C (35°F) for about 45 minutes.

PRESHAPE Using a dough sheeter, roll out the dough into a 60 × 30-centimeter (23 1/2 × 11 3/4-inch) rectangle.

CUT TO SIZE Cut the dough in half lengthwise, then place one on top of the other, with the two plain sides facing together so that the chocolate sides are on the outside of the dough.

PRESHAPE Using a dough sheeter, roll out the dough into a 100 × 30-centimeter (39 × 11 3/4-inch) rectangle.

CUT TO SIZE Cut six 100 × 5-centimeter (39 × 5-inch) strips.

SHAPE Fold the dough strips accordion style, place them on their side in greased 30 × 8 × 8-centimeter (11 3/4 × 3 1/4 × 3/14-inch) loaf pans. Insert a chocolate stick into the hollow of each fold.

FINAL PROOF At 27°C (80°F) for about 2 hours 30 minutes.

BAKE In a convection oven at 155°C (310°F), or in a deck oven at 180°C (355°F), for about 30 minutes.

FINISH Generously brush the brioches with the syrup.

COOL On a wire rack.

SPONGE BRIOCHES

MAKES 4 BRIOCHES

KNEADING INGREDIENTS

BRIOCHE DOUGH

Strong flour	670 G (1 LB 7 $\frac{5}{8}$ OZ)
Salt	18 G ($\frac{5}{8}$ OZ)
Superfine sugar	115 G (4 OZ)
Yeast	25 G ($\frac{7}{8}$ OZ)
Eggs	260 G (9 $\frac{1}{8}$ OZ)
Sponge levain	543 G (1 LB 3 OZ)
White rum	60 G (2 $\frac{1}{8}$ OZ)
Orange blossom water	30 G (1 OZ)

FINAL KNEADING

Superfine sugar	115 G (4 OZ)
Unsalted butter	260 G (9 $\frac{1}{8}$ OZ)

SPONGE LEVAIN

Strong flour	330 G (11 $\frac{5}{8}$ OZ)
Water	150 G (5 $\frac{1}{4}$ OZ)
Orange blossom water	50 G (1 $\frac{3}{4}$ OZ)
Yeast	13 G ($\frac{1}{2}$ OZ)

FOR THE SPONGE LEVAIN

In a stand mixer fitted with the hook attachment, beat all the sponge levain ingredients on speed 1 for about 5 minutes.
Shape into a compact ball, then let ferment at room temperature for 1 hour.

METHOD

BASE TEMPERATURE 48 to 52°C (120 to 125°F).
INCORPORATE In a stand mixer, mix all the kneading ingredients in the mixing bowl.
INITIAL MIX On speed 1 for about 3 minutes.
KNEAD On speed 1 for about 15 minutes.
INCORPORATE On speed 1, add the sugar, then the butter until the dough is smooth.
CONSISTENCY Soft dough.
DOUGH TEMPERATURE 23°C (75°F).
BULK FERMENT 2 hours.
WEIGHT Four 500-gram (1 lb 1 $\frac{5}{5}$-oz) dough pieces.
SHAPE Gently shape into balls.
REST At room temperature for about 30 minutes.
SHAPE 30-centimeter (11 $\frac{3}{4}$-inch)-diameter rings. Place them on baking sheets lined with parchment paper.
FINAL PROOF At 27°C (80°C) for about 1 hour 30 minutes, then at 3°C (35°F) for 12 hours.
GLAZE Egg.
SCORE Score the rings to make a spiral design and let rest at room temperature for 1 hour.
BAKE In a convection oven at 145°C (295°F), or in a deck oven at 180°C (355°F), for about 45 minutes.
COOL On a wire rack.

VEGAN SQUASH BRIOCHES

MAKES 5 BRIOCHES

KNEADING INGREDIENTS

BRIOCHE DOUGH

Strong flour	**1 KG (2 LB 3 ¼ OZ)**
Salt	**18 G (⅝ OZ)**
Superfine sugar	**120 G (4 ¼ OZ)**
Yeast	**30 G (1 OZ)**
Water	**300 G (10 ½ OZ)**
Cooked squash	**400 G (14 OZ)**

FINAL KNEADING

Grapeseed oil	**200 G (7 OZ)**

COOKED SQUASH

Winter squash	**500 G (1 LB 1 ⅝ OZ)**
Olive oil	**20 G (¾ OZ)**

TO FINISH

Confectioners' sugar	**AS NEEDED**

FOR THE COOKED SQUASH

Wash the squash, cut it in half, and remove the seeds.
Brush the squash with the 20 grams (¾ oz) of olive oil.
Place it on a baking sheet lined with parchment paper.
Bake in a convection oven at 150°C (300°F) for about 30 minutes.
Puree the cooked squash in a food processor. Set aside at 3°C (35°F).

METHOD

BASE TEMPERATURE	48 to 52°C (120 to 125°F).
INCORPORATE	In a stand mixer, mix all the kneading ingredients in the mixing bowl.
INITIAL MIX	On speed 1 for about 5 minutes.
KNEAD	On speed 2 for about 5 minutes.
INCORPORATE	On speed 1, add the grapseed oil until the dough is smooth.
CONSISTENCY	Medium-firm dough.
DOUGH TEMPERATURE	23°C (75°F).
BULK FERMENT	About 1 hour, then at 3°C (35°F) for 12 hours.
FOLD TO DEGAS	After 1 hour of bulk fermentation.
WEIGHT	Five 400-gram (14-oz) dough pieces.
PRESHAPE	Shape into balls.
REST	At room temperature for about 1 hour.
SHAPE	Shape into balls. Place them in 16-centimeter (6 ¼-inch)-diameter panettone molds.
FINAL PROOF	At 27°C (80°F) for about 3 hours.
GLAZE	Water.
FINISH	Sprinkle with confectioners' sugar.
BAKE	In a convection oven at 145°C (295°F), or in a deck oven 180°C (355°F), for about 30 minutes.
COOL	Upside down for 1 hour. Use the needles provided with the molds and insert through the bottom of the molds.

VEGAN DRIED FRUIT BRIOCHES

MAKES 30 BRIOCHES

KNEADING INGREDIENTS
VEGAN BRIOCHE DOUGH

Oat flour	900 G (1 LB 15 3/4 OZ)
Purple sweet potato powder	100 G (3 1/2 OZ)
Salt	20 G (3/4 OZ)
Superfine sugar	150 G (5 1/4 OZ)
Yeast	50 G (1 3/4 OZ)
Coconut milk	400 G (14 OZ)
Water	175 G (6 1/4 OZ)

FINAL KNEADING

Superfine sugar	150 G (5 1/4 OZ)
Vegan margarine	300 G (10 1/2 OZ)
Raisins	70 G (2 1/2 OZ)
Pistachios, chopped	70 G (2 1/2 OZ)
Hazelnuts, chopped	70 G (2 1/2 OZ)

BLACKBERRY CREAM

Blackberry puree	600 G (1 LB 6 1/8 OZ)
Superfine sugar	100 G (3 1/2 OZ)
Pectin NH	10 G (3/8 OZ)

TO FINISH

Vegan margarine, melted	200 G (7 OZ)
Superfine sugar	300 G (10 1/2 OZ)
Purple sweet potato powder	45 G (1 1/2 OZ)

FOR THE BLACKBERRY CREAM

Gently heat the blackberry puree. Add the sugar-pectin mixture. Stir, then bring to a boil. Set aside in a pastry bag at 3°C (35°F).

METHOD

BASE TEMPERATURE 44°C to 48°C (110 to 120°F).

INCORPORATE In a stand mixer, mix all the kneading ingredients in the bowl.

INITIAL MIX On speed 1 for about 3 minutes.

KNEAD On speed 1 for about 15 minutes until the dough is smooth.

INCORPORATE On speed 1, gradually add the sugar and margarine until the dough is smooth, then add the dried fruit.

CONSISTENCY Soft dough.

DOUGH TEMPERATURE 23°C (75°F).

BULK FERMENT About 30 minutes, then at 3°C (35°F) for 12 hours.

FOLD TO DEGAS Lightly after 30 minutes of bulk fermentation.

WEIGHT Thirty 80-gram (2 7/8-oz) dough pieces.

REST At room temperature for about 30 minutes.

SHAPE Gently shape into balls.

REST At room temperature for about 30 minutes.

SHAPE Small rings. Place them in greased 9.5-centimeter (3 3/4-inch)-diameter Kugelhopf molds.

FINAL PROOF At 27°C (80°F) for about 3 hours.

BAKE In a convection oven at 150°C (300°F), or in a deck oven at 180°C (355°F), for about 22 minutes.

COOL On a wire rack.

FINISH Brush the brioches with the melted margarine, then let harden.
Roll the brioches in the sugar-purple sweet potato powder mixture. Pipe 20 grams (3/4 oz) of the blackberry mixture into the center of the brioches.

MINI RASPBERRY BRIOCHES

MAKES 20 BRIOCHES

TURMERIC BRIOCHE DOUGH

Brioche dough *(see page 184)*	1 KG (2 LB 3 ¼ OZ)
Ground turmeric	5 G (3/16 OZ)

RASPBERRY CREAM

Raspberry puree	500 G (1 LB 1 ⅝ OZ)
Superfine sugar	100 G (3 ½ OZ)
Pectin NH	10 G (⅜ OZ)

CRAQUELIN

Strong flour	75 G (2 ⅝ OZ)
Superfine sugar	75 G (2 ⅝ OZ)
Almond flour	75 G (2 ⅝ OZ)
Unsalted butter	85 G (3 OZ)
Salt	1 G (1/32 OZ)

FOR THE TURMERIC BRIOCHE DOUGH

In a stand mixer fitted with the paddle attachment, beat the brioche dough and turmeric on speed 1 until smooth. Bulk ferment for about 30 minutes. Lightly fold to degas the dough, then proof at 3°C (35°F) for 12 hours.

FOR THE RASPBERRY CREAM

Combine the sugar and pectin. Gently heat the raspberry puree, add the powder mixture, and bring to a boil. Set aside at 3°C (35°F).

FOR THE CRAQUELIN

In the stand mixer fitted with the paddle attachment, beat all the ingredients until smooth.

Using a dough sheeter, roll out the dough between two guitar sheets to a thickness of 1.5 millimeters (1/16 inch), then place it in the freezer until ready to use. Using an 8-centimeter (3 ¼-inch)-diameter pastry cutter, cut out 20 disks.

METHOD

WEIGHT Twenty 50-gram (1 ¾-oz) dough pieces.

REST At room temperature for about 20 minutes.

SHAPE Shape into compact balls. Place them on baking sheets lined with parchment paper.

FINAL PROOF At 27°C (80°F) for about 2 hours.

FINISH Place the frozen *craquelin* disks on the brioches, pressing gently.

BAKE In a deck oven at 150°C (300°C) for about 15 minutes.

COOL On a wire rack.

TO FINISH When cool, pierce the top of each brioche.
Using a pastry bag, fill each brioche with 30 grams (1 oz) of raspberry cream. Pipe a little raspberry cream rosette on top of each brioche.

TROPICAL CROISSANTS

MAKES 30 CROISSANTS

LEAVENED LAMINATED DOUGH

Croissant dough *(see page 186)*	1.95 KG
Dry unsalted butter *(see page 10)*	500 G (1 LB 1 5/8 OZ)

TROPICAL CREAM

Superfine sugar	280 G (9 7/8 OZ)
Cornstarch	80 G (2 7/8 OZ)
Mango puree	580 G (1 LB 4 1/2 OZ)
Passion fruit puree	580 G (1 LB 4 1/2 OZ)
Limes, zest only	2

PASSION FRUIT WATER GLAZE

Confectioners' sugar	2 KG (4 LB 6 OZ)
Passion fruit puree	250 G (8 3/4 OZ)
Water	250 G (8 3/4 OZ)

TO FINISH

Lime zest	AS NEEDED

FOR THE TROPICAL CREAM

Combine the superfine sugar and cornstarch. In a saucepan, combine the two purees and the sugar mixture, then bring to a boil. Let cool. Add the lime zest to the cooled cream. Set aside at 3°C (35°F).

FOR THE PASSION FRUIT WATER GLAZE

Combine all the ingredients. Set aside at 3°C (35°F).

METHOD

TURNING (*TOURAGE*) Degas the dough. Encase the dry butter in the dough. Make two double turns *(see page 14)*.

REST At 1°C (35°F) for about 45 minutes.

CUT TO SIZE Using a dough sheeter, roll out the dough to a thickness of 3.5 millimeters (3/16 inch). Cut into thirty 9 × 25 centimeter (3 1/2 × 9 3/4-inch) triangles.

SHAPE Roll the croissants *(see page 186)*. Place them on baking sheets lined with parchment paper.

GLAZE Whisked egg.

FINAL PROOF At 27°C (80°F) for about 2 hours.

GLAZE Whisked egg.

BAKE In a convection oven at 170°C (340°F), or in a deck oven at 200°C (390°F), for about 16 minutes.

COOL On a wire rack.

TO FINISH After cooling, pierce the sides of the croissants. Using a pastry bag, fill the inside of each croissant with 45 grams (1 1/2 oz) of tropical cream. Brush the croissants with the passion fruit water glaze, then sprinkle with lime zest. Dry in a ventilated oven, with the vent open, at 90°C (195°F) for 4 minutes.

VANILLA CRUFFINS

MAKES 32 CRUFFINS

LEAVENED LAMINATED DOUGH

Croissant dough *(see page 186)*	**1.95 KG (4 1/4 LB)**
Dry butter *(see page 10)*	**500 G (1 LB 1 5/8 OZ)**

VANILLA CREAM

Milk	**700 G (1 LB 8 3/4 OZ)**
Whipping cream 35% fat	**300 G (10 1/2 OZ)**
Eggs	**100 G (3 1/2 OZ)**
Egg yolks	**40 G (1 3/8 OZ)**
Superfine sugar	**200 G (7 OZ)**
Cornstarch	**60 G (2 1/8 OZ)**
Vanilla beans	**4**
Butter	**120 G (4 1/4 OZ)**

TO FINISH

Confectioners' sugar	**AS NEEDED**

FOR THE VANILLA CREAM

In a saucepan, heat the milk, cream, and vanilla in a saucepan. In a bowl, whisk together the eggs, egg yolks, and sugar, then add the cornstarch. Stir the two mixtures together and boil for 1 minute.

Remove from the heat, add the butter, and stir again. Set aside at 3°C (35°F).

METHOD

TURNING (*TOURAGE*) Degas the dough. Encase the dry butter in the dough. Make one single and one double turn *(see page 14)*.

REST At 1°C (35°F) for about 45 minutes.

CUT TO SIZE Using a dough sheeter, roll out the dough to a thickness of 3 millimeters (1/8 inch), then make into a 144 × 30-centimeter (57 × 11 3/4-inch) rectangle.

Cut thirty-two 4.5 × 30-centimeter (3/16 × 11 3/4-inch) strips

SHAPE Roll up the strips, but not too tightly.

Place them in greased 8-centimeter (3 1/4-inch)-diameter, 6-centimeter (2 1/2-inch)-deep molds.

FINAL PROOF At 27°C (80°F) for about 2 hours 30 minutes.

BAKE In a convection oven at 160°C (320°F), or in a deck oven at 200°C (390°F), for about 16 minutes.

TO FINISH When cool, pierce the underside of each cruffin.

Using a pastry bag, fill the inside of each cruffin with 45 grams (1 1/2 oz) of vanilla cream. Sprinkle lightly with confectioners' sugar.

FLAKY CUBES

MAKES 12 CUBES

KNEADING INGREDIENTS LAMINATED CUBE DOUGH

Strong flour	**750 G (1 LB 10 ½ OZ)**
Bread flour (T65)	**250 G (8 ¾ OZ)**
Water	**420 G (14 ¾ OZ)**
Eggs	**50 G (1 ¾ OZ)**
Salt	**18 G (⅝ OZ)**
Superfine sugar	**130 G (4 ½ OZ)**
Yeast	**50 G (1 ¾ OZ)**
Butter	**140 G (5 OZ)**
Viennese fermented dough *(see page 28)*	**100 G (3 ½ OZ)**

FOLDING

Dry butter *(see page 10)*	**500 G (1 LB 1 ⅝ OZ)**

METHOD

BASE TEMPERATURE	46°C to 50°C (115 to 120°F).
INCORPORATE	In a stand mixer, mix all the kneading ingredients in the bowl.
INITIAL MIX	On speed 1 for about 3 minutes.
KNEAD	On speed 1 for about 8 minutes and on speed 2 for 3 minutes.
CONSISTENCY	Medium-firm dough.
DOUGH TEMPERATURE	23°C (75°F).
WEIGHT	One 1.9-kg (4 ¼-lb) dough piece.
PRESHAPE	Shape into a ball.
BULK FERMENT	About 20 minutes.
FOLD TO DEGAS	After 10 minutes of bulk fermentation.
PRESHAPE	Oval.
FINAL PROOF	In the freezer for about 30 minutes, then at 1°C (35°F) for 12 hours.
TURNING (TOURAGE)	Degas the dough. Encase the dry butter in the dough. Make one single turn and one double turn *(see page 14)*.
REST	At 1°C (35°F) for about 45 minutes.
CUT TO SIZE	Using a dough sheeter, roll out the dough to a thickness of 3.5 millimeters (3/16 inch), then into a 50 × 78-centimeter (19 ½ × 30 ½-inch) rectangle. Cut twelve 50 × 6.5-centimeter (19 ½ × 2 ⅝-inch) strips.
SHAPE	Roll up the strips, but not too tightly. Place them in greased 12-centimeter (4 ¾-inch)-square molds.
FINAL PROOF	At 27°C (80°F) for about 2 hours 30 minutes.
PRE-BAKE PREP	Place the lids on the molds.
BAKE	In a convection oven at 160°C (320°F), or a deck oven at 180°C (355°F), for about 25 minutes.
COOL	On a wire rack.

APPLE KOUIGN-AMANNS

MAKES 24 PASTRIES

KNEADING INGREDIENTS
KOUIGN-AMANN DOUGH

Strong flour	**1 KG (2 LB 3 ¼ OZ)**
Milk	**700 G (1 LB 8 ¾ OZ)**
Salt	**25 G (⅞ OZ)**
Yeast	**20 G (¾ OZ)**
Butter	**100 G (3 ½ OZ)**

FINAL KNEADING

Bassinage milk	**150 G (5 ¼ OZ)**

TURNING (*TOURAGE*)

Dry butter *(see page 10)*	**800 G (1 ¾ LB)**
Superfine sugar	**800 G (1 ¾ LB)**

FILLING

Diced apple	**440 G (15 ½ OZ)**
Superfine sugar	**88 G (3 OZ)**
Cornstarch	**12 G (⅜ OZ)**
Vanilla beans	**2**

FOR THE FILLING

Mix the diced apples with the sugar and set aside at room temperature for at least 2 hours. Drain the apples. Add the starch and vanilla to the strained apple juice. Stir to dissolve the starch. Add the apples and cook in a saucepan until thickened. Fill twenty-four 9 × 2-centimeter (3 ½ × ¾-inch) silicone molds. Set aside in the freezer.

METHOD

BASE TEMPERATURE 48 to 52°C (120 to 125°F).

INCORPORATE In a stand mixer, mix all the kneading ingredients in the bowl.

INITIAL MIX On speed 1 for about 3 minutes.

KNEAD On speed 2 for about 6 minutes.

INCORPORATE Add the bassinage milk in a thin stream.

CONSISTENCY Soft dough.

DOUGH TEMPERATURE 23°C (75°F).

PRESHAPE Shape into a ball.

BULK FERMENT About 1 hour.

WEIGHT One 2-kilogram (4 lb 6-oz) dough piece.

PRESHAPE Shape into a compact ball.

FINAL PROOF At 3°C (35°F) for about 12 hours.

TURNING (*TOURAGE*) Make a 40-centimeter (15 ½-inch) square with the dry butter, then encase the sugar inside the butter using an envelope fold. Encase the butter inside the rolled-out dough.
Make two double turns *(see page 14)*.

CUT TO SIZE Using a dough sheeter, roll out the dough into a 30 × 86-centimeter (11 ¾ × 34-inch) rectangle. Cut out twenty-four 7 × 14 centimeter (2 ¾ × 5 ½-inch) rectangles.

SHAPE Place a frozen apple insert at the base of each rectangle and roll up tightly, making sure the apple insert stays in the center. Place the rolls in greased 13 × 4.5 × 4 centimeter (5 × 1 ¾ × 1 ½-inch) loaf pans, making sure that the apples are at the bottom of the molds.

FINAL PROOF At 27°C (80°F) for about 1 hour.

BAKE In a convection oven at 165°C (330°F), or a deck oven at 180°C (355°F), for about 35 minutes.

COOL In the molds. When cool, heat the sides of the molds with a blowtorch and turn the kouign-amanns out onto a wire rack.

TROPICAL KOUIGN-AMANNS

MAKES 40 PASTRIES

KNEADING INGREDIENTS KOUIGN-AMANN DOUGH

Strong flour	1 KG (2 LB 3 1/4 OZ)
Milk	700 G (1 LB 8 3/4 OZ)
Salt	25 G (7/8 OZ)
Yeast	20 G (3/4 OZ)
Butter	100 G (3 1/2 OZ)
Limes, zest only	3

FINAL KNEADING

Bassinage rum	100 G (3 1/2 OZ)

TURNING (*TOURAGE*)

Dry butter *(see page 10)*	800 G (1 3/4 LB)
Brown sugar	800 G (1 3/4 LB)
Vanilla bean	1

FOR THE TURNING (*TOURAGE*)

Scrape out the vanilla seeds and stir the seeds into the sugar, mix well, and set aside.

METHOD

BASE TEMPERATURE	48 to 52°C (120 125°F).
INCORPORATE	In a stand mixer, mix all the kneading ingredients in the mixing bowl.
INITIAL MIX	On speed 1 for about 3 minutes.
KNEAD	On speed 2 for about 6 minutes.
INCORPORATE	Add the bassinage rum in a thin stream.
CONSISTENCY	Soft dough.
DOUGH TEMPERATURE	23°C (75°F).
PRESHAPE	Shape into a ball.
BULK FERMENT	About 1 hour.
WEIGHT	One 1.9-kilogram (4 lb 4 1/2-oz) dough piece.
PRESHAPE	Shape into a compact ball.
REST	At 3°C (35°F) for about 12 hours.
TURNING (TOURAGE)	After shaping the dry butter into a 40-centimeter (15 1/2-inch) square, encase the vanilla sugar inside the butter using an envelope fold. Encase the butter inside the rolled-out dough. Make one single turn and one double turn *(see page 14)*.
CUT TO SIZE	Using a dough sheeter, roll out the dough to a thickness of 6 mm (1/4 inch), then into a 38 × 92-centimeter (15 × 36-inch) rectangle. Cut out forty 9-centimeter (3 1/2-inch) squares.
SHAPE	Fold the corners of each square into the center and invert inside an 8-centimeter (3 1/4-inch)-diameter silicone mold.
FINAL PROOF	At 27°C (80°F) for about 1 hour.
BAKE	In a convection oven at 165°C (330°F), or a deck oven at 180°C (355°F), for about 35 minutes.
COOL	In the molds.

LAUGEN CROISSANTS

MAKES 24 CROISSANTS

KNEADING INGREDIENTS

LAUGEN CROISSANT DOUGH

Strong flour	**1 KG (2 LB 3 1/4 OZ)**
Milk	**310 G (11 OZ)**
Water	**310 G (11 OZ)**
Salt	**20 G (3/4 OZ)**
Superfine sugar	**50 G (1 3/4 OZ)**
Yeast	**50 G (1 3/4 OZ)**
Butter	**80 G (2 7/8 OZ)**

TURNING (*TOURAGE*)

Dry butter *(see page 10)*	**400 G (14 OZ)**

PRETZEL SOLUTION

Hot water	**1 KG (2 LB 3 1/4 OZ)**
Sodium hydroxide	**50 G (1 3/4 OZ)**

TO FINISH

Pretzel salt	**AS NEEDED**

FOR THE PRETZEL SOLUTION

Gently mix the hot water and sodium hydroxide together.
Cover the container with plastic wrap and set aside at room temperature.

METHOD

BASE TEMPERATURE 46°C to 50°C (115 to 120°F).

INCORPORATE In a stand mixer, mix all the kneading ingredients in the mixing bowl.

INITIAL MIX On speed 1 for about 3 minutes.

KNEAD On speed 1 for about 8 minutes and on speed 2 for 3 minutes.

CONSISTENCY Medium-firm dough.

DOUGH TEMPERATURE 23°C (75°F).

WEIGHT One 1.8-kilogram (4-lb) dough piece.

PRESHAPE Shape into a ball.

BULK FERMENT About 40 minutes.

FOLD TO DEGAS After 20 minutes of bulk fermentation.

PRESHAPE Oval.

FINAL PROOF In the freezer for about 30 minutes, then at 1°C (35°F) for 12 hours.

TURNING (TOURAGE) Degas the dough. Encase the dry butter in the dough. Make two single turns *(see page 14)*.

REST At 1°C (35°F) for about 45 minutes.

CUT TO SIZE Using a dough sheeter, roll out the dough to a thickness of 4 millimeters (3/16 inch). Cut into twenty-four 9.5 × 28-centimeter (3 3/4-inch × 11-inch) triangles.

SHAPE Croissant *(see page 186)*. Dip them in the pretzel solution for about 15 seconds. Place them on lightly oiled baking sheets.

FINAL PROOF At 27°C (80°F) for about 1 hour 30 minutes.

FINISH Sprinkle with pretzel salt.

BAKE In a deck oven at 210°C (410°F) for about 18 minutes. Keep the oven door slightly ajar for about 4 minutes before the end of the baking time.

COOL On a wire rack.

MONT-BLANCS

MAKES 14 PASTRIES

LEAVENED LAMINATED DOUGH		TO FINISH	
Croissant dough *(see page 186)*	**1.95 KG (4 1/4 LB)**	Neutral syrup *(see page 31)*	**AS NEEDED**
Dry butter *(see page 10)*	**500G (1 LB 1 5/8 OZ)**		

TURNING (*TOURAGE*) Degas the dough. Encase the dry butter in the dough. Make one single turn and one double turn *(see page 14)*.

REST At 1°C (35°F) for about 45 minutes.

CUT TO SIZE Using a dough sheeter, roll out the dough to a thickness of 4 millimeters (1/8 inch), then into a 63 × 54-centimeter (25 × 21-inch) rectangle. Cut fourteen 4.5 × 54-centimeter (1 3/4 × 21-inch) strips.

SHAPE Roll up the strips, but not too tightly.
Place them in greased 16-centimeter (6 1/4-inch)-diameter springform pans.

FINAL PROOF At 27°C (80°F) for about 2 hours 30 minutes.

BAKE In a convection oven at 150°C (300°F), or a deck oven at 180°C (355°F), for about 28 minutes.

FINISH Lightly brush the mont-blancs with neutral syrup.

COOL On a wire rack.

CHOCOLATE NESTS

MAKES 6 PASTRIES

PLAIN BRIOCHE DOUGH

(see page 184)	**900 G (1 LB 15 3/4 OZ)**

CHOCOLATE BROWNIE

Butter	**160 G (5 5/8 OZ)**
Dark couverture chocolate 63%	**160 G (5 5/8 OZ)**
Superfine sugar	**160 G (5 5/8 OZ)**
Eggs	**110 G (3 7/8 OZ)**
Strong flour	**65 G (2 1/4 OZ)**

FOR THE MACARONADE

Confectioners' sugar	**100 G (3 1/2 OZ)**
Almond flour	**100 G (3 1/2 OZ)**
Egg whites	**100 G (3 1/2 OZ)**

CHOCOLATE GANACHE

Whipping cream 35% fat	**150 G (5 1/4 OZ)**
Dark couverture chocolate 63%	**150 G (5 1/4 OZ)**

TO FINISH

Confectioners' sugar	**100 G (3 1/2 OZ)**
Almonds, chopped	**100 G (3 1/2 OZ)**

FOR THE CHOCOLATE BROWNIE

Melt the butter and chocolate together. Lightly whisk the eggs and sugar, then add the flour. Combine the two mixtures.
Spoon 80 grams (2 7/8 oz) of the batter into greased 12.5-centimeter (5-inch)-diameter savarin molds. Spoon 25 g (7/8 oz) of the batter into 5-centimeter (2-inch)-diameter silicone-coated hemisphere molds. Bake in a convection oven at 150°C (300°F) for about 15 minutes. Unmold 5 minutes after removing from the oven. Set aside in the freezer.

FOR THE MACARONADE

Mix all the ingredients together.

FOR THE CHOCOLATE GANACHE

Bring the cream to a boil, then pour it over the dark chocolate, stirring continuously. Use tempered.

METHOD

WEIGHT Six 150-gram (5 1/4-oz) dough pieces.
SHAPE Gently shape into balls.
REST At 3°C (35°F) for about 30 minutes.
SHAPE Use a rolling pin to roll the dough into 20-centimeter (8-inch)-diameter disks. Brush the egg around the edges of the disks, then place a brownie ring in the center. Fold the edges of the disks toward the center of the rings, then carefully seal, being careful to avoid piercing the dough. Turn them over and place in greased 14-centimeter (5 1/2-inch)-diameter springform pans.
FINAL PROOF At 27°C (80°F) for about 2 hours.
FINISH Prick the surface of the pastries to prevent a cavity from forming inside. Brush the edges of the pastries with the macaronade. Press the brownie hemispheres into the center of the pastries. Sprinkle chopped almonds around the edges of the rings, then dust with confectioners' sugar.
BAKE In a convection oven at 150°C (300°F), or a deck oven at 180°C (355°F), for about 22 minutes.
COOL On a wire rack.
FINISH Fill the center of the pastries with the chocolate ganache.

SAINT-ANTOINE ROLLS

MAKES 30 ROLLS

LEAVENED LAMINATED DOUGH

PLAIN DOUGH

Croissant dough *(see page 186)*	**1.7 KG (3 LB 12 OZ)**
Dry butter *(see page 10)*	**500 G (1 LB 1 ⅝ OZ)**

COCOA CROISSANT DOUGH

Croissant dough *(see page 186)*	**240 G (8 ½ OZ)**
Unsweetened cocoa powder	**24 G (⅞ OZ)**
Milk	**24 G (⅞ OZ)**
Butter	**12 G (⅜ OZ)**

FILLING

Chocolate sticks (5 g)	**30**
Candied orange strips	**30**

TO FINISH

Neutral syrup *(see page 31)*	**AS NEEDED**

FOR THE COCOA CROISSANT DOUGH

In a stand mixer fitted with the paddle attachment, beat the ingredients for the cocoa croissant dough on speed 1 until smooth. Bulk ferment for about 40 minutes, then at 1°C (35°F) for 12 hours.

METHOD

TURNING (*TOURAGE*) Degas the dough. Encase the dry butter in the dough. Make one single turn and one double turn *(see page 14)*. Moisten the surface of the dough, then place the rolled-out cocoa croissant dough—rolled to the same size as the kneaded dough—on top of the kneaded dough.

REST At 1°C (35°F) for about 45 minutes.

CUT TO SIZE Using a dough sheeter, roll out the dough to a thickness of 3.5 millimeters (³⁄₁₆ inch), then into a 42 × 80-centimeter (16 ½ × 31 ½-inch) rectangle.

Cut out thirty 14 × 8-centimeter (5 ½ × 3 ¼-inch) rectangles. Using a thin blade, such as a clean hobby knife, score the chocolate side, making cuts 1 millimeter (¹⁄₃₂ inch) deep and 1 centimeter (⅜ inch) apart.

SHAPE Turn the rectangles over, then roll up like a pain au chocolat, inserting one chocolate stick, then one candied orange strip. Place them on baking sheets lined with parchment paper.

GLAZE Whisked egg.

FINAL PROOF At 27°C (80°F) for about 2 hours.

GLAZE Whisked egg.

BAKE In a convection oven at 170°C (340°F), or in a deck oven at 200°C (390°F), for about 16 minutes.

FINISH Brush with neutral syrup.

COOL On a wire rack.

RASPBERRY AND ALMOND PAINS AU CHOCOLAT

MAKES 15 PASTRIES

INGREDIENTS

Day-old pains au chocolat *(see page 198)*	**15**
Neutral syrup *(see page 31)*	**150 G (5 1/4 OZ)**

ALMOND CREAM

(see page 30)	**600 G (1 LB 6 1/8 OZ)**

RASPBERRY CREAM

Raspberry puree	**240 G (8 1/2 OZ)**
Superfine sugar	**60 G (92 1/8 OZ)**
Cornstarch	**18 G (5/8 OZ)**

TO FINISH

Sliced almonds	**AS NEEDED**
Confectioners' sugar	**AS NEEDED**

FOR THE RASPBERRY CREAM

Combine the superfine sugar and cornstarch. Stir the raspberry puree with the dry mixture while cold, then bring to a boil. Set aside at 3°C (35°F).

METHOD

CUT TO SIZE Slice off the bottom of the pains au chocolat.

FILL Generously brush both sides of the cut with the neutral syrup. Using a pastry bag fitted with a basketweave tip, fill the lower section of the pains au chocolat with 20 grams (3/4 oz) of raspberry cream, then top with the upper section. Using a pastry bag fitted with a basketweave tip, cover the surface of the pains au chocolat with 40 grams (1 1/2 oz) of almond cream. Sprinkle the tops of the pains au chocolat with sliced almonds. Place them on baking sheets lined with parchment paper.

BAKE In a convection oven at 160°C (320°F), or in a deck oven at 180°C (355°C), for about 15 minutes.

COOL On a wire rack.

FINISH Sprinkle with confectioners' sugar.

WHITE CHOCOLATE AND CRANBERRY VIENNA BREAD

MAKES 15 PASTRIES

KNEADING INGREDIENTS WHITE CHOCOLATE AND CRANBERRY VIENNA DOUGH

Strong flour	**1 KG (2 LB 3 ¼ OZ)**
Milk	**640 G (1 LB 6 ½ OZ)**
Eggs	**110 G (3 ⅞ OZ)**
Salt	**18 G (⅝ OZ)**
Superfine sugar	**80 G (2 ⅞ OZ)**
Yeast	**18 G (⅝ OZ)**
Butter	**150 G (5 ¼ OZ)**

FINAL KNEADING

White chocolate 35% fat	**200 G (7 OZ)**
Dried cranberries	**200 G (7 OZ)**

MACARONADE

Almond flour	**150 G (5 ¼ OZ)**
Confectioners'sugar	**150 G (5 ¼ OZ)**
Egg whites	**120 G (4 ¼ OZ)**

TO FINISH

Sliced almonds	**AS NEEDED**
Confectioners' sugar	**AS NEEDED**

FOR THE MACARONADE

Mix all ingredients together. Set aside at 3°C (35°F).

METHOD

BASE TEMPERATURE	48 to 52°C (120 to 125°F).
INCORPORATE	In a stand mixer, mix all the kneading ingredients in the bowl.
INITIAL MIX	On speed 1 for about 3 minutes.
KNEAD	On speed 2 for about 7 minutes.
INCORPORATE	On speed 1, add the white chocolate and cranberries.
CONSISTENCY	Medium-firm dough.
DOUGH TEMPERATURE	23°C (75°F).
BULK FERMENT	About 20 minutes.
WEIGHT	Fifteen 160-gram (5 ⅝-oz) dough pieces.
PRESHAPE	Shape into balls.
REST	At 3°C (35°F) for about 12 hours.
SHAPE	Shape into balls. Place them in greased 12-centimeter (4 ¾-inch)-diameter springform molds.
FINAL PROOF	At 27°C (80°F) for about 2 hours.
FINISH	Cover the pastries with the macaronade, then sprinkle with sliced almonds and dust generously with confectioners' sugar.
BAKE	In a convection oven at 150°C (300°F), or in a deck oven at 180°C (355°F), for about 16 minutes.
COOL	On a wire rack.

SUISSES WITH CHOCOLATE AND HAZELNUT SPREAD

MAKES 30 PASTRIES

PLAIN LEAVENED LAMINATED DOUGH

Croissant dough *(see page 186)*	**1.7 KG (3 ¾ LB)**
Dry butter *(see page 10)*	**500 G (1 LB 1 ⅝ OZ)**

COCOA CROISSANT DOUGH

Croissant dough *(see page 186)*	**240 G (8 ½ OZ)**
Unsweetened cocoa powder	**24 G (⅞ OZ)**
Milk	**24 G (⅞ OZ)**
Butter	**12 G (⅜ OZ)**

CHOCOLATE TOPPING

Chocolate hazelnut spread	**650 G (1 LB 7 OZ)**
Almond flour	**195 G (6 ⅞ OZ)**
Egg whites	**130 G (4 ½ OZ)**

TO FINISH

Neutral syrup *(see page 31)*	**AS NEEDED**

FOR THE CHOCOLATE TOPPING

Mix all the ingredients together.

FOR THE COCOA CROISSANT DOUGH

In a stand mixer fitted with the paddle attachment, beat the ingredients on speed 1 until smooth.
Bulk ferment for about 40 minutes, then at 1°C (35°F) for 12 hours.

METHOD

TURNING (TOURAGE) Degas the dough. Encase the dry butter in the dough. Make one single turn and one double turn *(see page 14)*. Moisten the surface of the dough, then place the rolled-out cocoa croissant dough, rolled to the same size as the kneaded dough, on top of the kneaded dough.

REST At 1°C (35°F) for about 45 minutes.

CUT TO SIZE Using a dough sheeter, roll out the dough to a thickness of 3 millimeters (⅛ inch), then into a 26 × 160-centimeter (10 ¼ × 64-inch) rectangle. Cut out thirty-two 26 × 5-centimeter (10 ¼ × 2-inch) rectangles.

SHAPE With the chocolate side down and using a pastry bag, pipe 30 grams (1 oz) of chocolate filling onto the bottom half of the rectangles. Using a brush, lightly moisten the edges around the filling. Fold the top over and seal firmly. Turn the dough pieces over and, using a sharp blade, such as a clean hobby knife, gently score the surface of the pastries to make the desired pattern. Place them on baking sheets lined with parchment paper.

GLAZE Whisked egg.

FINAL PROOF At 27°C (80°F) for about 2 hours.

GLAZE Whisked egg.

BAKE In a convection oven at 170°C (340°F), or in a deck oven at 200°C (410°F), for about 16 minutes.

FINISH Brush with neutral syrup.

COOL On a wire rack.

APPLE SWIRLS

MAKES 32 PASTRIES

KNEADING INGREDIENTS
ORANGE BLOSSOM BRIOCHE DOUGH

Strong flour	1 KG (2 LB 3 ¼ OZ)
Eggs	600 G (1 LB 6 ⅛ OZ)
Orange blossom water	70 G (2 ½ OZ)
Yeast	35 G (1 ¼ OZ)
Salt	20 G (¾ OZ)
Superfine sugar	140 G (5 OZ)
Viennese fermented dough *(see page 28)*	100 G (3 ½ OZ)

FINAL KNEADING

Unsalted butter	450 G (1 LB)

FILLING

Plain pastry cream *(see page 30)*	650 G (1 LB 7 OZ)

BAKED APPLES

Apples	1.5 KG (3 LB 5 OZ)

LEMON SUGAR

Granulated sugar	250 G (8 ¾ OZ)
Lemon, zest only	1

TO FINISH

Melted butter	200 G (7 OZ)

FOR THE BAKED APPLES

Wash, peel, core, and dice the apples and place them on a baking sheet lined with a silicone mat. Bake in a convection oven, with the vent open, at 150°C (300°F) for about 30 minutes.

FOR THE LEMON SUGAR

Combine the sugar and lemon zest.

METHOD

BASE TEMPERATURE 48 to 52°C (120 to 125°F).

INCORPORATE In a stand mixer, mix all the kneading ingredients in the mixing bowl.

INITIAL MIX On speed 1 for about 5 minutes.

KNEAD On speed 2 for about 5 minutes.

INCORPORATE On speed 1, add the butter until the dough is smooth.

CONSISTENCY Medium-firm dough.

DOUGH TEMPERATURE 23°C (75°F).

FINAL PROOF At 1°C (35°F) for about 2 hours.

PRESHAPE Using a dough sheeter, roll out the dough to a thickness of 3 millimeters (⅛ inch), then into a 40 × 120-centimeter (15 ½ × 47-inch) rectangle. Using the dough sheeter, roll the scraps to a thickness of 1 millimeter (1/32 inch) and set aside at 1°C (35°F).

SHAPE Moisten the lower 4 centimeters (1 ½ inches) of the dough. Using a spatula, spread the pastry cream over the remaining dough, then sprinkle with the diced apples.
Roll up the dough to form a cylinder, then seal with the moistened part.

CUT TO SIZE Cut into 4-centimeter (1 ¼-inch) spiral slices. Using a pastry cutter, cut out 7-centimeter (2 ¾-inch)-diameter disks from the scraps. Place the disks, then the spirals, in greased 10-centimeter (4-inch)-diameter springform pans.

FINAL PROOF At 27°C (80°F) for about 2 hours 30 minutes.

BAKE In a convection oven at 150°C (300°F), or in a deck oven at 180°C (355°F), for about 15 minutes.

FINISH Brush the swirls with melted butter, then roll in the lemon sugar.

COOL On a wire rack.

ALMOND BRAIDS

MAKES 4 LOAVES

PLAIN BRIOCHE DOUGH

(see page 184)	**1 KG (2 LB 3 ¼ OZ)**

ALMOND PASTE

Almond flour	**140 G (5 OZ)**
Superfine sugar	**140 G (5 OZ)**
Beurre	**140 G (5 OZ)**
Eggs	**70 G (2 ½ OZ)**
Cornstarch	**14 G (½ OZ)**
Vanilla beans	**2**

TO FINISH

Sliced almonds	**AS NEEDED**

FOR THE ALMOND PASTE

In a stand mixer fitted with the paddle attachment, beat the almond flour, superfine sugar, butter, starch, and vanilla. Gradually add the eggs and beat well. Set aside at 3°C (35°F).

METHOD

WEIGHT One 1-kilogram (2 lb 3 ¼-oz) dough piece.

PRESHAPE Using a dough sheeter, roll out the dough into a 24 × 120-centimeter (9 ½ × 47-inch) rectangle.

CUT TO SIZE Cut twelve 24 × 10-centimeter (9 ½ × 4-inch) strips.

FILL Spread 40 gram (1 ⅜ oz) of almond paste on each strip, making sure to spread it on the upper part of the length of each strip.

REST In the freezer for about 10 minutes, until the almond paste hardens.

SHAPE Roll the dough pieces into 30-centimeter (11 ¾-inch)-long ropes, making sure that the almond paste stays in the center of the rope, then shape into a loose three-strand braid. Place them in greased 28 × 8 × 6-centimeter (11 × 3 ¼ × 2 ½-inch) loaf pans.

FINAL PROOF At 27°C (80°F) for about 2 hours 30 minutes.

GLAZE Brushed egg.

FINISH Sprinkle with sliced almonds.

BAKE In a convection oven at 150°C (300°F), or in a deck oven at 180°C (355°F), for about 24 minutes.

COOL On a wire rack.

• • VI
ENNO
ISER
IE • •
FROM

ARO
UND
THE
WO
RLD

THE HISTORY OF VIENNOISERIE FROM AROUND THE WORLD

BOLLERS

Although these rolls, or buns, are popular in most Scandinavian countries, they are originally from Norway. What makes them distinctive is that cardamom is added to the dough. Undoubtedly Norway's most popular viennoiserie, *bollers* come in several variations, including *raisinbolle* and *Sjokoladebolle*. Eaten at any time of day, they are particularly enjoyed for breakfast.

KOREAN BRIOCHES

These brioches are said to have been invented in Japan in 1875 by Yasubei Kimura, a samurai who lost his job when the Imperial Army came into power. They are also popular in South Korea, where they are called *danpatbbang*. The filling is usually a red bean paste, but white beans, green beans, or chestnuts are also used.

CINNAMON ROLL

Originating in Sweden, cinnamon rolls, or buns, has been celebrated in the country on every October 4 since 1999. They are also popular throughout Scandinavia and North America. In Norway they are called *kanelbulle*, while in Finland they are known as *korvapuusti*. In these countries, cardamom is often added to the dough.

COLOMBA EASTER BREAD

A religious symbol, an emblem of peace, *Colomba* is traditionally enjoyed in Italy at the end of the Easter meal. The story goes that to appease the wrath of Albuin, King of the Lombards, who was about to raze the city of Pavia to the ground, a pastry chef offered him a delicious dove-shaped cake. It has a soft, pillowy texture that is similar to panettone. Some pastry chefs add chocolate, hazelnuts, or other ingredients.

CRAQUELINS

Originally from Belgium, they are also popular in northern France. The name comes from the Dutch *crakelinc*, meaning "dry cookie that crunches under your teeth." The first mention of a craquelin as a cake dates back to 1265.

FLÛTES AU SEL

Savory cookies in the shape of straight or twisted sticks, *flûtes au sel* are enjoyed as an aperitif in French-speaking Switzerland, particularly in the canton of Vaud. They are usually plain, but they can be sprinkled with poppy seeds, sesame seeds, or even cheese.

HOT CROSS BUNS

Hot cross buns, which are originally from Great Britain, are said to have been invented in the fourteenth century by a monk called Thomas Rockcliffe, at St. Albans Abbey in England. Originally called Alban buns, they were distributed to the poor on Good Friday. They are still popular at that particular time of year, particularly in English-speaking countries. The cross on top of the bun symbolizes the Crucifixion.

SALÉES AU SUCRE

To speak of something "salted with sugar" might seem paradoxical, but there is an explanation for the origin of this name. In the seventeenth century, in the canton of Vaud in Switzerland, a *salée* was, in fact, a cake. *Salées* were made with cheese, lard and cumin, wine, and, why not, sugar? *Salée au sucre* is a round cake with a sweet leavened crust that is filled with a mixture of sugar and cream. Total happiness.

SOBOROS

Originating in South Korea, *soboros* are one of the most emblematic of Korean baked goods. Their distinctive feature is the streusel that completely covers them; the word *soboro* refers to this streusel, which is usually made with peanut butter.

TAILLÉS AUX GREUBONS

Created in the late nineteenth century, these golden rectangular *taillés aux greubons*, also known as *grattons*, are savory pastries from the Vaud region in Switzerland. They are made with leavened laminated dough and *greubons* (cracklings or scratchings), pork fat residue left over from melted lard during the lard-making process. Served with white wine, *taillés aux greubons* are enjoyed as an aperitif in the wine cellars and *carnotzets* of the Vaud.

BOLLERS

MAKES 25 ROLLS

KNEADING INGREDIENTS

BOLLER DOUGH

Strong flour	**1 KG**
Eggs	**100 G (3 ½ OZ)**
Milk	**550 G (1 LB 3 ⅜ OZ)**
Salt	**18 G (⅝ OZ)**
Superfine sugar	**120 G (4 ¼ OZ)**
Yeast	**25 G (⅞ G)**
Ground cardamom	**8 G (¼ OZ)**

FINAL KNEADING

Unsalted butter	**200 G (7 OZ)**

GLAZE

Whisked eggs	**AS NEEDED**

METHOD

BASE TEMPERATURE	48°C to 52°C (120 to 125°F).
INCORPORATE	In a stand mixer, mix all the kneading ingredients in the mixing bowl.
INITIAL MIX	On speed 1 for about 5 minutes.
KNEAD	On speed 2 for about 5 minutes.
INCORPORATE	On speed 1, add the butter until the dough is smooth.
CONSISTENCY	Medium-firm dough.
DOUGH TEMPERATURE	23°C (75°F).
BULK FERMENT	About 45 minutes.
WEIGHT	Twenty-five 80-gram (2 ⅞-oz) dough pieces.
PRESHAPE	Shape into balls.
REST	At room temperature for about 20 minutes.
SHAPE	Shape into balls. Place them on baking sheets lined with parchment paper.
GLAZE	Whisked egg.
FINAL PROOF	At 27°C (80°F) for about 1 hour 30 minutes.
GLAZE	Whisked egg.
BAKE	In a convection oven at 150°C (300°F), or a deck oven at 180°C (355°F), for about 15 minutes.
COOL	On a wire rack.

KOREAN BRIOCHES

MAKES 57 BRIOCHES

KNEADING INGREDIENTS
KOREAN BRIOCHE DOUGH

Strong flour	1 KG (2 LB 3 ¼ OZ)
Eggs	240 G (1 ⅜ OZ)
Milk	200 G (7 OZ)
Water	200 G (7 OZ)
Salt	18 G (⅝ OZ)
Superfine sugar	180 G (6 ⅜ OZ)
Yeast	40 G (1 ⅜ OZ)
Instant dry milk powder	20 G (¾ OZ)
Viennese fermented dough *(see page 28)*	210 G

FINAL KNEADING

Unsalted butter	180 G (6 ⅜ OZ)

RED BEAN PASTE

Red kidney beans	1.25 KG (2 ¾ LB)
Soaking water	2 KG (4 LB 6 OZ)
Cooking water	2.5 KG (5 ½ LB)
Granulated sugar	1 KG (2 LB 3 ¼ OZ)
Glucose	250 G (8 ¾ OZ)

TO FINISH

Walnuts (shelled)	AS NEEDED

FOR THE RED BEAN PASTE

Soak the beans in room-temperature soaking water for 12 hours. Drain.
In a saucepan, add them to the cooking water, bring to a boil, then cook over low heat for about 40 minutes. Drain. In a saucepan, combine the cooked beans, superfine sugar, and glucose, then cook over low heat, stirring regularly, for about 40 minutes. Puree half of the mixture in a food processor, then stir it into the remaining beans. Set aside at 3°C (35°F).

METHOD

BASE TEMPERATURE 48°C to 52°C (120 to 125°F).
INCORPORATE In a stand mixer, mix all the kneading ingredients in the bowl.
INITIAL MIX On speed 1 for about 5 minutes.
KNEAD On speed 2 for about 5 minutes.
INCORPORATE On speed 1, add the butter until the dough is smooth.
CONSISTENCY Medium-firm dough.
DOUGH TEMPERATURE 23°C (75°F).
BULK FERMENT About 1 hour.
WEIGHT Fifty-seven 40-gram (1 ⅜-oz) dough pieces.
PRESHAPE Shape into balls.
REST At room temperature for about 15 minutes.
SHAPE Using a rolling pin, gently roll out the balls to form 7-centimeter (2 ¾-inch)-diameter disks.
Place 60-gram (2 ⅛-oz) balls of red bean paste in the center of the disks, then fold over the edges to form balls. Place on baking sheets lined with parchment paper and, using a rolling pin with rounded ends, gently press the centers of the balls to form rings.
GLAZE Whisked egg.
FINAL PROOF At 27°C (80°F) for about 1 hour 15 minutes.
GLAZE Whisked egg.
FINISH Insert a walnut kernel in the center of each ring.
BAKE In a convection oven at 150°C (300°F), or a deck oven at 180°C (355°F), for about 14 minutes.
COOL On a wire rack.

CINNAMON ROLLS

MAKES 28 ROLLS

KNEADING INGREDIENTS

CINNAMON ROLL DOUGH

Strong flour	500 G (1 LB 1 ⅝ OZ)
Bread flour (T65)	500 G (1 LB 1 ⅝ OZ)
Eggs	420 G (14 ¾ OZ)
Milk	200 G (7 OZ)
Salt	18 G (⅝ OZ)
Superfine sugar	200 G (7 OZ)
Yeast	40 G (1 ⅜ OZ)

FINAL KNEADING

Unsalted butter	500 G (1 LB 1 ⅝ OZ)

CINNAMON TOPPING

Philadelphia® cream cheese	500 G (1 LB 1 ⅝ OZ)
Confectioners' sugar	75 G (2 ⅝ OZ)
Sweetened condensed milk	50 G (1 ¾ OZ)
Ground cinnamon	38 G (1 ⅜ OZ)

CINNAMON WATER GLAZE

Confectioners' sugar	1.5 KG (5 LB 5 OZ)
Water	375 G (13 ¼ OZ)
Ground cinnamon	12 G (⅜ OZ)

FOR THE CINNAMON TOPPING

In a stand mixer fitted with the paddle attachment, beat all the ingredients until smooth.
Set aside at 3°C (35°F).

FOR THE CINNAMON WATER GLAZE

Mix all the ingredients together.

METHOD

BASE TEMPERATURE 48°C to 50°C (120 to 125°F).

INCORPORATE In a stand mixer, mix all the kneading ingredients in the mixing bowl.

INITIAL MIX On speed 1 for about 5 minutes.

KNEAD On speed 2 for about 5 minutes.

INCORPORATE On speed 1, add the butter until the dough is smooth.

CONSISTENCY Medium-firm dough.

DOUGH TEMPERATURE 23°C (75°F).

BULK FERMENT After kneading, at 3°C (35°F) about 12 hours.

PRESHAPE Using a dough sheeter, roll out the dough to a thickness of 2.5 millimeters (⅛ inch), then into a 40 × 140-centimeter (15 ½ × 55-inch) rectangle.

SHAPE Moisten the bottom 2 centimeters (¾ inch) of the dough with water. Using a spatula, spread the cinnamon filling evenly over the remaining dough. Roll up the dough into a 140-centimeter (55-inch)-long rope, then seal with the moistened area.

CUT TO SIZE Cut into 5-centimeter (2-inch)-wide slices and place them in greased 10-centimeter (4-inch)-diameter, 4-centimeter (1 ½-inch)-deep springform pans.

FINAL PROOF At 27°C (80°F) for about 3 hours.

BAKE In a convection oven at 150°C (300°F), or a deck oven at 180°C (355°F), for about 14 minutes.

COOL On a wire rack.

FINISH Glaze the cinnamon rolls with the cinnamon water glaze.
Dry in a convection oven, with the vent open, at 90°C (195°F) for 2 minutes.

COLOMBA EASTER BREAD

MAKES 19 LOAVES

LEVAIN REFRESHMENT

Stiff levain *(see page 8 and Note below)*	**500 G (1 LB 1 5/8 OZ)**
Water at 38°C (100°F)	**2 KG (4 LB 6 OZ)**
Superfine sugar	**6 G (3/16 OZ)**

FIRST REFRESHMENT

Reactivated stiff levain	**500 G (1 LB 1 5/8 OZ)**
Oat flour	**450 G (15 7/8 OZ)**
Water at 24°C (75°F)	**135 G (4 3/4 OZ)**

SECOND REFRESHMENT

Stiff levain from the first refreshment	**500 G (1 LB 1 5/8 OZ)**
Oat flour	**450 G (15 7/8 OZ)**
Water at 24°C (75°F)	**180 G (6 3/8 OZ)**

THIRD REFRESHMENT

Stiff levain from the second refreshment	**500 G (1 LB 1 5/8 OZ)**
Oat flour	**450 G (15 7/8 OZ)**
Water at 24°C (75°F)	**180 G (6 3/8 OZ)**

FOURTH REFRESHMENT

Superfine sugar	**600 G (1 LB 6 1/8 OZ)**
Water at 24°C (75°F)	**1 KG (2 LB 5 1/2 OZ)**
Egg yolks 1	**250 G (8 3/4 OZ)**
Stiff levain from the third refreshment	**600 G (1 LB 6 1/8 OZ)**
Oat flour	**2.1 KG (4 LB 10 OZ)**
Egg yolks 2	**300 G (10 1/2 OZ)**
Unsalted butter	**900 G (1 LB 15 3/4 OZ)**

NOTE:

Before making *colomba*, it is a good idea to make the first stiff levain refreshment once a day for 5 days, letting it rest in a container with water at room temperature. Numerous refreshments of the levain—and keeping it in water at room temperature—will activate fermentation and remove excess acidity.

FOR REACTIVATING THE LEVAIN

Let the levain rest in the water and sugar for 30 minutes.

FOR THE FIRST REFRESHMENT

In a stand mixer on speed 1, beat all of the ingredients.
Let ferment at 28°C (80°F) in a container with water at 24°C (75°F) for about 3 hours.

FOR THE SECOND REFRESHMENT

In a stand mixer on speed 1, beat all of the ingredients.
Let ferment at 28°C (80°F) in a container with water at 24°C (75°F) for about 3 hours.

FOR THE THIRD REFRESHMENT

In a stand mixer on speed 1, beat all of the ingredients.
Let ferment at 28°C (80°F) in a container with water at 24°C (75°F) for about 3 hours.

FOR THE FOURTH REFRESHMENT

Using a spiral mixer on speed 1, beat the sugar and water.
Add 1 egg yolk, then the levain from the third refreshment and beat on speed 1 for 2 minutes.
Add the flour and knead on speed 2 until the dough comes away from the sides of the bowl.
Add the remaining egg yolk on speed 2.
Mix until smooth, then add the butter.
Place in a buttered stainless steel container, fold to degas, butter the surface of the dough, and let rest at 27°C (80°F) for about 12 hours, until it triples in volume.

FINAL PROOF

Levain from the fourth refreshment	5. 8 KG (12 3/4 LB)
Oat flour	820 G (1 LB 12 7/8 OZ)
Egg yolks	600 G (1 LB 6 1/8 OZ)
Water	90 G 3 1/8 OZ)
Superfine sugar	600 G (1 LB 6 1/8 OZ)
Honey	200 G (7 OZ)
Salt	50 G (1 3/4 OZ)
Vanilla beans	2
Pastry cream	170 G (6 OZ)
Unsalted butter	1.1 KG (2 LB 5 1/1 OZ)

FILLING

Candied citron, diced	400 G (14 OZ)
Candied orange, diced	1 KG (2 LB 3 1/4 OZ)
Raisins	1.15 KG (2 1/2 LB)
Water	575 G 1 LB 4 1/4 OZ)
Orange zest	3

MACARONADE

Almond flour	390 G (13 3/4 OZ)
Cornstarch	350 G (12 3/8 OZ)
Confectioners' sugar	775 G (1 LB 11 3/8 OZ)
Egg whites	390 G (13 3/4 OZ)

TO FINISH

Confectioners' sugar	AS NEEDED

FOR THE TOPPING

The day before preparing the *colomba*, macerate the raisins, water, and orange zest for at least 12 hours.

FOR THE MACARONADE

The day before preparing the *colomba*, stir all the ingredients together.

METHOD

BASE TEMPERATURE	48°C to 52°C (120 to 125°F).
INCORPORATE	Using the spiral mixer, mix the fourth refreshment and the flour in the bowl.
INITIAL MIX	On speed 1 for about 3 minutes.
INCORPORATE	Add the egg yolks and water.
KNEAD	On speed 2 for about 5 minutes, until the dough comes away from the sides of the bowl.
INCORPORATE	On speed 1, gradually add the sugar, honey, salt, vanilla, pastry cream, and butter. When the dough is smooth, on speed 1, add the filling in two batches.
CONSISTENCY	Soft dough.
DOUGH TEMPERATURE	24°C (75°F).
BULK FERMENT	About 45 minutes.
WEIGHT	Nineteen 650-gram (1 lb 7-oz) dough pieces.
PRESHAPE	Shape into balls.
REST	At room temperature for about 30 minutes.
PRESHAPE	Shape into balls a second time.
REST	At room temperature for about 15 minutes.
SHAPE	Gently stretch out two sides of the dough pieces to fit the shape of the mold. Place the dough pieces in 21 × 28-centimeter (8 ¼ × 11-inch) *colomba* dove molds.
FINAL PROOF	At 27°C (80°F) for 7 to 8 hours.
FINISH	Spread the macaronade over the surface of the *colomba* and sprinkle generously with confectioners' sugar.
BAKE	In a convection oven at 150°C (300°F), or a deck oven at 180°C (355°F), for about 40 minutes.
COOL	Inverted, for at least 2 hours. Use the needles provided and insert through the bottom of the molds.

CRAQUELINS

MAKES 12 ROLLS

KNEADING INGREDIENTS

CRAQUELIN DOUGH

Strong flour	**1 KG (2 LB 3 ¼ OZ)**
Milk	**550 G (1 LB 3 ⅜ OZ)**
Egg yolks	**110 G (3 ⅞ OZ)**
Salt	**18 G (⅝ OZ)**
Superfine sugar	**50 G (1 ¾ OZ)**
Yeast	**15 G**
Liquid levain *(see page 9)*	**200 G (7 OZ)**

FINAL KNEADING

Unsalted butter	**300 G (10 ½ OZ)**
Pearl sugar	**340 G (12 OZ)**

METHOD

BASE TEMPERATURE 48°C to 52°C (120 to 125°F).

INCORPORATE In a stand mixer, mix all the kneading ingredients in the mixing bowl.

INITIAL MIX On speed 1 for about 5 minutes.

KNEAD On speed 2 for about 3 minutes.

INCORPORATE On speed 1, add the butter until the dough is smooth. Remove 600 grams (1 lb 6 ⅛ oz) of dough, then add the pearl sugar to the remaining dough and beat on speed 2.

CONSISTENCY Medium-firm dough.

DOUGH TEMPERATURE 23°C (75°F).

BULK FERMENT About 1 hour 30 minutes.

WEIGHT Twelve 165-gram dough (5 ⅞-oz) pieces for the *craquelin* dough and twelve 50-gram (1 ¾-oz) pieces for plain dough.

PRESHAPE Shape into balls.

REST At 3°C (35°F) for bout 20 minutes.

SHAPE Roll the plain dough into 12-centimeter (4 ¾-inch)-diameter disks. Roll the *craquelin* dough pieces into balls, then place them seam side up on the dough disks.
Fold the edges of the disks over the balls to close them. Place in greased 12-centimeter (4 ¾-inch-diameter molds.

FINAL PROOF At 3°C (35°F) for about 12 hours, then at 27°C (80°F) for 3 hours.

GLAZE Whisked egg.

COOL At 3°C (35°F) for about 10 minutes.

SCORE Cross cut.

BAKE In a convection oven at 160°C (320°F), or in a deck oven at 190°C (375°F) for about 20 minutes.

COOL On a wire rack.

FLÛTES AU SEL

MAKES 146 FLUTES

KNEADING INGREDIENTS
LEAVENED LAMINATED DOUGH

Strong flour	**1 KG (2 LB 3 ¼ OZ)**
Water	**275 G (9 ¾ OZ)**
Milk	**275 G (9 ¾ OZ)**
Salt	**18 G (⅝ OZ)**
Superfine sugar	**80 G (2 ⅞ OZ)**
Yeast	**30 G (1 OZ)**
Viennese fermented dough *(see page 28)*	**200 G (7 OZ)**
Unsalted butter	**150 G (5 ¼ OZ)**

TURNING (*TOURAGE*)

Dry butter	**360 G (12 ⅝ OZ)**

TO FINISH

Fleur de sel	**AS NEEDED**

METHOD

BASE TEMPERATURE 46°C to 50°C (115 to 120°F).

INCORPORATE In a stand mixer, mix all the kneading ingredients in the mixing bowl.

INITIAL MIX On speed 1 for about 3 minutes.

KNEAD On speed 1 for about 7 minutes and on speed 2 for 2 minutes.

CONSISTENCY Firm dough.

DOUGH TEMPERATURE 23°C (75°F).

WEIGHT One 2-kilogram (4 lb 7-oz) dough piece.

PRESHAPE Shape into balls.

BULK FERMENT About 40 minutes.

PUNCH DOWN After 20 minutes of bulk fermentation.

SHAPE Oval.

FINAL PROOF At 1°C (35°F) for about 2 hours.

TURNING (TOURAGE) Degas the dough. Encase the dry butter in the dough. Make two double turns *(see page 14)*.

REST At 1°C (35°F) for about 1 hour.

CUT Using a dough sheeter, roll out the dough into a 36 × 110-centimeter (14 × 43-inch) rectangle, then cut into 36 × 1.5-centimeter (110 × ⅝-inch) strips.

SHAPE Twist the strips and place them on greased or parchment-lined baking sheets.
Cut the twists in half to make 15-centimeter (6-inch)-long flutes.

FINAL PROOF A 27°C (80°F) for about 2 hours.

GLAZE Whisked egg.

FINISH Sprinkle the flutes with fleur de sel.

BAKE In a convection oven at 170°C (340°F), or in a deck oven at 200°C (390°F) for about 17 minutes.

COOL On a wire rack.

HOT CROSS BUNS

MAKES 32 BUNS

KNEADING INGREDIENTS
HOT CROSS BUN DOUGH

Strong flour	1 KG (2 LB 3 ¼ OZ)
Eggs	110 G (3 ⅞ OZ)
Milk	500 G (1 LB 1 ⅝ OZ)
Salt	18 G (⅝ OZ)
Superfine sugar	110 G (3 ⅞ OZ)
Honey	50 G (1 ¾ OZ)
Yeast	20 G (¾ OZ)
Ground cinnamon	10 G (⅜ OZ)
Ground anise seed	5 G (3/16 OZ)
Ground cardamom	5 G (3/16 OZ)
Unsalted butter	160 G (5 ⅝ OZ)
Liquid levain *(see page 9)*	250 G (8 ¾ OZ)

FINAL KNEADING

Raisins	200 G (7 OZ)
Candied orange, diced	200 G (7 OZ)
Orange zest	1
Lemon zest	1

CROSS ICING

Bread flour (T65)	50 G (1 ¾ OZ)
Water	53 G (1 ⅞ OZ)

TO FINISH

Neutral syrup *(see page 31)*	AS NEEDED

FOR THE ICING TO FINISH

Mix all the ingredients together. Set aside at 3°C (35°F).

METHOD

BASE TEMPERATURE	48°C to 52°C (120 to 125°F).
INCORPORATE	In a stand mixer, mix all the kneading ingredients in the mixing bowl.
INITIAL MIX	On speed 1 for about 8 minutes.
KNEAD	On speed 2 for about 5 minutes.
INCORPORATE	Add the raisins, diced candied orange, and orange and lemon zests.
CONSISTENCY	Medium-firm dough.
DOUGH TEMPERATURE	23°C (75°F).
BULK FERMENT	About 2 hours 30 minutes.
WEIGHT	80-gram (2 ⅞-oz) dough pieces.
SHAPE	Shape into balls. Place them on baking sheets lined with parchment paper.
FINAL PROOF	At 3°C (35°F) for about 12 hours, then at 27°C (80°F) for 2 hours.
PRE-BAKE PREP	Using a pastry bag, pipe the icing in a cross shape on top of the dough pieces.
BAKE	In a convection oven at 160°C (320°F), or in a deck oven 190°C (375°F) for about 15 minutes.
FINISH	Brush with neutral syrup.
COOL	On a wire rack.

SALÉES AU SUCRE

MAKES 18 TARTS

PLAIN BRIOCHE DOUGH	
(see page 184)	**1 KG (2 LB 3 ¼ OZ)**

CREAM FILLING	
Whipping cream 35% fat	**550 G (1 LB 3 ⅜ OZ)**
Superfine sugar	**150 G (5 ¼ OZ)**
Strong flour	**40 G (1 ⅜ OZ)**

FOR THE CREAM FILLING

In a stand mixer fitted with the whisk attachment, whisk all the ingredients together.

METHOD

PRESHAPE Using a dough sheeter, roll out the dough into a 58 × 70-centimeter (23 × 27 ½-inch) rectangle. Use a roller docker or fork to prick the dough.
Cut into eighteen 13-centimeter (5-inch)-diameter disks using a plain round pastry cutter.

REST At 3°C (35°F) for about 1 hour.

SHAPE Line greased 11-centimeter (4 ¼-inch)-diameter flared tartlet pans with the dough disks.

FINAL PROOF At 3°C (35°F) for about 12 hours, then at 27°C (80°F) for about 2 hours.

GLAZE Whisked egg, along the perimeter of the tartlets.

FINISH Fill the tartlet shells with 40 gram (1 ⅜ oz) of the cream mixture.

BAKE In a convection oven at 160°C (320°F), or in a deck oven at 190°C (375°F, for about 12 minutes.

COOL On a wire rack.

SOBOROS

MAKES 51 PASTRIES

KNEADING INGREDIENTS

SOBORO DOUGH

Strong flour	1 KG (2 LB 3 1/4 OZ)
Eggs	240 G (8.5 OZ)
Milk	200 G (7 OZ)
Water	200 G (7 OZ)
Salt	18 G (5/8 OZ)
Superfine sugar	180 G (6 3/8 OZ)
Yeast	40 G (1 3/8 OZ)
Instant dry milk powder	20 G (3/4 Oz)

FINAL KNEADING

Unsalted butter	180 G (6 3/8 OZ)

PEANUT STREUSEL

Unsalted butter, softened	175 G (6 1/4 OZ)
Peanut butter	150 G (5 1/4 OZ)
Salt	3 G (1/8 OZ)
Superfine sugar	220 G (7 3/4 OZ)
Glucose	20 G (3/34 OZ)
Eggs	75 G (2 5/8 OZ)
Bread flour (T65)	500 G (1 LB 1 5/8 OZ)
Baking powder	10 G (3/8 OZ)
Baking soda	4 G (1/8 OZ)
Unsalted peanuts, chopped	225 G (7/8 OZ)

SHAPING INGREDIENTS

Whisked egg yolks	AS NEEDED

FOR THE PEANUT STREUSEL

In a stand mixer fitted with the paddle attachment, cream the butter and peanut butter. Add the salt, sugar, glucose, and eggs and beat until smooth. Add the sifted flour, baking powder, and baking soda, beating slowly to obtain a fine crumbly mixture, then add the chopped peanuts. Set aside at 3°C (35°F).

METHOD

BASE TEMPERATURE	48°C to 52°C (120 to 125°F).
INCORPORATE	In a stand mixer, mix all the kneading ingredients in the mixing bowl.
INITIAL MIX	On speed 1 for about 5 minutes.
KNEAD	On speed 2 for about 5 minutes.
INCORPORATE	On speed 1, add the butter until the dough is smooth.
CONSISTENCY	Medium-firm dough.
DOUGH TEMPERATURE	23°C (75°F).
BULK FERMENT	About 1 hour.
WEIGHT	Fifty-one 40-gram (1 3/8-oz) dough pieces.
PRESHAPE	Shape into balls.
REST	At room temperature for about 15 minutes.
SHAPE	Shape into balls. Moisten the surface of the balls with egg yolks, then roll them in the peanut crumbs. Place them on baking sheets lined with parchment paper.
FINAL PROOF	At 27°C (80°F) for about 1 hour 15 minutes.
BAKE	In a convection oven at 150°C (300°F), or a deck oven at 180°C (355°F), for about 15 minutes.
COOL	On a wire rack.

TAILLÉS AUX GREUBONS

MAKES 30 STICKS

KNEADING INGREDIENTS LEAVENED LAMINATED DOUGH

Strong flour	**1 KG (2 LB 3 ¼ OZ)**
Water	**500 G (1 LB 1 ⅝ OZ)**
Salt	**18 G (⅝ OZ)**
Yeast	**40 G (1 ⅜ OZ)**
Viennese fermented dough *(see page 28)*	**200 G (7 OZ)**
Unsalted butter	**50 G (1 ¾ OZ)**

FINAL KNEADING

Greubons (cracklings)	**500 G (1 LB 1 ⅝ OZ)**

TURNING (*TOURAGE*)

Dry butter *(see page 10)*	**360 G**

TO FINISH

Egg yolks	**AS NEEDED**

METHOD

BASE TEMPERATURE 46°C to 50°C (115 to 120°F).

INCORPORATE In a stand mixer, mix all the kneading ingredients in the mixing bowl.

INITIAL MIX On speed 1 for about 3 minutes.

KNEAD On speed 1 for about 7 minutes and 2 minutes on speed 2.

INCORPORATE On speed 1, add the cracklings.

CONSISTENCY Firm dough.

DOUGH TEMPERATURE 23°C (75°F).

WEIGHT One 2.3-kilogram (5 lb 1-oz) dough piece.

PRESHAPE Shape into balls.

BULK FERMENT About 1 hour.

PUNCH DOWN After 30 minutes of bulk fermenting.

SHAPE Oval.

FINAL PROOF At 1°C (35°F) for about 2 hours.

TURNING (TOURAGE) Degas the dough. Encase the dry butter in the dough. Make two double turns *(see page 14)*.

REST At 1°C (35°F) for about 1 hour.

TURNING (TOURAGE) Make one double turn *(see page 14)*.

REST At 1°C (35°F) for about 1 hour.

CUT Using a dough sheeter, roll out the dough to a thickness of 5 millimeters (3/16 inch), then into a 60 × 45-centimeter (23 ½ × 17 ½-inch) rectangle. Cut out thirty 6 × 15-centimeter (2 ½ × 6-inch) rectangles. Place them on baking sheets lined with parchment paper.

FINAL PROOF At 27°C (80°F) for about 2 hours.

GLAZE Egg yolk.

BAKE In a convection oven at 190°C (375°F), or in a deck oven at 220°C (430°F) for about 17 minutes.

COOL On a wire rack.

MOUNA

WITH ROOTS IN PIED NOIR (ALGERIAN-BORN FRENCH PEOPLE) AND ALGERIAN CUISINE, PARTICULARLY THAT OF ORAN, THESE PASTRIES ARE TRADITIONALLY MADE DURING EASTER. IN FACT, ON EASTER MONDAY, THE INHABITANTS OF ORAN WOULD GATHER ON THE MOUNTAIN NEAR FORT LAMOUNE, ENJOY A PICNIC, AND, FOR DESSERT, ENJOY THIS DELICIOUS BRIOCHE SCENTED WITH CITRUS FRUIT AND ORANGE BLOSSOM WATER. WHEN THE PIED NOIRS WERE REPATRIATED IN THE 1960S, THEY BROUGHT THE *MOUNA* WITH THEM WHEN THEY ARRIVED IN THE SOUTH OF FRANCE.

MAKES 1 LOAF (1.5 KG/3 LB 5 OZ OF DOUGH)

KNEADING INGREDIENTS

Strong flour	**1 KG (2 LB 3 ¼ OZ)**
Eggs	**200 G (7 OZ)**
Milk	**250 G (8 ¾ OZ)**
Orange blossom water	**50 G (1 ¾ OZ)**
Salt	**22 G (¾ OZ)**
Superfine sugar	**200 G (7 OZ)**
Yeast	**25 G (⅞ OZ)**
Liquid levain	**300 G (10 ½ OZ)**

FINAL KNEADING

Unsalted butter, melted	**400 G (14 OZ)**
Lemons, zest only	**2**
Oranges, zest only	**2**
Green anise seeds	**10 G (⅜ OZ)**

TO FINISH

Granulated sugar	**AS NEEDED**

METHOD

BASE TEMPERATURE	48 to 52°C (120 to 125°F).
INCORPORATE	In a stand mixer, mix all the kneading ingredients in the bowl.
INITIAL MIX	On speed 1 for about 5 minutes.
KNEAD	On speed 2 for about 5 minutes.
INCORPORATE	On speed 1, add the melted butter until the dough is smooth. Add the zests and green anise seeds.
CONSISTENCY	Medium-firm dough.
DOUGH TEMPERATURE	23°C (35°F).
BULK FERMENT	About 2 hours 30 minutes.
WEIGHT	One 1.5-kilogram (3 lb 5-oz) dough piece.
PRESHAPE	Oval.
REST	At 3°C (35°F) for 2 hours.
SHAPE	40 centimeters (15 ½ inches) long. Place the dough in a greased 40 × 12 × 12-centimeter (15 ½ × 4 ¾ × 4 ¾-inch) loaf pan.
FINAL PROOF	At 3°C (35°F) for about 12 hours, then at 27°C (80°F) for about 3 hours.
GLAZE	Whisked egg.
FINISH	Using a knife, score a sausage cut on the top of the loaf, then sprinkle with granulated sugar.
BAKE	In a convection oven at 145°C (295°F), or in a deck oven at 180°C (365°F), for about 50 minutes.
COOL	On a wire rack.

STOLLEN

ORIGINALLY FROM GERMANY, THIS FRUIT BREAD IS ALSO KNOWN AS *CHRISTSTOLLEN*. A PARTICULARITY OF THIS DENSE TRADITIONAL CHRISTMAS BREAD IS THAT IT WILL KEEP FOR SEVERAL WEEKS. MADE WITH CANDIED FRUIT, ALCOHOL, AND ALMOND PASTE, IT IS ONE OF GERMANY'S FAVORITE CHRISTMAS DESSERTS.

MAKES 8 LOAVES

KNEADING INGREDIENTS

Strong flour	1 KG (2 LB 3 1/4 OZ)
Milk	450 G (15 7/8 OZ)
Salt	22 G (3/4 OZ)
Superfine sugar	80 G (1 LB 1 5/8 OZ)
Honey	40 G (1 3/8 OZ)
Yeast	20 G (3/4 OZ)
Liquid levain	300 G (10 1/2 OZ)
Unsalted butter	100 G (3 1/2 OZ)

FINAL KNEADING

Unsalted butter	300 G (10 1/2 OZ)
Macerated fruit	1.125 KG (2 3/4 LB)

MACERATED FRUIT

Dried currants	500 G (1 LB 1 5/8 OZ)
Candied orange, diced	250 G (8 3/4 OZ)
Candied lemon, diced	250 G (8 3/4 OZ)
Kirsch	130 G (4 1/2 OZ)
Orange, zest only	1
Lemon, zest only	1

ALMOND PASTE

Almond paste 50%	400 G (14 OZ)

TO FINISH

Unsalted butter, melted	200 G (7 OZ)
Superfine sugar	100 G (3 1/2 OZ)
Confectioners' sugar	AS NEEDED

FOR THE MACERATED FRUIT

Let the currants, diced candied orange, and diced candied lemon macerate in the kirsch and zests for 12 hours.

METHOD

BASE TEMPERATURE 48 to 52°C (120 to 125°F).

INCORPORATE In a stand mixer, mix all the kneading ingredients in the mixing bowl.

INITIAL MIX On speed 1 for about 3 minutes.

KNEAD On speed 1 for about 20 minutes.

INCORPORATE On speed 1, add the butter until the dough is smooth. Add the currants and candied fruit.

CONSISTENCY Medium-firm dough.

DOUGH TEMPERATURE 23°C (35°F).

BULK FERMENT About 2 hours.

WEIGHT Eight 430-gram (15 1/8-oz) dough pieces.

PRESHAPE Shape into balls.

REST About 45 minutes.

SHAPE Using a rolling pin, gently press each dough piece two-thirds of the way down, and place a line of almond paste in the hollow. Fold the smaller section over the almond paste and press again in the middle of the dough. Place in greased 18 × 8 × 8-centimeter (7 × 3 1/4 × 3 1/4-inch) loaf pans.

FINAL PROOF About 3 hours.

BAKE In a deck oven at 170°C (340°F) for about 35 minutes.

FINISH Dip the stollens in the melted butter and let them soak up the butter for 5 minutes. Roll each stollen in the superfine sugar, then sprinkle with confectioners' sugar.

COOL On a wire rack.

CRAMIQUES

BELGIAN *CRAMIQUES* ARE ALSO KNOWN AS *KRAMIEK* IN FLEMISH. POPULAR IN NORTHERN FRANCE AS WELL, THIS RAISIN-STUDDED SWEET BREAD, WHICH IS TOPPED WITH PEARL SUGAR, IS A FAVORITE BREAKFAST ITEM IN BELGIUM.

MAKES 10 SQUARES

KNEADING INGREDIENTS

Strong flour	**1 KG (2 LB 3 ¼ OZ)**
Eggs	**600 G (1 LB 6 ⅛ OZ)**
Salt	**22 G (¾ OZ)**
Superfine sugar	**100 G (3 ½ OZ)**
Yeast	**20 G (¾ OZ)**
Liquid levain	**300 G (10 ½ OZ)**

FINAL KNEADING

Unsalted butter	**400 G (14 OZ)**
Macerated raisins	**630 G (1 LB 6 ¼ OZ)**
Brown sugar	**400 G (14 OZ)**

MACERATED RAISINS

Raisins	**500 G (1 LB 1 ⅝ OZ)**
Water	**180 G (6 ⅜ OZ)**

TO FINISH

Brown sugar	**AS NEEDED**

FOR THE MACERATED RAISINS

Bring the water to a boil.
Pour the hot water over the raisins and set aside.

METHOD

BASE TEMPERATURE	48 to 52°C (120 to 125°F).
INCORPORATE	In a stand mixer, mix all the kneading ingredients in the bowl.
INITIAL MIX	On speed 1 for about 5 minutes.
KNEAD	On speed 2 for about 5 minutes.
INCORPORATE	On speed 1, add the butter until the dough is smooth. Add the macerated raisins, then the brown sugar.
CONSISTENCY	Medium-firm dough.
DOUGH TEMPERATURE	23°C (35°F).
BULK FERMENT	About 2 hours 30 minutes.
WEIGHT	Ten 345-gram (12 ⅛-oz) dough pieces.
PRESHAPE	Shape into balls.
REST	About 30 minutes.
SHAPE	Place them in 10-centimeter (4-inch) square pans, greased and lined with parchment paper.
FINAL PROOF	At 27°C (80°F) for about 2 hours 30 minutes.
GLAZE	Whisked egg.
SCORE	Using a baker's alme, make an "X" on the surface of the dough pieces and sprinkle with brown sugar.
BAKE	In a convection oven at 145°C (295°F), or in a deck oven at 180°C (365°F), for about 25 minutes.
COOL	On a wire rack.

LIÈGE WAFFLES

THE RECIPE FOR LIÈGE WAFFLES IS SAID TO HAVE BEEN INVENTED IN THE EIGHTEENTH CENTURY BY THE PRINCE OF LIÈGE'S COOK. HE CAME UP WITH THE IDEA OF COOKING BRIOCHE DOUGH—SPRINKLED WITH PEARL SUGAR—IN A WAFFLE IRON, WHICH RESULTED IN THIS MELT-IN-YOUR-MOUTH YET CRISPY DELICACY. THE WAFFLES BECAME A HIT, AND THEY ARE NOW PART OF THE CULINARY TRADITION IN THE LIÈGE REGION.

MAKES 31 WAFFLES

KNEADING INGREDIENTS

Strong flour	**1 KG (2 LB 3 ¼ OZ)**
Eggs	**300 G (10 ½ OZ)**
Milk	**300 G (10 ½ OZ)**
Salt	**18 G (⅝ OZ)**
Invert sugar	**80 G (1 LB 1 ⅝ OZ)**
Yeast	**60 G (2 ⅛ OZ)**
Viennese fermented dough *(see page 28)*	**250 G (8 ¾ OZ)**

FINAL KNEADING

Unsalted butter	**500 G (1 LB 1 ⅝ OZ)**
Brown sugar	**600 G (1 LB 6 ⅛ OZ)**

METHOD

BASE TEMPERATURE	46 to 50°C (115 to 120°F).
INCORPORATE	In a stand mixer, mix all the kneading ingredients in the bowl.
INITIAL MIX	On speed 1 for about 3 minutes.
KNEAD	On speed 2 for about 5 minutes.
INCORPORATE	On speed 1, add the butter until the dough is smooth.
CONSISTENCY	Medium-firm dough.
DOUGH TEMPERATURE	23°C (35°F).
INCORPORATE	Add the brown sugar after 20 minutes of bulk fermentation.
BULK FERMENT	About 1 hour.
WEIGHT	Thirty-one 100-gram (3 ½-oz) dough pieces.
PRESHAPE	Shape into balls.
FINAL PROOF	About 1 hour.
COOK	In large-cavity waffle makers, preheated to 180°C (365°F), for about 3 minutes.
COOL	On a wire rack.

DONUTS

INVENTED IN THE UNITED STATES, THESE LITTLE FRIED RINGS OF DOUGH ARE INCREDIBLY POPULAR. THEY COME IN MYRIAD VERSIONS WITH GLAZES IN EVERY POSSIBLE COLOR. TODAY, FEW NORTH AMERICAN BAKERS MAKE THEM FROM SCRATCH, BECAUSE READY-TO-USE MIXES HAVE BEEN THE NORM FOR DECADES.

MAKES 22 DONUTS

KNEADING INGREDIENTS

Strong flour	**1 KG (2 LB 3 1/4 OZ)**
Eggs	**250 G (8 3/4 OZ)**
Milk	**350 G (12 3/8 OZ)**
Salt	**20 G (3/4 OZ)**
Superfine sugar	**100 G (3 1/2 OZ)**
Yeast	**10 G (3/8 OZ)**
Viennese fermented dough *(see page 28)*	**200 G (7 OZ)**
Baking powder	**10 G (3/8 OZ)**
Vanilla extract	**5 G (3/16 OZ)**
Vanilla bean	**1**

FINAL KNEADING

Unsalted butter	**200 G (7 OZ)**

TO FINISH

Oil	**AS NEEDED**
Superfine sugar	**AS NEEDED**

METHOD

BASE TEMPERATURE 48 to 52°C (120 to 125°F).

INCORPORATE In a stand mixer, mix all the kneading ingredients in the bowl.

INITIAL MIX On speed 1 for about 5 minutes.

KNEAD On speed 2 for about 5 minutes.

INCORPORATE On speed 1, add the butter until the dough is smooth.

CONSISTENCY Medium-firm dough.

DOUGH TEMPERATURE 23°C (35°F).

BULK FERMENT About 40 minutes.

PRESHAPE Using a dough sheeter, roll out the dough to a thickness of 6 millimeters (1/4 inch).

CUT Using a 9-centimeter (3 1/2-inch) pastry cutter, cut out disks, then make a hole in the center of the disks using a 4-centimeter (1 1/2-inch) cutter. Place the dough rings on guitar sheets.

FINAL PROOF At 27°C (80°F) for 1 hour.

COOK In oil heated to 180°C (365°F), fry for about 1 minute on each side.

COOL On a wire rack.

FINISH Roll the donuts in the superfine sugar.

PANETTONE

ORIGINALLY FROM ITALY, THIS SWEET BREAD IS CHARACTERIZED BY A FERMENTATION BASED ON USING ONLY A LEVAIN. GENEROUSLY STUDDED WITH CANDIED FRUIT, ITS FLAVOR AND TEXTURE ARE INCOMPARABLE, MAKING IT A FAVORITE CHRISTMAS DESSERT BOTH IN ITALY AND FOR MANY PEOPLE OF ITALIAN DESCENT AROUND THE WORLD.

MAKES 17 LOAVES

KNEADING INGREDIENTS

LEVAIN REFRESHMENT

Stiff levain	**600 G (1 LB 6 ⅛ OZ)**
Water at 38°C (100°F)	**1 KG (2 LB 3 ¼ OZ)**
Superfine sugar	**5 G (3/16 OZ)**

FIRST REFRESHMENT

Reactivated stiff levain	**600 G (1 LB 6 ⅛ OZ)**
Oat flour	**600 G (1 LB 6 ⅛ OZ)**
Water at 30°C (85°F)	**180 G (6 ⅜ OZ)**

SECOND REFRESHMENT

Stiff levain from the first refreshment	**600 G (1 LB 6 ⅛ OZ)**
Oat flour	**600 G (1 LB 6 ⅛ OZ)**
Water at 30°C (85°F)	**300 G (10 ½ OZ)**

THIRD REFRESHMENT

Stiff levain from the second refreshment	**1 KG (2 LB 3 ¼ OZ)**
Oat flour	**1 KG (2 LB 3 ¼ OZ)**
Water at 30°C (85°F)	**500 G (1 LB 1 ⅝ OZ)**

FOURTH REFRESHMENT

Superfine sugar	**875 G (1 LB 14 ⅞ OZ)**
Water at 30°C (86°F)	**500 G (1 LB 1 ⅝ OZ)**
Egg yolks	**625 G (1 LB 6 OZ)**
Stiff levain from the third refreshment	**1.5 KG (3 LB 7 OZ)**
Oat flour	**2 KG (4 LB 6 OZ)**
Egg yolks	**500 G (1 LB 1 ⅝ OZ)**
Water	**350 G (12 ⅜ OZ)**
Unsalted butter	**1.125 KG (2 ½ LB)**

LEVAIN REFRESHMENT

Soak the levain in the water mixed with the sugar for 30 minutes.

FOR THE FIRST REFRESHMENT

In a stand mixer on speed 1, beat all the ingredients. Let ferment at 30°C (85°F) for 3 hours.

FOR THE SECOND REFRESHMENT

In the stand mixer on speed 1, beat all the ingredients. Let ferment at 30°C (85°F) for 3 hours.

FOR THE THIRD REFRESHMENT

In the stand mixer on speed 1, beat all the ingredients. Let ferment for 2 to 3 hours.

FOR THE FOURTH REFRESHMENT

In the stand mixer on speed 1, mix the 875 grams (1 lb 14 ⅞ oz) of sugar and the 500 grams (1 lb 1 ⅝ oz) of water at 30°C (85°F). Add the 625 grams (1 lb 6 oz) of egg yolks, then the 1.5 kilograms (3 lb 5 oz) of levain from the third refreshment and, on speed 1, beat for 2 minutes. On speed 2, add the 2 kilograms (4 lb 6 oz) of flour and knead until the dough comes away from the sides the bowl. On speed 1, add the 500 grams (1 lb 1 ⅝ oz) egg yolks, followed by the 350 grams (12 ⅜ oz) of water. When the dough is smooth, add the butter and knead again until smooth. Place in a buttered stainless steel container and fold to degas once. Brush the surface of the dough with melted butter and let ferment at 27°C (80°F) until tripled in volume (about 12 hours).

FINAL KNEADING PANETTONE DOUGH

Levain from the fourth refreshment	7.475 KG (16 ½ LB)
Oat flour	1.125 KG (2 ½ LB)
Egg yolks	450 G (15 ⅞ OZ)
Superfine sugar	325 G (11 ½ OZ)
Honey	100 G (3 ½ OZ)
Unsalted butter	600 G (1 LB 6 ⅛ OZ)
Salt	90 G (3 ⅛ OZ)
Vanilla beans	5
Pastry cream	170 G (6 OZ)

MACERATED RAISINS

Raisins	1 KG (2 LB 3 ¼ OZ)
Orange juice	300 G (10 ½ OZ)
Oranges, zest only	5

FILLING

Candied citron, diced	1 KG (2 LB 3 ¼ OZ)
Candied orange, diced	1 KG (2 LB 3 ¼ OZ)
Macerated raisins	1.3 KG (2 LB 14 OZ)

MACARONADE

Ground hazelnuts	800 G (1 ¾ LB)
Cornstarch	100 G (3 ½ OZ)
Superfine sugar	650 G (1 LB 7 OZ)
Egg whites	600 G (1 LB 6 ⅛ OZ)

TO FINISH

Confectioners' sugar	AS NEEDED

FOR THE MACERATED RAISINS

Macerate the raisins in the water and orange zest for at least 12 hours.

FOR THE MACARONADE

Mix all ingredients together.

METHOD

BASE TEMPERATURE	48 to 52°C (120 to 125°F).
INCORPORATE	In a spiral mixer, mix the fourth refreshment and the flour in the bowl.
INITIAL MIX	On speed 1 for about 3 minutes.
INCORPORATE	Add the egg yolks.
KNEAD	On speed 2 for about 5 minutes, until the dough comes away from the sides of the bowl.
INCORPORATE	On speed 1, add the sugar, honey, butter, salt, vanilla bean (split and scraped), and pastry cream. When the dough is smooth, on speed 1, add the filling in two batches.
CONSISTENCY	Soft dough.
DOUGH TEMPERATURE	24°C (75°F).
BULK FERMENT	About 1 hour.
WEIGHT	Seventeen 800-gram (1 ¾-lb) dough pieces.
PRESHAPE	Shape into balls.
REST	About 15 minutes.
SHAPE	Shape into balls, then place the dough pieces in 21-centimeter (8 ¼-inch) diameter, 6-centimeter (2 ½-inch) deep panettone pans.
FINAL PROOF	At 27°C (80°F) for about 6 to 7 hours.
FINISH	Spread the macaronade over the surface of the panettones and sprinkle generously with confectioners' sugar.
BAKE	In a convection oven at 150°C (300°F) for about 40 minutes.
COOL	Inverted for at least 2 hours. Insert the needles provided with the molds through the base of the molds.

PANDORO

MAKES 20 LOAVES

KNEADING INGREDIENTS

LEVAIN REFRESHMENT

Stiff levain	200 G (7 OZ)
Water at 38°C (100°F)	1 KG (2 LB 3 1/4 OZ)
Superfine sugar	3 G (1/8 OZ)

FIRST REFRESHMENT

Reactivated stiff levain	110 G (3 7/8 OZ)
Oat flour	140 G (1 3/8 OZ) (5 OZ)
Water at 26°C (80°F)	60 G (2 1/8 OZ)

SECOND REFRESHMENT

Stiff levain from the first refreshment	300 G (10 1/2 OZ)
Oat flour	370 G (13 OZ)
Water at 26°C (80°F)	160 G (5 5/8 OZ)

THIRD REFRESHMENT

Stiff levain from the second refreshment	800 G (1 3/4 LB)
Oat flour	800 G (1 3/4 LB)
Water at 26°C (80°F)	340 G (12 OZ)

FOURTH REFRESHMENT

Stiff levain from the third refreshment	600 G (1 LB 6 1/8 OZ)
Oat flour	2 KG (4 LB 6 OZ)
Eggs	1.74 KG (3 LB 13 OZ)
Superfine sugar	600 G (1 LB 6 1/8 OZ)
Unsalted butter	900 G (1 LB 15 3/4 OZ)

FINAL KNEAD

PANDORO DOUGH

Stiff levain from the fourth refreshment	6. 675 KG (14 3/4 LB)
Oat flour	1 KG (2 LB 3 1/4 OZ)
Instant dry milk powder	120 G (4 1/4 OZ)
Liquid malt	35 G (1 1/4 OZ)
Eggs	1 KG (2 LB 3 1/4 OZ)
Salt	55 G (2 OZ)
Emulsified butters	1. 83 KG (4 LB)

EMULSIFIED BUTTERS

Unsalted butter	1.1 KG (2 LB 3 1/4 OZ)
Cocoa butter	120 G (4 1/4 OZ)
Vanilla beans	2
Superfine sugar	620 G (1 LB 5 7/8 OZ)
Honey	120 G (4 1/4 OZ)

TO FINISH

Confectioners' sugar	AS NEEDED

FOR REACTIVATING THE LEVAIN

Soak the levain in the water and sugar for 30 minutes.

FOR THE FIRST REFRESHMENT

In a stand mixer on speed 1, beat all the ingredients. Let ferment at 26°C (80°F) for about 3 hours.

FOR THE SECOND REFRESHMENT

In the stand mixer on speed 1, beat all the ingredients. Let ferment at 26°C (80°F) for about 3 hours.

FOR THE THIRD REFRESHMENT

In the stand mixer on speed 1, beat all the ingredients. Let ferment at 26°C (80°F) for about 3 hours.

FOR THE FOURTH REFRESHMENT

In the stand mixer on speed 1, beat the third refreshment, the flour and eggs, then, on speed 2, knead until the dough comes away from the sides of the bowl. On speed 1, add the sugar in two batches, then add the butters until the dough is smooth. Place in a buttered stainless steel container and fold to degas once. Brush the surface of the dough with melted butter and let ferment at 27°C (80°F) until tripled in volume (about 12 hours).

FOR THE EMULSIFIED BUTTERS

Melt the cocoa butter. In the stand mixer fitted with the paddle attachment, emulsify the butters, vanilla, sugar, and honey.

METHOD

BASE TEMPERATURE	48 to 52°C (120 to 125°F).
INCORPORATE	In a spiral mixer, mix the fourth refreshment, oat flour, milk powder, and liquid malt in the bowl.
FIRST MIX	On speed 1 for about 3 minutes.
INCORPORATE	Add the eggs and salt.
KNEAD	On speed 2 for about 5 minutes, until the dough comes away from the sides of the bowl.
INCORPORATE	When the dough is smooth, on speed 1, add the emulsified butters.
CONSISTENCY	Soft dough.
DOUGH TEMPERATURE	26°C (80°F).
BULK FERMENT	About 30 minutes.
PUNCH DOWN	After 15 minutes.
WEIGHT	Twenty 500-gram (1 lb 1 ⅝-oz) dough pieces.
PRESHAPE	Shape into balls.
REST	About 30 minutes.
SHAPE	Shape into balls and place the dough pieces in the pregreased 14-centimeter (5 ½-inch) diameter, 14-centimeter (5 ½-inch)-deep pandoro pans.
FINAL PROOF	At 27°C (80°F) for about 6 to 7 hours.
BAKE	In a convection oven at 140°C (285°F) for about 30 minutes.
COOL	In the pans for at least 2 hours.
FINISH	Sprinkle the pandoros with confectioners' sugar.

MELON PAN

MELON PAN IS ONE OF THE MOST POPULAR BAKED GOODS IN JAPAN. EATEN AT ALL HOURS OF THE DAY, YOU CAN FIND THESE ROLLS EVERYWHERE. SOFT ON THE INSIDE AND CRISP ON THE OUTSIDE, THEIR ROUNDED SHAPE WITH A PATTERN OF SQUARES IS REMINISCENT OF A HALF CANTALOUPE MELON, HENCE THE NAME.

MAKES 60 ROLLS

KNEADING INGREDIENTS

Strong flour	1 KG (2 LB 3 ¼ OZ)
Water	450 G (15 ⅞ OZ)
Eggs	150 G (5 ¼ OZ)
Salt	18 G (⅝ OZ)
Superfine sugar	200 G (7 OZ)
Yeast	30 G (1 OZ)
Viennese fermented dough *(see page 28)*	400 G (14 OZ)
Instant dry milk powder	30 G (1 OZ)
Unsalted butter	150 G (5 ¼ OZ)

SWEET PASTRY DOUGH

Strong flour	875 G (1 LB 14 ⅞ OZ)
Baking powder	9 G (5/16 OZ)
Unsalted butter	310 G (11 OZ)
Superfine sugar	310 G (11 OZ)
Eggs	310 G (11 OZ)

FOR THE SWEET PASTRY DOUGH

Sift the flour and baking powder together. In a stand mixer fitted with the paddle attachment, beat the butter and sugar. Add the eggs, then the flour and baking powder, and beat until smooth. Weigh out sixty 30-gram (1-oz) dough pieces. Shape into balls, then flatten between two guitar sheets to a diameter of 7 centimeters (2 ¾ inches).

METHOD

BASE TEMPERATURE 46 to 50°C (115 to 120°F).

INCORPORATE In the stand mixer, mix all the kneading ingredients in the bowl.

INITIAL MIX On speed 1 for about 3 minutes.

KNEAD On speed 2 for about 8 minutes.

CONSISTENCY Medium-firm dough.

DOUGH TEMPERATURE 23°C (35°F).

BULK FERMENT About 1 hour.

WEIGHT Sixty 40-gram (1 ⅜-oz) dough pieces.

PRESHAPE Shape into balls.

REST About 15 minutes.

SHAPE Shape into balls, then cover the dough pieces with the disks of sweet pastry dough.
Gently roll so that the sweet pastry dough covers the dough balls perfectly. Using a bowl scraper or a special melon pan mold, score the sweet pastry dough in a diamond pattern. Place them on baking sheets lined with parchment paper.

FINAL PROOF At 27°C (80°F) for about 2 hours.

BAKE In a deck oven at 200°C (390°F) for about 15 minutes.

COOL On a wire rack.

CONCHAS

FROM MEXICO, THESE ROLLS ARE CHARACTERIZED BY THEIR SHELL-LIKE SHAPE, HENCE THEIR NAME *CONCHA,* MEANING "SHELL" IN SPANISH. THE COME IN ALL COLORS AND ARE ONE OF THE MOST POPULAR BRIOCHES IN MEXICO. A SPECIAL CUTTING TOOL IS AVAILABLE TO MAKE SHAPING CONCHAS EASIER.

MAKES 50 ROLLS

KNEADING INGREDIENTS

Strong flour	**1 KG (2 LB 3 1/4 OZ)**
Milk	**300 G (10 1/2 OZ)**
Eggs	**250 G (8 3/4 OZ)**
Egg yolks	**40 G (1 3/8 OZ)**
Salt	**18 G (5/8 OZ)**
Superfine sugar	**150 G (5 1/4 OZ)**
Yeast	**40 G (1 3/8 OZ)**
Viennese fermented dough *(see page 28)*	**250 G (8 3/4 OZ)**
Unsalted butter	**200 G (7 OZ)**

SWEET COCOA PASTRY DOUGH

Strong flour	**200 G (7 OZ)**
Unsweetened cocoa powder	**50 G**
Confectioners' sugar	**250 G (8 3/4 OZ)**
Unsalted butter	**250 G (8 3/4 OZ)**
Ground black pepper	**AS NEEDED**
Ground cinnamon	**AS NEEDED**

FOR THE SWEET COCOA PASTRY DOUGH

Using a stand mixer fitted with the paddle attachment, beat all the ingredients together. Weigh out fifty 15-gram (1/2-oz) dough pieces. Shape into balls, then flatten gently to a diameter of 6 centimeters (2 1/2 inches).

METHOD

BASE TEMPERATURE 44 to 48°C (115 to 120°F).

INCORPORATE In the stand mixer, mix all the kneading ingredients in the bowl.

INITIAL MIX On speed 1 for about 3 minutes.

KNEAD On speed 2 for about 9 minutes.

CONSISTENCY Medium-firm dough.

DOUGH TEMPERATURE 23°C (35°F).

BULK FERMENT About 1 hour.

WEIGHT Fifty 45-gram (1 1/2-oz) dough pieces.

PRESHAPE Shape into balls.

REST 30 minutes.

SHAPE Shape into balls, then place the sweet cocoa pastry dough on top.
Press gently to ensure that both doughs are the same diameter. Using a bowl scraper, score a scallop pattern on the sweet cocoa pastry dough. Alternatively, use a special "concha" cutter. Place them on baking sheets lined with parchment paper.

FINAL PROOF At 27°C (80°F) for about 2 hours.

BAKE In a deck oven at 200°C (390°F) for about 15 minutes.

COOL On a wire rack.

PAN DE MUERTO

HAILING FROM MEXICO, *PAN DE MUERTO* MEANS "BREAD OF THE DEAD." EVERY YEAR, ON THE DAY OF THE DEAD, THESE ROLLS ARE MADE AND GIVEN AS AN OFFERING TO THE DEPARTED. THE MAIN ROLL REPRESENTS THE BODY, THE BALL ON THE TOP IS THE SKULL, AND THE OTHER PIECES OF DOUGH EVOKE THE BONES OF THE DECEASED.

MAKES 6 ROLLS

KNEADING INGREDIENTS

Strong flour	**1 KG (2 LB 3 ¼ OZ)**
Eggs	**250 G (8 ¾ OZ)**
Egg yolks	**80 G (1 LB 1 ⅝ OZ)**
Milk	**200 G (7 OZ)**
Orange blossom water	**30 G (1 OZ)**
Salt	**18 G (⅝ OZ)**
Superfine sugar	**150 G (5 ¼ OZ)**
Yeast	**40 G (1 ⅜ OZ)**
Orange, zest only	**1**

FINAL KNEADING

Unsalted butter	**200 G (7 OZ)**

TO FINISH

Unsalted butter, melted	**AS NEEDED**
Superfine sugar	**AS NEEDED**

METHOD

BASE TEMPERATURE	48 to 52°C (120 to 125°F).
INCORPORATE	In a stand mixer, mix all the kneading ingredients in the bowl.
INITIAL MIX	On speed 1 for about 3 minutes.
KNEAD	On speed 2 for about 6 minutes.
INCORPORATE	On speed 1, add the butter until the dough is smooth.
CONSISTENCY	Medium-firm dough.
DOUGH TEMPERATURE	23°C (35°F).
BULK FERMENT	About 1 hour.
WEIGHT	Six 225-gram (8-oz) dough pieces, eighteen 30-gram (1-oz) dough pieces, and six 10-gram (⅜-oz) dough pieces.
SHAPE	Roll the 225-gram (8-oz) and 10-gram (⅜-oz) dough pieces into balls. Stretch out the 30-gram (1-oz) dough pieces to lengthen them.
REST	About 30 minutes.
SHAPE	Gently roll the 225-gram (8-oz) dough pieces into balls and place them on baking sheets lined with parchment paper. Make strings of six beads from each of the 30-gram (1-oz) dough pieces. Place three strings of beads on each 225-gram (8-oz) ball in a star shape. Place a 10-gram (⅜-oz) ball where the strings of beads overlap each other.
FINAL PROOF	At 27°C (80°F) for about 2 hours.
BAKE	In a convection oven at 150°C (300°C) for about 25 minutes.
COOL	On a wire rack.
TO FINISH	Dip the rolls in the melted butter and let them soak in the butter for 5 minutes. Roll in the superfine sugar.

BABKA

MAKES 4 LOAVES

BRIOCHE DOUGH

(see page 184)	1 KG (2 LB 3 1/4 OZ)

CHOCOLATE PRALINE

Milk couverture chocolate 44%	110 G (3 7/8 OZ)
Unsalted butter	100 G (3 1/2 OZ)
Confectioners' sugar	40 G (1 3/8 OZ)
Unsweetened cocoa powder	25 G (7/8 OZ)
Hazelnut praline	130 G (4 1/2 OZ)

FILLING

Milk couverture chocolate 44%	160 G (5 5/8 OZ)

WATER GLAZE

Water	120 G (4 1/4 OZ)
Unsweetened cocoa powder	15 G (1/2 OZ)
Confectioners' sugar	675 G (1 LB 7 3/4 OZ)

FOR THE CHOCOLATE PRALINE

Melt the chocolate and butter. Remove from the heat and stir in the remaining ingredients.

FOR THE WATER GLAZE

Mix all the ingredients together, then blend with an immersion blender until smooth. To make glazing the loaves easier, it is best to make more glaze than you will actually need.

METHOD

WEIGHT Four 250-gram (8 3/4-oz) dough pieces.

PRESHAPE Rectangle.

SHAPE Roll out the dough into a 22 × 34-centimeter (8 3/4 × 13 1/2-inch) rectangle.
Spread 100 grams (3 1/2 oz) of chocolate praline over the surface of the dough, keeping a strip free for sealing. Sprinkle the dough pieces with 40 grams (1 3/8 oz) of the chopped milk chocolate. Roll the dough lengthwise, then cut in half lengthwise. Twist the two strands together. Place in greased 18 × 8 × 8 centimeter (7 × 3 1/4 × 3 1/4-inch) loaf pans lined with parchment paper.

FINAL PROOF At 3°C (35°F) for about 12 hours, then at 27°C (80°F) for about 3 hours.

BAKE In a convection oven at 150°C (300°F) for about 30 minutes.

FINISH Glaze the loaves with the water glaze.

BAKE To dry the glaze, place the loaves in a convection oven, with the vent open, at 90°C (195°F) for about 4 minutes.

COOL On a wire rack.

BUTTER BRAIDS

POPULAR IN SWITZERLAND, THESE LOAVES HAVE BECOME A SUNDAY BREAKFAST STAPLE. LEGEND HAS IT THAT BUTTER BRAIDS WERE INVENTED TO REPLACE THE OFFERINGS THAT YOUNG WOMEN MADE OF THEIR TRESSES TO PAGAN DEITIES.

MAKES 4 LOAVES

KNEADING INGREDIENTS

Strong flour	**1 KG (2 LB 3 ¹⁄₄ OZ)**
Water	**275 G (9 ³⁄₄ OZ)**
Milk	**275 G (9 ³⁄₄ OZ)**
Salt	**18 G (⁵⁄₈ OZ)**
Superfine sugar	**40 G (1 ³⁄₈ OZ)**
Yeast	**30 G (1 OZ)**
Viennese fermented dough *(see page 28)*	**250 G (8 ³⁄₄ OZ)**
Unsalted butter	**200 G (7 OZ)**

METHOD

BASE TEMPERATURE	46 to 50°C (115 to 120°F).
INCORPORATE	In a stand mixer, mix all the kneading ingredients in the bowl.
INITIAL MIX	On speed 1 for about 3 minutes.
KNEAD	On speed 2 for about 6 minutes.
CONSISTENCY	Medium-firm dough.
DOUGH TEMPERATURE	23°C (35°F).
BULK FERMENT	About 45 minutes.
WEIGHT	Four 250-gram (8 ³⁄₄-oz) dough pieces.
SHAPE	Elongated, 15 centimeters (6 inches) long.
REST	At 3°C (35°F) for about 1 hour.
SHAPE	Shape into 55-centimeter (21 ¹⁄₂-inch)-long strands, tapered at the ends. Use two strands of dough to make a deep, two-strand braid.
GLAZE	Whisked egg.
FINAL PROOF	At 3°C (35°F) for about 12 hours, then at 27°C (80°F) for about 30 minutes.
GLAZE	Whisked egg.
BAKE	In a deck oven at 220°C (430°F) for about 30 minutes.
COOL	On a wire rack.

RUSSIAN BRAIDS

MAKES 8 LOAVES

KNEADING INGREDIENTS

BRIOCHE DOUGH

Strong flour	1 KG (2 LB 3 ¼ OZ)
Eggs	650 G (1 LB 7 OZ)
Salt	18 G (⅝ OZ)
Superfine sugar	150 G (5 ¼ OZ)
Yeast	25 G (⅞ OZ)
Viennese fermented dough *(see page 28)*	250 G (8 ¾ OZ)

FINAL KNEADING

Unsalted butter	500 G (1 LB 1 ⅝ OZ)

ALMOND FILLING

Confectioners' sugar	650 G (1 LB 7 OZ)
Unblanched almond flour	650 G (1 LB 7 OZ)
Strong flour	200 G (7 OZ)
Eggs	500 G (1 LB 1 ⅝ OZ)
Rum	50 G (1 ¾ OZ)

WATER GLAZE

Water	240 G (8 ½ OZ)
Rum	30 G (1 OZ)
Confectioners' sugar	1.35 KG

FOR THE ALMOND FILLING

Combine the sugar and almond flour. Mix all the ingredients together.

FOR THE WATER GLAZE

Mix all the ingredients together, then blend using an immersion blender.
Note: To make glazing the loaves easier, it is best to make more glaze than you will actually need.

METHOD

BASE TEMPERATURE	48 to 52°C (120 to 125°F).
INCORPORATE	In a stand mixer, mix all the kneading ingredients in the bowl.
INITIAL MIX	On speed 1 for about 5 minutes.
KNEAD	On speed 2 for about 5 minutes.
INCORPORATE	On speed 1, add the butter until the dough is smooth.
CONSISTENCY	Medium-firm dough.
DOUGH TEMPERATURE	23°C (35°F).
BULK FERMENT	About 30 minutes.
WEIGHT	Eight 320-gram (11 ¼-oz) dough pieces.
SHAPE	Shape the dough pieces into rectangles that are as even as possible.
REST	At 3°C (35°F) for about 2 hours.
SHAPE	Roll out the dough pieces into 40 × 30-centimeter (15 ½ × 11 ¾-inch) rectangles. Spread 250 grams (8 ¾ oz) of the almond filling over the dough, keeping a strip free for sealing. Roll the dough pieces widthwise. Cut the dough strands in half lengthwise and twist the two strands together. Place in greased 30 × 8 × 8-centimeter (11 ¾ × 3 ¼ × 3 ¼-inch) loaf pans lined with parchment paper.
FINAL PROOF	At 3°C (35°F) for about 12 hours, then at 27°C (80°F) for about 3 hours.
BAKE	In a convection oven at 150°C (300°F) for about 30 minutes.
FINISH	While hot, glaze the loaves with the water glaze.
BAKE	To dry the glaze, place the loaves in a convection oven, with the vent open, at 90°C (195°F) for about 4 minutes.
COOL	On a wire rack.

FAN
CY

VIE
NNO
ISE
RIE

PISTACHIO AND BLACK CURRANT ACCORDIONS

MAKES 12 PASTRIES

PLAIN BRIOCHE DOUGH

(see page 184)	**800 G (1 ¾ LB)**

ALMOND AND PISTACHIO PASTE

Almond paste 50%	**180 G (6 ⅜ OZ)**
Pistachio paste	**30 G (1 OZ)**
Egg white	**18 G (⅝ OZ)**

ALMOND PASTE AND BLACK CURRANT PASTE

Almond paste 50%	**180 G (6 ⅜ OZ)**
Black currant puree	**40 G (1 ⅜ OZ)**

TO FINISH

Neutral syrup *(see page 31)*	**AS NEEDED**

FOR THE ALMOND AND PISTACHIO PASTE

In a stand mixer fitted with the paddle attachment, loosen the almond paste with the pistachio paste and the eggs **(1)**. Set aside in a pastry bag fitted with a 10-millimeter (1/3-inch) plain tip.

FOR THE ALMOND AND BLACK CURRANT PASTE

In the stand mixer fitted with the paddle attachment, loosen the almond paste with the black currant puree **(2)**. Set aside in a pastry bag fitted with a 10-millimeter (1/3-inch) plain tip.

METHOD

WEIGHT One 800-gram (1 3/4-lb) dough piece.

PRESHAPE Using a dough sheeter, roll out the dough into a 56 × 44-centimeters (22 × 17 1/2-inch) rectangle.

REST In the freezer for about 15 minutes.

SHAPE Pipe a line of pistachio almond paste 3 centimeters (1 1/4 inches) from the top edge of the dough **(3)**, lightly moisten with glaze, and fold to encase the paste **(4, 5)**. Turn the dough over and pipe a line of black currant almond paste, lightly moisten with glaze, and fold to encase the paste **(6)**. Repeat four times to obtain five lines of each color, using the entire rectangle of dough **(7, 8, 9)**.

REST In the freezer for about 30 minutes.

CUT TO SIZE Using a knife, cut the dough into 12 even pieces **(10)**. Place the accordions in greased 12 × 5.5 × 5-centimeter (4 3/4 × 2 1/4 × 2-inch) flared loaf pans **(11)**.

GLAZE Whisked egg **(12)**.

FINAL PROOF At 27°C (80°F) for about 2 hours 30 minutes.

BAKE In a convection oven at 145°C (295°F), or in a deck oven at180°C (355°F), for about 15 minutes.

TO FINISH Brush with neutral syrup.

COOL On a wire rack.

1

2

3

4

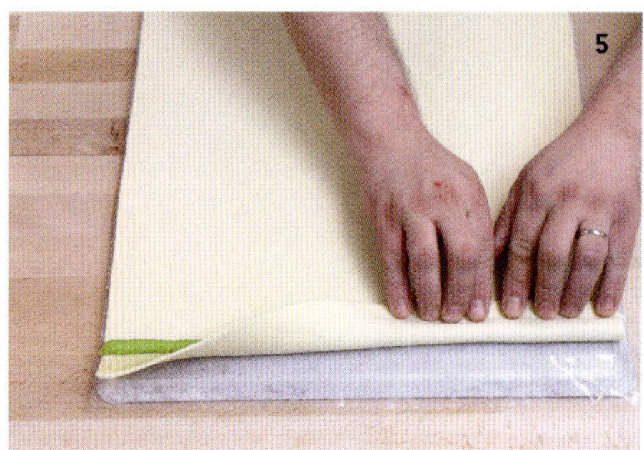
5

6

7

8

9

10

11

12

VANILLA AND STRAWBERRY RINGS

MAKES 12 RINGS

PLAIN LEAVENED LAMINATED DOUGH

Croissant dough *(see page 186)*	500 G (1 LB 2 OZ)
Dry butter *(see page 10)*	180 G (6 3/8 OZ)

RED CROISSANT DOUGH

Croissant dough *(see page 186)*	96 G (3 3/8 OZ)
Red food coloring	4 G (1/8 OZ)

FILLING

Vanilla pastry cream *(see page 30)*	240 G (8 1/2 OZ)

STRAWBERRY CREAM

Strawberry puree	150 G (5 1/4 OZ)
Superfine sugar	40 G (1 3/8 OZ)
Custard powder	16 G (5/8 OZ)

STRAWBERRY JELLY

Strawberry puree	170 G (6 OZ)
Superfine sugar	70 G (2 1/2 OZ)
Pectin NH	3 G (1/8 OZ)

TO FINISH

Neutral syrup *(see page 31)*	AS NEEDED

FOR THE RED CROISSANT DOUGH

In a stand mixer fitted with the paddle attachment, beat the ingredients for the red croissant dough on speed 1 until smooth. Bulk ferment about 40 minutes, then at 1°C (35°F) for 12 hours.

FOR THE STRAWBERRY CREAM

Combine the sugar and custard powder.
Gently heat the strawberry puree.
Add the sugar and custard mixture and bring to a boil.
Set aside at 3°C (35°F).

FOR THE STRAWBERRY VANILLA INSERTS

Pipe 20 grams (3/4 oz) of pastry cream **(1)** into 5-centimeter (2-inch)-diameter silicone molds and top with 15 gram (1/2 oz) of strawberry cream **(2)**. Set aside in the freezer.

FOR THE STRAWBERRY JELLY

Combine the sugar and pectin. Gently heat the strawberry puree. Add the sugar and pectin mixture and bring to a boil. Set aside at 3°C (35°F).

METHOD

TURNING (*TOURAGE*) Degas the dough. Encase the dry butter in the dough. Make two single turns *(see page 14)*. Moisten the surface of the dough **(3)**, then roll out the red croissant dough to the size of the turning (*tourage*) dough **(4)**.

REST At 1°C (35°F) for 45 minutes.

PRESHAPE Using a dough sheeter, roll out the dough to a thickness of 3 millimeters (3/16 inch), then into a 30 × 50-centimeter (11 3/4 × 19 1/2-inch) rectangle.

REST In the freezer for about 15 minutes.

CUT TO SIZE Cut out twelve 4 × 18-centimeter (1 1/2 × 7-inch) rectangles and twelve 3.5 × 8-centimeter (1 3/8 × 3 1/4-inch) rectangles. Roll out the dough scraps to a thickness of 1 millimeter (1/32 inch), chill in the freezer for 10 minutes, then cut out twelve 6-centimeter (2 1/2-inch)-diameter disks.

FILL Pipe strawberry cream along the center of the 4 × 18-centimeter (1 1/2 × 7-inch) rectangles **(5)**.

SHAPE Moisten the edges of the rectangles, then roll them up **(6)**. Score with a sausage cut **(7, 8)**. Shape into rings **(9)** and seal with the previously moistened 3.5 × 8-centimeter (1 3/8 × 3 1/4-inch) rectangles **(10, 11)**. Place the 6-centimeter (2 1/2-inch) disks of dough in previously greased 10-centimeter (4-inch)-diameter molds **(12)**, then add the rings.

FINAL PROOF At 27°C (80°F) for about 2 hours 30 minutes.

PREBAKE PREP Place a strawberry vanilla cream insert in the middle **(13)**.

BAKE In a convection oven at 170°C (340°F) for about 14 minutes.

TO FINISH Brush with neutral syrup.

COOL On a wire rack.

TO FINISH Gently heat the strawberry jelly, then fill the centers of the pastries.

1

2

3

4

5

6

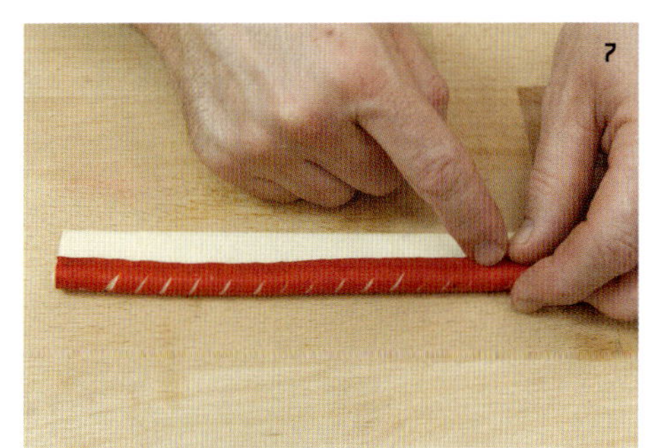
7

8

9

10

11

12

13

CHOCOLATE AND PRALINE CHALICES

MAKES 12 PASTRIES

BRIOCHE DOUGH

(see page 184)	**800 G (1 ¾ LB)**

COCOA BRIOCHE DOUGH

Brioche dough *(see page. 184)*	**200 G (7 OZ)**
Unsweetened cocoa powder	**20 G (¾ OZ)**
Milk	**20 G (¾ OZ)**

CHOCOLATE ALMOND-HAZELNUT MIXTURE

Milk couverture chocolate 40%	**100 G (3 ½ OZ)**
Dark couverture chocolate 60%	**75 G (2 ⅝ OZ)**
Almond-hazelnut praline	**175 G (2 ⅝ OZ)**

PRALINE CREAM

Milk	**155 G**
Superfine sugar	**30 G (1 OZ)**
Egg yolks	**30 G (1 OZ)**
Cornstarch	**15 G (½ OZ)**
Pectin NH	**8 G (¼ OZ)**
Almond and hazelnut praline	**85 G (3 OZ)**

TO FINISH

Neutral syrup	**AS NEEDED**

FOR THE COCOA BRIOCHE DOUGH

In a stand mixer fitted with the paddle attachment, beat all the ingredients on speed 1 until smooth. Bulk ferment for about 20 minutes.
Shape into a square, then let rest at 3°C (35°F) for 12 hours.

FOR THE CHOCOLATE ALMOND-HAZELNUT MIXTURE

Melt the chocolates and praline, then stir. Pipe 28 grams (1 oz) into 6-centimeter (2 ½-inch)-diameter silicone-coated savarin molds **(1)**. Set aside at 3°C (35°F).

FOR THE PRALINE CREAM

Heat the milk. Mix the eggs, sugar, and dry ingredients together. Combine the two mixtures and bring to a boil for about 30 seconds (the cream should be slightly undercooked). Remove from the heat and stir in the praline. Pipe 20 grams (¾ oz) into 4-centimeter (1 ½-inch)-diameter silicone hemisphere molds **(2)**. Set aside in the freezer.

METHOD

PRESHAPE Encase the cocoa dough in the plain dough **(3, 4)**.

SHAPE THE DOUGH Using a dough sheeter, roll out the dough to a thickness of 3 mm (⅛ inch), then into a 40 × 60-centimeter (15 ½ × 23 ½-inch) rectangle.

REST In the freezer for about 30 minutes.

CUT TO SIZE Using a pastry cutter, cut out twelve 11-centimeter (4 ¼-inch)-diameter disks **(5)**. Using a spiral cutter, cut 12 curves into the disks **(6, 7)**.

SHAPE Place a chocolate-praline insert in the center of each disk, then fold the curved sections of dough over the insert **(8, 9)**. Place in greased 9-centimeter (3 ½-inch) flared molds.

FINAL PROOF At 27°C (80°F) for about 2 hours 30 minutes.

PREBAKE PREP Gently place a praline cream hemisphere in the center of each pastry **(10)**.

BAKE In a convection at 145°C (295°F) for 15 minutes.

FINISH Brush with neutral syrup **(11)**.

COOL On a wire rack.

CHOCORANGES

MAKES 12 PASTRIES

LEAVENED LAMINATED DOUGH

Croissant dough *(see page 186)*	**720 G (1 LB 9 3/8 OZ) (3/4 OZ)**
Dry butter *(see page 10)*	**180 G (6 3/8 OZ)**

ORANGE FILLING

Almond flour	**65 G (2 1/4 OZ)**
Superfine sugar	**80 G (2 7/8 OZ)**
Eggs	**120 G (4 1/4 OZ)**
Orange juice	**40 G (1 3/8 OZ)**
Orange, zest only	**1**
Brown butter	**85 G (3 OZ)**

CHOCOLATE MIRROR GLAZE

Water	**100 G (3 1/2 OZ)**
Superfine sugar	**180 G (6 3/8 OZ)**
Whipping cream 35% fat	**85 G (3 OZ)**
Unsweetened cocoa powder	**65 G (2 1/4 OZ)**
Unflavored jelly powder	**10 G (3/8 OZ)**
Cold water for the jelly	**50 G (1 3/4 OZ)**

TO FINISH

Confectioners' sugar	**AS NEEDED**
Gold leaf	**AS NEEDED**

FOR THE ORANGE BATTER

Mix all the ingredients together, stirring in the warm brown butter last. Pour the batter into 6-centimeter (2 ½-inch)-diameter silicone molds **(1)**.
Set aside in the freezer.

FOR THE CHOCOLATE MIRROR GLAZE

Soak the jelly in the cold water.
Bring the remaining ingredients to a boil, add the jelly and the soaking water, then bring to a boil for about 1 minute.
Cover with plastic wrap in direct contact and set aside at 3°C (35°F).
Use at 35°C (95°F).

METHOD

TURNING (*TOURAGE*) Degas the dough. Encase the dry butter in the dough. Make two double turns *(see page 14)*.

REST At 1°C (35°F) for about 45 minutes.

PRESHAPE Using a dough sheeter, roll out the dough to a thickness of 4 millimeters (3/16 inch), then into a 37 × 28-centimeter (14 ½ × 11-inch) rectangle

REST In the freezer for about 15 minutes.

CUT TO SIZE Using a 9-centimeter (3 ½-inch)-diameter pastry cutter, cut out 12 disks, then make a hole in the center of each one with a 5-centimeter (2-inch)-diameter pastry cutter **(2)**.
Roll out the dough scraps to a thickness of 1.5 millimeters (1/32 inch), chill in the freezer for 10 minutes, then cut into twelve 9-centimeter (3 ½-inch)-diameter disks **(3)**.

SHAPE Place the twelve 1.5-millimeter (1/32-inch)-thick disks on a baking sheet lined with parchment paper, then place a glazed ring on top of each one **(4, 5)**.

GLAZE Whisked egg.

FINAL PROOF At 27°C (80°F) for about 2 hours.

GLAZE Whisked egg **(6)**.

PREBAKE PREP Place a frozen orange filling in the center of each pastry **(7)**.

BAKE In a convection oven at 170°C (340°F), or a deck oven at 200°C (390°F), for about 17 minutes.

COOL On a wire rack.

TO FINISH Sprinkle with confectioners' sugar **(8)**. Pour the chocolate mirror glaze into the centers **(9)**. Place a piece of gold leaf on top **(10)**.

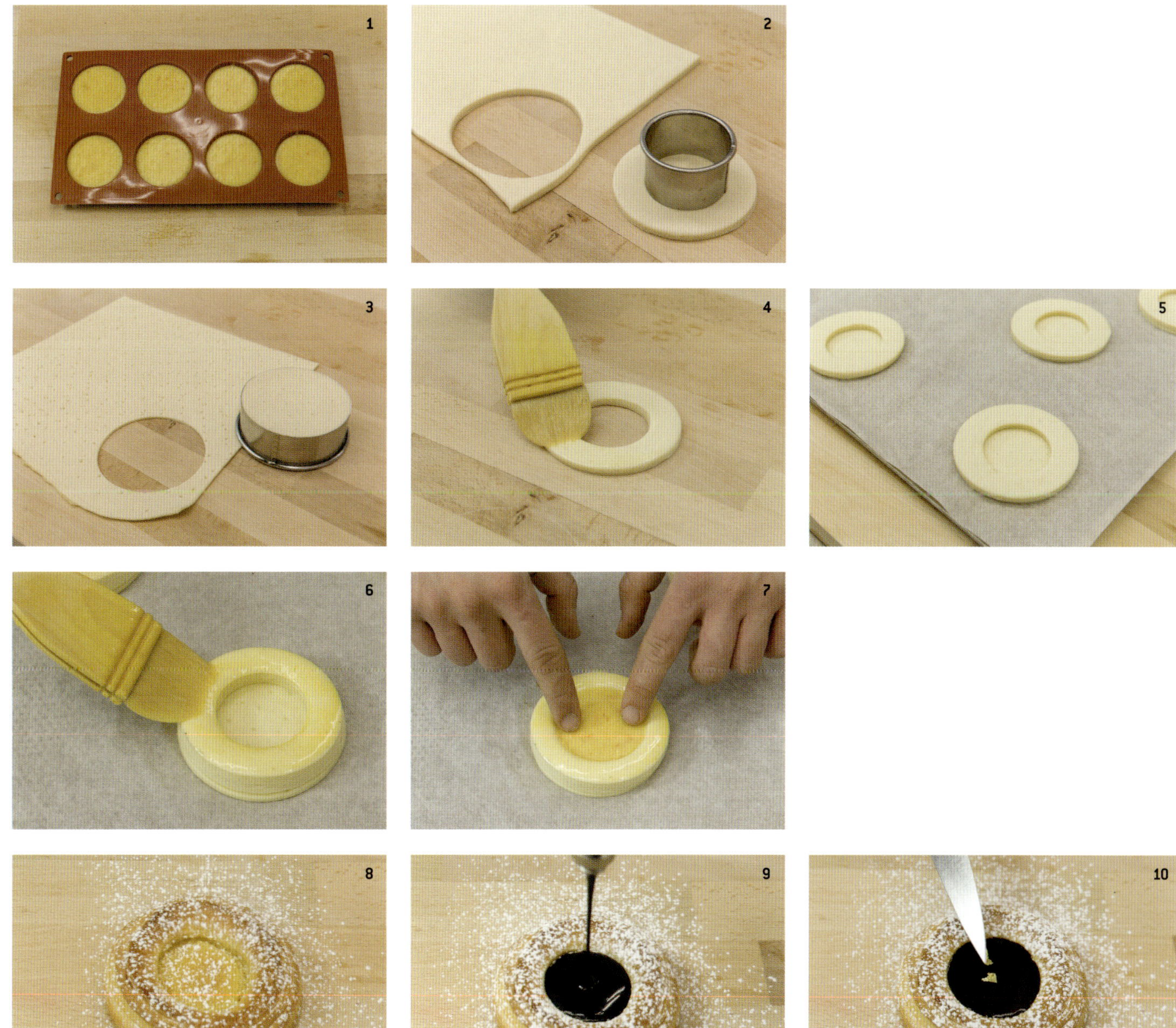
1
2
3
4
5
6
7
8
9
10

CHOCOLATE CROWNS

MAKES 3 CROWNS

PLAIN LEAVENED LAMINATED DOUGH

Lightly kneaded croissant dough *(see page 186)*	660 G (1 LB 7 ¼ OZ)
Dry butter *(see page 10)*	190 G (6 ¾ OZ)

COCOA CROISSANT DOUGH

Lightly kneaded croissant dough *(see page 186)*	100 G (3 ½ OZ)
Unsweetened cocoa powder	10 G (⅜ OZ)
Water	10 G (⅜ OZ)
Butter	10 G (⅜ OZ)

FILLING

Chocolate sticks 3.5 × 1 cm (1 ⅜ × ⅜ inch) *(see page 31)*	45

TO FINISH

Neutral syrup *(see page 31)*	AS NEEDED

COCOA CROISSANT DOUGH

In a stand mixer fitted with the paddle attachment on speed 1, beat the ingredients for the cocoa croissant dough until smooth. Bulk ferment for about 40 minutes, then rest at 1°C (35°F) 12 hours.

METHOD

KNEADING THE CROISSANT DOUGH

LIGHTLY KNEADED On speed 1 for about 10 minutes.

WEIGHT One 660-gram (1 lb 7 1/4-oz) piece lightly kneaded croissant dough and one 130-gram (4 1/2-oz) piece cocoa dough.

PRESHAPE Shape into balls.

BULK FERMENT About 40 minutes.

FOLD TO DEGAS After 20 minutes of bulk fermentation.

PRESHAPE Oval.

FINAL PROOF About 30 minutes in the freezer, then at 1°C (35°F) for 12 hours.

TURNING (TOURAGE) Degas the dough. Encase the dry butter in the dough. Make one double turn *(see page 14)*. Moisten the surface of the dough, then roll out the cocoa croissant dough to the size of the rolled-out dough **(1)**.

REST At 1°C (35°F) for about 45 minutes.

PRESHAPE Using a dough sheeter, roll out the dough to a thickness of 8 millimeters (5/16 inch) **(2)**. Cut the dough in half lengthwise **(3)**. Moisten the white sides **(4)** and lay one on top of the other **(5)**.

REST At 1°C (35°F) for about 45 minutes.

PRESHAPE Using a dough sheeter, roll out the dough to a thickness of 3 millimeters (3/16 inch), then into a 140 × 12-centimeters (55 × 4 3/4-inch) rectangle.

CUT TO SIZE Cut three strips lengthwise **(6)**.

SHAPE Make an accordion with each strip **(7)**. Place the dough pieces around 8-centimeter (3 1/4-inch)-diameter ring molds on baking sheets lined with parchment paper **(8)**. Evenly arrange the folds around the ring molds, then place 20-centimeter (8-inch) **(9)** ring molds on the outside of the folds. Insert a chocolate stick **(10)** into each loop.

FINAL PROOF At 27°C (80°F) for about 2 hours.

BAKE In a convection oven at 170°C (340°F) for about 18 minutes.

FINISH Brush with neutral syrup **(11)**.

COOL On a wire rack.

1
2
3
4
5
6
7
8
9
10
11

TROPICAL RINGS

MAKES 12 RINGS

TURMERIC CROISSANT DOUGH

Croissant dough *(see page 186)*	500 G (1 LB 2 OZ)
Ground turmeric	4 G (1/8 OZ)
Water	4 G (1/8 OZ)

COCOA CROISSANT DOUGH

Croissant dough *(see page 186)*	170 G (6 OZ)
Unsweetened cocoa powder	15 G (1/2 OZ)
Milk	15 G (1/2 OZ)
Butter	7 G (1/4 OZ) (1/4 OZ)

TURNING (*TOURAGE*)

Dry butter	200 G (7 OZ)

GOOEY BROWNIE

Milk couverture chocolate 40%	50 G (1 3/4 OZ)
Dark couverture chocolate 65%	50 G (1 3/4 OZ)
Unsalted butter	60 G (2 1/8 OZ)
Superfine sugar	50 G (1 3/4 OZ)
Eggs	50 G (1 3/4 OZ)
Strong flour	24 G (7/8 OZ)

FOR THE MANGO-PASSION FRUIT-LIME JELLY

Mango puree	150 G (5 1/4 OZ)
Passion fruit puree	75 G (2 5/8 OZ)
Lime juice	30 G (1 OZ)
Sugar	37 G (1 3/8 OZ)
Pectin NH	2.5 G (1/16 OZ)

TO FINISH

Neutral syrup	AS NEEDED

FOR THE TURMERIC CROISSANT DOUGH

In a stand mixer fitted with the hook, knead the ingredients for the turmeric croissant dough on speed 1 until smooth.
Bulk ferment for about 20 minutes, then at 1°C (35°F) for 12 hours.

FOR THE COCOA CROISSANT DOUGH

In the stand mixer fitted with the paddle attachment on speed 1, beat the ingredients for the cocoa croissant dough until smooth. Divide into two 103-gram (3 5/8-oz) dough pieces. Using guitar sheets, shape into 15-centimeter (6-inch) squares. Bulk ferment at 1°C (35°F) for 12 hours.

FOR THE GOOEY BROWNIE

Melt the milk and dark chocolates with the butter. Gently whisk the egg and sugar, then whisk in the flour. Combine the two mixtures. Pipe 23 grams (7/8 oz) of the batter into greased 4-centimeter (1 1/2-inch) ring molds, placed on a silicone mat **(1)**. Bake in a convection oven at 170°C (340°F) for 7 minutes. Set the disks aside in the freezer.

FOR THE MANGO-PASSION FRUIT-LIME JELLY

Combine the sugar and pectin. Heat the purees and lemon juice, add the dry ingredients, then bring to a boil for about 30 seconds. Set aside.

METHOD

TURNING (*TOURAGE*) Degas the dough pieces. Encase the dry butter in the turmeric dough. Make one single turn *(see page 14)*. Using a dough sheeter, roll out to a thickness of about 5 millimeters (3/16 inch), then into a 15 × 45 (6 × 17 1/2-inch) rectangle **(2)**. Divide the turmeric dough into three pieces, then stack the turmeric and cocoa doughs, making sure to end with a layer of turmeric dough **(3, 4)**.

REST At 1°C (35°F) for about 1 hour.

PRESHAPE Roll out to a thickness of 8 millimeters (5/16 inch), then into a 15 × 40-centimeter (6 × 15 1/2-inch) rectangle. Cut 5-millimeter (3/16-inch) strips and place them on the moistened dough **(5, 6)**. Seal with the rolling pin **(7)**. Using the dough sheeter, roll out to a thickness of 2 millimeters (1/16 inch), then into a 25 × 100 centimeter (9 3/4 × 39-inch) rectangle in the same direction as the laminated dough.

SHAPE Using a pastry cutter, cut out twelve 5 × 20-centimeter (2 × 8-inch) parallelograms, then fold them in on themselves lengthwise, sealing the base with a small rolling pin **(8, 9)**. Shape into rings **(10)**.
Use the scraps to make the 6-centimeter (2 1/2-inch)-diameter pastry disks. Place the disks in greased 8-centimeter (3 1/4-inch)-diameter circular molds. Place a brownie on each disk, smooth side up. Place the rings around the brownies **(11, 12, 13)**.

FINAL PROOF At 27°C (80°F) for about 2 hours 30 minutes.

BAKE In a convection oven at 170°C (340°F) for about 13 minutes.

FINISH Unmold, then brush with neutral syrup.
Bake in a convection oven at 170°C (340°F) for an additional 1 minute.
Using a piston, pour 14 grams (1/2 oz) of mango-passion-lime coulis in the center of each pastry **(14)**.

COOL On a wire rack.

1
2
3
4
5
6
7
8
9
10
11
12
13
14

PRALINE AND MANGO SPOONS

MAKES 12 SPOONS

LEAVENED LAMINATED DOUGH

Croissant dough *(see page 186)*	**600 G (1 LB 6 1/8 OZ)**
Dry butter *(see page 10)*	**180 G (6 3/8 OZ)**

CRÈME BRÛLÉE WITH PRALINE INSERTS

Whipping cream 35% fat	**125 G (4 3/8 OZ)**
Milk	**125 G (4 3/8 OZ)**
Almond-hazelnut praline	**25 G (7/8 OZ)**
Egg yolks	**50 G (1 3/4 OZ)**
Superfine sugar	**25 G (7/8 OZ)**

MANGO JELLY FILLING

Mango puree	**150 G (5 1/4 OZ)**
Superfine sugar	**70 G (2 1/2 OZ)**
Pectin NH	**3 G (1/8 OZ)**

TO FINISH

Whole toasted hazelnuts	**12**

FOR THE CRÈME BRÛLÉE WITH PRALINE INSERTS

In a saucepan, bring the cream, milk, and almond-hazelnut praline to a boil, then let infuse until cool.
Blanch the eggs yolks and sugar a little.
Whisk in the milk, cream, and almond-hazelnut praline infusion **(1)**.
Let rest at 3°C (35°F) for 12 hours **(2)**.
Pour 28 grams (1 oz) of batter into 8 × 4.5-centimeter (3 1/4 × 1 3/4-inch) silicone quenelle molds **(3)**. Bake in a convection oven at 90°C (195°F) for about 45 minutes.
Set aside in the freezer.

FOR THE MANGO JELLY

Combine the sugar and pectin.
Gently heat the mango puree.
Stir in the sugar and pectin mixture and bring to a boil.
Pour 16 grams (5/8 oz) of the mixture into 6 × 4-centimeter (2 1/2 × 1 1/2-inch) oval silicone molds **(4)**. Set aside in the freezer.

METHOD

TURNING (*TOURAGE*) Degas the dough. Encase the dry butter in the dough. Make one single turn and one double turn *(see page 14)*.

REST At 1°C (35°F) for about 45 minutes.

PRESHAPE Using a dough sheeter, roll out the dough to a thickness of 4.5 millimeters (3/16 inch), then into a 30 × 40-centimeter (11 3/4 × 15 1/2-inch) rectangle.

REST In the freezer for about 15 minutes.

CUT TO SIZE Using a knife and a template, cut out 12 spoons, then place them on greased supports **(5, 6)**.

FINAL PROOF At 27°C (80°F) for about 2 hours 30 minutes.

GLAZE Whisked egg **(7)**.

PREBAKE PREP Gently press a toasted hazelnut on the handle of each spoon **(8)**. Gently degas the center of the spoons and add the frozen praline crème brûlée insert **(9)**.

BAKE In a convection at 170°C (340°F) for 15 minutes.

TO FINISH Remove from oven and place a frozen mango jelly on each spoon **(10)**.

COOL On supports.

1

2

3

4

5

6

7

8

9

10

RASPBERRY LYCHEE FLOWERS

MAKES 12 FLOWERS

BRIOCHE DOUGH

(see page 184)	800 G (1 ¾ LB)

BEET BRIOCHE DOUGH

Brioche dough *(see page. 184)*	450 G (15 ⅞ OZ)
Beet powder	30 G (1 OZ)
Water	10 G (⅜ OZ)
Strong flour	30 G (1 OZ)

RASPBERRY VISITANDINES

Mixed almond flour	30 G (1 OZ)
Confectioners' sugar	78 G (2 ¾ OZ)
Strong flour	24 G (⅞ OZ)
Brown butter	60 G (2 ⅛ OZ)
Frozen raspberry pieces	60 G (2 ⅛ OZ)
Vanilla bean	1 G (1/32 OZ)
Egg whites	70 G (2 ½ OZ)

RASPBERRY LYCHEE JELLY

Raspberry puree	85 G (3 OZ)
Lychee puree	60 G (2 ⅛ OZ)
Sugar	18 G (⅝ OZ)
Pectin NH	4.5 G (⅛ OZ)

FOR THE BEET BRIOCHE DOUGH

In a stand mixer fitted with the hook, knead all the ingredients on speed 1 until smooth. Bulk ferment about 20 minutes, then rest at 3°C (35°F) for 12 hours.

FOR THE RASPBERRY VISITANDINES

Combine the brown butter and the seeds from the scraped vanilla bean. In the stand mixer fitted with the paddle attachment, beat all the ingredients, adding in the brown butter and vanilla last. Spoon 20 g (3/4 oz) of the mixture into 7-centimeter (2 3/4-inch)-diameter silicone savarin molds, then sprinkle with 5 grams (3/16 oz) of raspberry pieces **(1)**. Bake in a convection oven at 170°C (340°F) for 7 minutes. Set aside in the freezer.

FOR THE RASPBERRY LYCHEE JELLY

Heat the purees, then stir in the sugar and pectin. Bring to a boil. Using a piston, pour into 2.5-centimeter (1-inch)-diameter silicone hemisphere molds **(2)**. Set aside in the freezer.

METHOD

PRESHAPE Using a dough sheeter, roll out the plain dough to a thickness of 2.7 millimeters (1/8 inch), then roll out the beet dough to a thickness of 1 millimeter (1/32 inch).

CUT TO SIZE Using a flower pastry cutter, cut out twelve flowers from each dough **(3, 4)**, as well as twelve 5-centimeter (2-inch)-diameter disks from the beet dough.

REST In the freezer for about 30 minutes.

SHAPE Use a petal cutter to cut out the beet flowers, then place them on top of the plain dough **(5, 6, 7)**. Place the visitandines on the plain dough, followed by the 5-centimeter (2-inch) disks. Fold the petals over the disks **(8, 9, 10)**. Turn over onto baking sheets lined with parchment paper, then place in greased flower molds **(11, 12)**.

FINAL PROOF At 27°C (80°F) for about 2 hours 30 minutes.

PREBAKE PREP Place a raspberry-lychee insert in the center of each pastry, dome side down, pressing it gently all the way to the bottom.

BAKE In a convection oven at 145°C (295°F) for 15 minutes.

FINISH Brush with neutral syrup, then place a raspberry-lychee insert in the center of the pastry, dome side up **(13)**.

COOL On a wire rack.

1
2
3
4
5
6
7
8
9
10
11
12
13

FLAKY BLACK CURRANT DOMES

MAKES 12 PASTRIES

LEAVENED LAMINATED DOUGH

Croissant dough *(see page 186)*	720 G (1 LB 9 3/8 OZ)
Dry butter *(see page 10)*	180 G (6 3/8 OZ)

ALMOND LIME CREAM

Almond flour	55 G (2 OZ)
Butter	55 G (2 OZ)
Superfine sugar	55 G (2 OZ)
Egg	42 G (1 1/2 OZ)
Cornstarch	12 G (3/8 OZ)
Black currant powder	3 G (1/8 OZ)
Lime, zest only	1

BLACK CURRANT JELLY DISKS

Black currant puree	80 G (2 7/8 OZ)
Superfine sugar	20 G (3/4 OZ)
Pectin NH	1.6 G (1/16 OZ)

TO FINISH

Neutral syrup *(see page 31)*	AS NEEDED

FOR THE ALMOND LIME CREAM

Whisk all the ingredients together until smooth **(1)**. Pipe 17 grams (5/8 oz) of the cream into 5-centimeter (2-inch)-diameter silicone molds **(2)**.
Set aside in the freezer.

FOR THE BLACK CURRANT JELLY DISKS

Combine the sugar and the pectin.
Stir the sugar and pectin mixture into the cold black currant puree, then bring to a boil. Pour the mixture into 3-centimeter (1 1/4-inch)-diameter silicone molds **(3)**. Set aside in the freezer.

METHOD

TURNING (*TOURAGE*) Degas the dough. Encase the dry butter in the dough. Make two double turns *(see page 14)*.
When making the second turn, stretch the dough to a 12 × 25-centimeter (4 3/4 × 9 3/4-inch) rectangle **(4)**.

REST At 1°C (35°F) for about 45 minutes.

PRESHAPE Using a dough sheeter, roll out the dough to a thickness of 5 millimeters (3/16 inch), then into a 15 × 55-centimeter (6 × 21 1/2-inch) rectangle.

REST In the freezer for about 15 minutes.

CUT TO SIZE Cut twelve 1.2 × 52-centimeter (1/2 × 20 1/2-inch) strips **(5)**. Trim the ends of the strips diagonally **(6)**.
Roll out the dough scraps to a thickness of 1 millimeter (1/32 inch), use a roller docker or fork to prick the dough **(7)**, then place on a greased sheet of parchment paper.

SHAPE Lightly moisten the dough strips, then roll them up **(8)**. Place the rolls on an oiled silicone mat. Place a 1.9-centimeter (3/4-inch)-tall block in each corner of the silicone mat, then cover with a well-greased aluminum sheet **(9)**.

FINAL PROOF At 27°C (80°F) for about 2 hours.

CHILL At 1°C (35°F) for about 10 minutes.

PREBAKE PREP Using an 8-centimeter (3 1/4-inch)-diameter pastry cutter, cut 12 disks from the pricked and rested scraps **(10)**. Place the rolls of pastry in domed molds **(11)**, then top with the frozen almond cream inserts **(12)**. Cover with the pastry disks **(13)** and place a sheet of parchment paper and then a baking tray over the molds.

BAKE In a convection oven at 170°C (340°F) for about 18 minutes.

TO FINISH Place a frozen black currant jelly disk in the center of each dome **(14)**, then brush with neutral syrup.

COOL On a wire rack.

1
2
3
4
5
6
7
8
9
10
11
12
13
14

BLACK CURRANT AND LEMON DOMES

MAKES 12 PASTRIES

PLAIN BRIOCHE DOUGH

(see page 184)	**660 G (1 LB 7 ¼ OZ)**

FILLING

Black currants, frozen	**180 G (6 ⅜ OZ)**
Pearl sugar	**72 G (2 ½ OZ)**

LEMON MACARONADE

Raw almond flour	**100 G (3 ½ OZ)**
Egg whites	**75 G (2 ⅝ OZ)**
Superfine sugar	**70 G (2 ½ OZ)**
Lemon, zest only	½

TO FINISH

Sliced almonds	**AS NEEDED**
Confectioners' sugar	**AS NEEDED**

FOR THE LEMON MACARONADE

Combine all the ingredients **(1)**. Set aside at 3°C (35°F).

PREP THE RING MOLDS

Butter 7-centimeter (2 ¾-inch)-diameter, 6-centimeter (2 ½-inch)-deep ring molds and line with sliced almonds **(2)**.

METHOD

WEIGHT Twelve 55-gram (2-oz) dough pieces.

PRESHAPE Shape into balls.

REST At room temperature for about 45 minutes.

SHAPE Use a rolling pin to roll out the dough into 9-centimeter (3 ½-inch)-diameter disks. Top each disk with 15 grams (½ oz) of frozen black currants and 6 grams (3/16 oz) of pearl sugar **(3)**.
Shape into balls, making sure the filling stays evenly distributed throughout the dough **(4, 5, 6)**. Place a ball in each ring mold on baking sheets lined with parchment paper **(7)**.

FINAL PROOF At 27°C (80°F) for 3 hours.

TO FINISH Pipe the lemon macaronade over the top **(8)**, then sprinkle with sliced almonds **(9)** and confectioners' sugar **(10)**.

BAKE In a convection oven at 145°C (295°F), or in a deck oven at 180°C (355°F), for about 20 minutes.

COOL On a wire rack.

1
2
3
4
5
6
7
8
9
10

RASPBERRY AND PISTACHIO DOMES

MAKES 12 PASTRIES

TURMERIC BRIOCHE DOUGH

Plain brioche dough *(see page 184)*	600 G (1 LB 6 1/8 OZ)
Ground turmeric	3 G (1/8 OZ)

RASPBERRY JELLY FILLING

Raspberry puree	200 G (7 OZ)
Superfine sugar	120 G (4 1/4 OZ)
Pectin NH	4 G (1/8 OZ)

RASPBERRY AND PISTACHIO SPONGE CAKES

Butter, melted and cooled	60 G (2 1/8 OZ)
Superfine sugar	60 G (2 1/8 OZ)
Eggs	80 G (2 7/8 OZ)
Strong flour	60 G (2 1/8 OZ)
Baking powder	1 G (1/32 OZ)
Pistachio paste	40 G (1 3/8 OZ)

PLAIN CIGARETTE BATTER

Egg whites, at room temperature	150 G (5 1/4 OZ)
Superfine sugar	130 G (1 OZ) (4 1/2 OZ)
Strong flour	80 G (2 7/8 OZ)
Butter, melted and cooled	80 G (2 7/8 OZ)

PISTACHIO CIGARETTE BATTER

Plain cigarette batter	100 G (3 1/2 OZ)
Pistachio paste	50 G (1 3/4 OZ)

TO FINISH

Neutral topping	AS NEEDED
Crushed peeled pistachios	50 G (1 3/4 OZ)

FOR THE TURMERIC BRIOCHE DOUGH

In a stand mixer fitted with the hook, knead the brioche dough and turmeric on speed 1 until smooth. Bulk ferment for about 30 minutes. Lightly fold to degas the dough, then proof at 3°C (35°F) for 12 hours.

RASPBERRY JELLY FILLING

Combine the sugar and pectin. Gently heat the raspberry puree. Whisk in the sugar and pectin mixture **(1)**, then bring to a boil. Set aside in a pastry bag at 3°C (35°F).

FOR THE RASPBERRY AND PISTACHIO SPONGE CAKES

In the stand mixer fitted with the paddle attachment, gently cream the butter and sugar, then add the eggs. Gently fold in the sifted dry mixture. Fold in the pistachio paste until smooth **(2)**.

Spoon 25 grams (⅞ oz) of the batter into 6-centimeter (2 ½-inch)-diameter silicone molds **(3)**. Pipe a ring of raspberry jelly in the center **(4)**. Bake in a convection oven at 150°C (300°F) for 13 minutes. Set aside in the freezer.

FOR THE CIGARETTE BATTER

Stir the warm egg whites and sugar together. Add the flour, then stir in the cold butter, melted. Separate 100 grams (3 ½ oz) of the plain cigarette batter and stir in 50 grams (1 ¾ oz) of the colored pistachio paste **(5)**.

Place a lightly greased silicone mat on a rimless aluminum sheet, then place the trefoil stencil on it. Spread the pistachio cigarette batter over the trefoil stencil **(6)**, then carefully lift it off **(7)**. Set aside in the freezer for 1 hour.

Spread the plain cigarette batter over the frozen trefoils **(8)**.

Bake in a convection oven at 150°C (300°F) for 7 minutes.

Cut twelve 2.5 × 28-centimeter (1 × 11-inch) strips **(9)**.

Wrap the strips around the bottom edge of 9.5-centimeter (3 ¾-inch)-diameter silicone hemisphere molds that have a pyramid in the center, using toothpicks to hold the strips in place **(10)**.

METHOD

WEIGHT Twelve 50-gram (1 ¾-oz) dough pieces.

REST At room temperature for about 20 minutes.

PRESHAPE Gently shape into balls.

REST At 3°C (35°F) for about 45 minutes.

SHAPE Use a rolling pin, roll out the dough pieces into 10-centimeter (4-inch)-diameter disks.
Lightly moisten the edges of the disks.
Place a frozen pistachio-raspberry sponge cake in the center of each disk **(11)**.
Wrap the dough disks around the sponge cakes, and place them in the 9.5-centimeter (3 ¾-inch)-diameter silicone hemisphere molds with a pyramid in the center **(12)**.

FINAL PROOF At 27°C (80°F) for about 2 hours 30 minutes.

BAKE Remove the toothpicks. Cover the pastries with a micro-perforated silicone mat **(13)** and a wire rack. Bake in a convection oven at 150°C (300°F) for about 12 minutes.

COOL On a wire rack.

FINISH Brush with neutral glaze, sprinkle with chopped pistachios, then place a raspberry jelly filling in each pastry **(14)**.

1
2
3
4
5
6
7
8
9
10
11
12
13
14

CARAMELIZED MARRON AND BLACK CURRANT DOMES

MAKES 12 PASTRIES

LEAVENED LAMINATED DOUGH

Croissant dough *(see page 186)*	700 G (1 LB 8 3/4 OZ)
Dry butter *(see page 10)*	200 G (7 OZ)

MARRON AND BLACK CURRANT SPONGE CAKE

Chestnut (marron) paste	160 G (5 5/8 OZ)
Butter	50 G (1 3/4 OZ)
Superfine sugar	50 G (1 3/4 OZ)
Egg	50 G (1 3/4 OZ)
Strong flour	10 G (3/8 OZ)
Baking powder	3.5 G (1/8 OZ)
Chestnuts (marrons) in syrup	60 G (2 1/8 OZ)
Frozen black currants	60 G (2 1/8 OZ)

BLACK CURRANT JELLY FILLING

Black currant puree	65 G (2 1/4 OZ)
Superfine sugar	14 G (1/2 OZ)
Pectin NH	0.6 G (1/64 OZ)

DRY CARAMEL

Superfine sugar	100 G (3 1/2 OZ)

MARRON AND BLACK CURRANT SPONGE CAKE

In a stand mixer fitted with the paddle attachment, loosen the chestnut paste with the butter. Combine the sugar and eggs. Stir in the sugar and egg mixture, then add the sifted dry ingredients. Whisk until smooth. Add the chestnuts in syrup. Pour 25 grams (7/8 oz) of batter into each 5-centimeter (2-inch)-diameter silicone hemisphere mold, then sprinkle with 5 grams (3/16 oz) of black currants. Cover with a greased silicone mat. Bake in a convection oven at 170°C (340°F) for 13 minutes. Set aside in the freezer.

FOR THE BLACK CURRANT JELLY FILLING

Combine the sugar and pectin. Gently heat the black currant puree. Add the dry ingredients, then bring to a boil. Set aside in a pastry bag at 3°C (35°F).

FOR THE DRY CARAMEL

Melt the superfine sugar over low heat until a brown runny caramel forms. When cool, puree in a food processor before using.

METHOD

TURNING (TOURAGE) Degas the dough. Encase the dry butter in the dough. Make two single turns *(see page 14)*.

REST At 1°C (35°F) for about 1 hour.

PRESHAPE Roll out to a thickness of 8 millimeters (1/4 inch), then into a 15 × 40-centimeters (6 × 15 1/2-inch) rectangle. Cut out 5-millimeter (3/16-inch) strips, then place them on the moistened dough **(1, 2)**.

CUT TO SIZE Using a zigzag cutter, cut out 12 strips **(4)**. Cut through the downward-facing points and use the pieces to form a star **(5, 6)**. Roll out the dough scraps to 1 millimeter (1/32 inch), use a roller docker or a fork to prick them, then set aside at 1°C (33.8°F).

SHAPE Using a 3-centimeter (1 1/4-inch) diameter pastry cutter, gently score the center of the stars, then fold the tips toward the marked circle **(7, 8)**. Place the stars in domed molds, then insert the marron and black currant sponge cakes. Cut 8-centimeter (3 1/4-inch)-diameter disks from the pricked dough and place them on top the sponge cakes **(9, 10, 11)**.

FINAL PROOF At 27°C (80°F) for about 2 hours 30 minutes.

PREBAKE PREP Cover the molds with a sheet of parchment paper, then top with a baking sheet.

BAKE Bake in a convection oven at 170°C (340°F) for about 20 minutes

FINISH Unmold. Sprinkle with the processed dry caramel, then place a black currant jelly filling in the center of each pastry **(12, 13)**. Bake for an additional 2 minutes.

COOL On a wire rack.

1
2
3
4
5
6
7
8
9
10
11
12
13

STRIPED ÉCLAIRS

MAKES 12 ÉCLAIRS

PLAIN BRIOCHE DOUGH

(see page 184)	**800 G (1 ¾ LB)**

PISTACHIO AND BLUEBERRY FINANCIER

Almond flour	**40 G (1 ⅜ OZ)**
Confectioners' sugar	**32 G (1 ⅛ OZ)**
Egg whites	**30 G (1 OZ)**
Strong flour	**12 G (⅜ OZ)**
Butter, melted	**24 G (⅞ OZ)**
Pistachio paste	**18 G (⅝ OZ)**
Dried blueberries	**90 G**

CIGARETTE BATTER

Confectioners' sugar	**54 G (1 ⅞ OZ)**
Egg whites, at room temperature	**56 G (2 OZ)**
Cornstarch	**36 G (1 ¼ OZ)**
Strong flour	**36 G (1 ¼ OZ)**
Butter, softened	**27 G (1 OZ)**
Pistachio paste	**20 G (¾ OZ)**
Blueberry powder	**10 G (⅜ OZ)**

FOR THE PISTACHIO AND BLUEBERRY FINANCIER

Combine all the ingredients except for the dried blueberries. Place the dough in 9 × 2-centimeter (3 ½ × ¾-inch) silicone molds and arrange the dried blueberries on top **(1)**. Bake in a convection oven at 150°C (300°F) for 8 minutes. Set aside in the freezer.

FOR THE CIGARETTE BATTER

Mix all the ingredients except the pistachio paste and blueberry powder together. Separate 40 grams (1 ⅜ oz) of the plain dough and add 10 grams (⅜ oz) of blueberry powder to it. Mix together well and set aside. Add 20 grams (¾ oz) pistachio paste to the remaining plain dough, mix well, then set aside in a pastry bag. Using a spatula, spread the blueberry cigarette batter on a silicone mat using molds **(2)**, then cover with the pistachio paste **(3)**. Bake in a convection oven at 150°C (300°F) for 4 minutes. Set aside in the freezer.

METHOD

WEIGHT One 550-gram (1 lb 3 ⅜-oz) dough piece and one 250-gram (5 ¼-oz) dough piece **(4)**.

PRESHAPE Using a dough sheeter, roll the 550-gram (1 lb 3 ⅜-oz) dough piece into a 47 × 33-centimeter (18 ½ × 13-inch) rectangle, then roll the 250-gram (5 ¼-oz) dough piece into an 18 × 44-centimeter (7 × 17 ½-inch) rectangle.

REST In the freezer for about 15 minutes.

CUT TO SIZE Cut twelve 3.9 × 33-centimeter (1 ½ × 13-inch) strips from the 550-gram (1 lb 3 ⅜-oz) dough rectangle **(5)**, then cut 6 × 11-centimeter (2 ½ × 4 ¼-inch) rectangles from the 250-gram (5 ¼-oz) dough rectangle **(6)**.

SHAPE Place a frozen pistachio and blueberry financier on each rectangle. Wrap the dough around it to make a cylinder **(7)**, then place on a silicone mat **(8)**. Place the 3.9 × 33-centimeter (1 ½ × 13-inch) strips of dough on microperforated silicone mats **(9)**.

FINAL PROOF At 27°C (80°F) for about 2 hours 30 minutes.

COOL At 3°C (35°F) for about 20 minutes.

PREBAKE PREP Line the molds with the pastry strips **(10)**, then insert in the pistachio and blueberry cylinders **(11)**. Place a piece of striped frozen cigarette batter on top **(12)**.

BAKE Cover with a sheet of parchment paper, then a rimmed baking sheet covered with salt **(13)** and bake in a convection oven at 140°C (285°F) for about 14 minutes.

COOL On a wire rack.

1

2

3

4

5

6

7

8

9

10

11

12

13

TRAFFIC LIGHTS

MAKES 12 PASTRIES

LEAVENED LAMINATED DOUGH

Croissant dough *(see page 186)*	**720 G (1 LB 9 3/8 OZ)**
Dry butter *(see page 10)*	**180 G (6 3/8 OZ)**

CRÈME BRÛLÉE WITH PISTACHIO

Milk	**30 G (1 OZ)**
Whipping cream 35% fat	**30 G (1 OZ)**
Egg yolks	**18 G (5/8 OZ)**
Superfine sugar	**12 G (3/8 OZ)**
Pistachio paste	**6 G (3/16 OZ)**

RASPBERRY JELLY FILLING

Raspberry puree	**144 G (5 1/8 OZ)**
Superfine sugar	**42 G (1 1/2 OZ)**
Pectin 325 NH 95	**2.5 G (1/16 OZ)**
Xanthan gum	**1 G (1/32 OZ)**

MINI DRIED APRICOTS

Dried apricots in syrup	**6**

TO FINISH

Neutral syrup *(see page 31)*	**AS NEEDED**

FOR THE CRÈME BRÛLÉE WITH PISTACHIO

Mix together the egg yolks, sugar, and pistachio paste, then stir in the milk and cream.
Let rest at 3°C (35°F) for 12 hours, then pour into 3-centimeter (1 ¼-inch)-diameter silicone hemisphere molds **(1)**.
Bake in a convection oven at 90°C (195°F) for about 45 minutes.
Set aside in the freezer.

FOR THE RASPBERRY JELLY FILLING

Combine the sugar, pectin, and xanthan gum.
Bring the raspberry puree to a boil, add the dry ingredients, and cook for 1 minute **(2)**.
Pour the mixture into 4-centimeter (1 ½-inch)-diameter silicone molds **(3)**. Set aside in the freezer.

FOR THE MINI DRIED APRICOTS

Using a 20-millimeter plain tip, cut little disks from the mini apricots **(4)**.

METHOD

TURNING (TOURAGE) Degas the dough. Encase the dry butter in the dough. Make two double turns *(see page 14)*.

REST At 1°C (35°F) for about 45 minutes.

PRESHAPE Using a dough sheeter, roll out the dough to a thickness of 4 millimeters (3/16 inch), then into a 42 × 28-centimeter (16 ½ × 11-inch) rectangle.

REST In the freezer for about 15 minutes.

CUT TO SIZE Using a "traffic light" pastry cutter **(5)**, cut out 12 pieces and place them on baking sheets lined with parchment paper.

FINAL PROOF At 27°C (80°F) for about 2 hours.

GLAZE Whisked egg.

PREBAKE PREP Gently degas the dough in the area that will be filled. Place an apricot disk **(6)**, a frozen crème brûlée disk **(7)**, and a frozen raspberry jelly disk into the cavities **(8)**.

BAKE In a convection oven at 170°C (340°F), or a deck oven at 200°C (390°F), for about 17 minutes.

TO FINISH Brush with neutral syrup.

COOL On a wire rack.

1

2

3

4

5

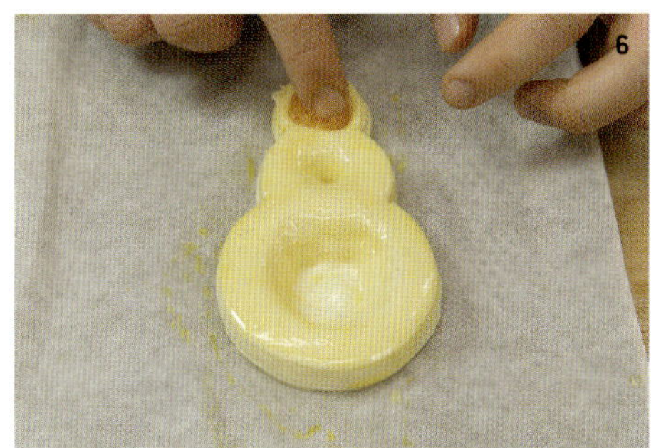
6

7

8

BLACK CURRANT AND LEMON FLOWERS

MAKES 3 PASTRIES

PLAIN BRIOCHE DOUGH

(see page 184)	**450 G (15 ⅞ OZ)**

VIOLET BRIOCHE DOUGH

Brioche dough *(see page 184)*	**180 G (6 ⅜ OZ)**
Blueberry powder	**13 G (⅛ OZ)**
Water	**13 G (⅛ OZ)**

ALMOND AND BLACK CURRANT PASTE

Almond paste 50%	**225 G (8 OZ)**
Egg white	**12 G (⅜ OZ)**
Black currant puree	**63 G (2 ¼ OZ)**

LEMON CREAM

Lemon juice	**45 G (1 ½ OZ)**
Milk	**21 G (¾ OZ)**
Butter	**6 G (3/16 OZ)**
Eggs	**21 G (¾ OZ)**
Superfine sugar	**30 G (1 OZ)**
Custard powder	**6 G (3/16 OZ)**
Yellow pectin	**4 G (⅛ OZ)**
Feuilletine flakes	**AS NEEDED**

TO FINISH

Neutral syrup *(see page 31)*	**AS NEEDED**

FOR THE VIOLET BRIOCHE DOUGH

In a stand mixer fitted with the paddle attachment, beat the brioche dough and blueberry powder-water mixture on speed 1 until smooth.
Bulk ferment for about 30 minutes. Lightly fold to degas the dough, then proof at 3°C (35°F) for 12 hours.

FOR THE ALMOND AND BLACK CURRANT PASTE

In the stand mixer fitted with the paddle attachment, beat the almond paste with the egg white. Add the black currant puree and beat until smooth. Set aside in a pastry bag at 3°C (35°F).

FOR THE LEMON CREAM

Heat the lemon juice, milk, and butter together.
Cream the remaining ingredient, except for the feuillentine flakes. Combine the two mixtures and boil for 1 minute **(1)**. Pipe the cream into 5-centimeter (2-inch)-diameter silicone hemisphere molds **(2)**, then sprinkle with the feuillentine flakes **(3)**. Set aside in the freezer.

METHOD

WEIGHT One 210-gram (7 ⅜-oz) plain dough piece and two 120-gram (4 ¼-oz) plain dough pieces, then two 100-gram (3 ½-oz) violet brioche dough pieces **(4)**.

REST About 10 minutes in the freezer.

PREP THE DOUGH PIECES Using a rolling pin, roll out the dough pieces into 18 × 12-centimeter (7 × 4 ¾-inch) rectangles.

REST In the freezer for about 15 minutes.

ASSEMBLY Moisten and layer the five dough pieces, starting with a 210-gram (7 ⅜-oz) plain dough piece and alternating the plain and purple dough pieces **(5, 6)**.

PRESHAPE Using a dough sheeter, roll out the dough into a 42 × 16-centimeter (16 ½ × 6 ¼-inch) rectangle.

REST In the freezer for about 15 minutes.

CUT TO SIZE Cut out eighteen 2.5 × 16-centimeter (1 × 6 ¼-inch) strips **(7)**.

SHAPE Moisten the top of the strips, then fold them over to make the petals **(8)**. Arrange six petals on a baking sheet lined with parchment paper to make a flower **(9)**. Place a ring mold around each flower, then pipe 15 grams (½ oz) of almond and black currant paste into each petal **(10)**.

FINAL PROOF At 27°C (80°F) for about 2 hours.

PREBAKE PREP Place a dome of frozen lemon cream in the center of each flower **(11)**.

BAKE Cover with a sheet of parchment paper, then a rimmed baking sheet covered with salt **(12)** and bake in a convection oven at 150°C (300°F) for about 25 minutes.

FINISH Brush with neutral syrup **(13)**.

COOL On a wire rack.

1

2

3

4

5

6

7

8

9

10

11

12

13

CHERRY AND PISTACHIO FLOWERS

MAKES 12 PASTRIES

LEAVENED LAMINATED DOUGH

Croissant dough *(see page 186)*	**780 G (1 LB 11 ½ OZ)**
Dry butter *(see page 10)*	**190 G (6 ¾ OZ)**

PISTACHIO CRÈME BRÛLÉE

Whipping cream 35% fat	**116 G (⅝ OZ)**
Egg yolks	**34 G (1 ¼ OZ)**
Confectioners' sugar	**24 G (⅞ OZ)**
Pistachio paste	**12 G (⅜ OZ)**

CHERRY CREAM

Cherry puree	**200 G (7 OZ)**
Superfine sugar	**50 G (1 ¾ OZ)**
Cornstarch	**8 G (¼ OZ)**

TO FINISH

Neutral syrup *(see page 31)*	**AS NEEDED**
Chopped pistachios	**AS NEEDED**

FOR THE PISTACHIO CRÈME BRÛLÉE

Combine the egg yolks, confectioners' sugar, and pistachio paste, then stir in the whipping cream. Pour 15 grams (½ oz) of the mixture into 6-centimeter (2 ½-inch)-diameter silicone molds **(1)**, then bake in a convection oven at 90°C (195°F) for about 45 minutes. Set aside. The cherry cream will be added later.

FOR THE CHERRY CREAM

Combine the sugar and starch. Stir the cold cherry puree with the dry ingredients, then bring to a boil. Pour 20 grams (¾ oz) of cherry cream over each crème brûlée **(2)**, then set aside in the freezer.

METHOD

TURNING (TOURAGE)	Degas the dough. Encase the dry butter in the dough. Make two double turns *(see page 14)*.
REST	At 1°C (35°F) for about 45 minutes.
PRESHAPE	Using a dough sheeter, roll out the dough to a thickness of 4.5 millimeters (3/16 inch), then into a 43 × 32-centimeter (17 × 12 ½-inch) rectangle.
REST	In the freezer for about 15 minutes.
CUT TO SIZE	Using a 10.5-centimeter (4 ⅛-inch)-diameter flower cutter, cut out 12 flowers **(3)**, then using two teardrop-shaped cutters, cut out the center of petals **(4)**. Roll out the dough scraps to a thickness of 1 millimeter (1/32 inch), chill in the freezer for 10 minutes, then cut out 12 flowers.
SHAPE	Place a frozen cherry and pistachio disk on each cut-out flower, then cover with a thin, moistened dough flower **(5)**. Carefully turn the flowers over, use a pastry cutter to seal them **(6)**, then place them on baking sheets lined with parchment paper.
FINAL PROOF	At 27°C (80°F) for about 2 hours.
GLAZE	Egg **(7)**.
BAKE	In a convection oven at 170°C (340°F) for about 16 minutes.
TO FINISH	Brush with the neutral syrup, then place a few chopped pistachios in the center **(8)**.
COOL	On a wire rack.

1

2

3

4

5

6

7

8

ORANGE BLOSSOM AND PRALINE FLOWERS

MAKES 3 FLOWERS

LEAVENED LAMINATED DOUGH

Croissant dough *(see page 186)*	**700 G (1 LB 8 3/4 OZ)**
Dry butter *(see page 10)*	**200 G (7 OZ)**

TOPPING

Ground pralines	**AS NEEDED**
Crushed pralines	**AS NEEDED**
Whole pink pralines	**3**

BLOOD ORANGE WATER GLAZE

Blood orange juice	**135 G (4 3/4 OZ)**
Blood oranges, zest only	**3**
Confectioners' sugar	**675 G (2 5/8 OZ)**

FOR THE BLOOD ORANGE WATER GLAZE

Mix all the ingredients together. Set aside at 3°C (35°F).

METHOD

TURNING (TOURAGE) Degas the dough. Encase the dry butter in the dough. Make two single turns *(see page 14)*.

REST At 1°C (35°F) for about 1 hour.

PRESHAPE Roll out the dough into a 40-centimeter (15 ½-inch) square. Cut in half to obtain two 20 × 40-centimeter (8 × 15 ½-inch) rectangles **(1)**. Moisten the surface of the rectangles, then sprinkle one rectangle generously with the ground pralines **(2)**. Place the other rectangle of dough, moistened side down, on top of the one with the ground pralines **(3)**. Roll out the dough to a thickness of 5 millimeters (3/16 inch), then into a 24 × 40-centimeter (9 ½ × 15 ½-inch) rectangle.

CUT TO SIZE Cut out eighteen 4 × 12-centimeter (1 ½ × 4 ¾-inch) strips **(4)**.

SHAPE Lay six strips one top of the other, staggering each one by 1 centimeter (3/8 inch) **(5)**. Roll up the overlapping strips, then fold the remaining parts over the top **(7)**. Turn the flowers over and gently press the center with a rolling pin **(8)**. Place on baking sheets lined with parchment paper, then arrange in greased flower molds **(9)**.

FINAL PROOF At 27°C (80°F) for about 2 hours 30 minutes.

BAKE In a convection oven at 170°C (340°F) for about 23 minutes.

FINISH While still hot, glaze the pastries with the blood orange water glaze, then carefully turn over to remove the excess **(10)**. Sprinkle with crushed pralines and place a whole praline in the center **(11)**.

COOL On a wire rack.

1
2
3
4
5
6
7
8
9
10
11

BLUEBERRY FLOWERS

MAKES 12 PASTRIES

PLAIN LEAVENED LAMINATED DOUGH

Croissant dough *(see page 186)*	400 G (14 OZ)
Dry butter *(see page 10)*	150 G (5 ¼ OZ)

COCOA CROISSANT DOUGH

Croissant dough *(see page 186)*	90 G (3 ⅛ OZ)
Cocoa powder	7 G (¼ OZ)
Butter	3.5 G (⅛ OZ)
Water	3.5 G (1.8 OZ)

ALMOND, APRICOT, AND BLUEBERRY FILLING

Almond paste 50%	250 G (5 ¼ OZ)
Blueberry puree	50 G (1 ¾ OZ)
Apricots in syrup	12

TO FINISH

Neutral syrup	AS NEEDED

FOR THE COCOA CROISSANT DOUGH

In a stand mixer fitted with the paddle attachment, beat the ingredients for the cocoa croissant dough on speed 1 until smooth. Bulk ferment about 40 minutes, then rest at 1°C (35°F) 12 hours.

FOR THE ALMOND, APRICOT, AND BLUEBERRY FILLING

In the stand mixer fitted with the paddle attachment, beat the almond paste and blueberry puree until smooth. Pipe 25 grams (⅞ oz) of the mixture into 5-centimeter (2-inch)-diameter silicone hemisphere molds **(1)**. Using a 3-centimeter (1 ⅛-inch)-square pastry cutter, make apricot squares. Place an apricot square in the center of each hemisphere **(2)**. Set aside in the freezer.

METHOD

TURNING (TOURAGE) Degas the dough. Encase the dry butter in the dough. Make one single turn and one double turn *(see page 14)*. Moisten the surface of the dough piece **(3)**, then place the piece of cocoa croissant dough on top, previously rolled out to the size of the kneaded dough piece **(4)**.

REST At 1°C (35°F) for about 45 minutes.

PRESHAPE Using a dough sheeter, roll out the dough to a thickness of 3 millimeters (3/16 inch), then into a 35 × 30-centimeter (1 ¼ × 11 ¾-inch) rectangle.

SHAPE Moisten the surface of the dough on the white side, except for the center **(5)**. Roll up the dough **(6)** from one side, then the other, making the shape of a pair of glasses **(7)**.

REST In the freezer for about 15 minutes.

CUT TO SIZE Cut into 12 pairs of glasses. To make a flower, divide each pair of glasses in half, leaving 1 centimeter (⅜ inch) uncut in the middle **(8, 9)**. Place in greased 10-centimeter (4-inch)-diameter stainless steel hemispheres **(10)**.

FINAL PROOF At 27°C (80°F) for about 2 hours 30 minutes.

GLAZE Whisked egg.

PREBAKE PREP Place a frozen almond-apricot-blueberry hemisphere in the center of each flower **(11)**.

BAKE In a convection oven at 160°C (320°F) for about 22 minutes.

COOL In the molds.

TO FINISH Brush with the neutral syrup **(12, 13)**.

1
2
3
4
5
6
7
8
9
10
11
12
13

FLAKY CRESCENTS

MAKES 12 PASTRIES

LEAVENED LAMINATED DOUGH

Lightly kneaded croissant dough *(see page 186)*	640 G (1 LB 6 1/2 OZ)
Dry butter *(see page 10)*	160 G (5 5/8 OZ)

FILLING

Vanilla pastry cream *(see page 30)*	195 G (6 7/8 OZ)

RASPBERRY CREAM

Raspberry puree	80 G (2 7/8 OZ)
Superfine sugar	40 G (1 3/8 OZ)
Cornstarch	8 G (1/4 OZ)
Yellow pectin	3 G (1/8 OZ)

TO FINISH

Neutral syrup *(see page 31)*	AS NEEDED

FOR THE RASPBERRY CREAM

Combine the sugar, starch, and yellow pectin. Stir the cold raspberry puree and dry ingredients, then bring to a boil. Set aside in a pastry bag at 3°C (35°F).

METHOD

KNEADING THE CROISSANT DOUGH

LIGHT KNEADING On speed 1 for about 10 minutes.

PRESHAPE Shape into balls.

BULK FERMENT About 40 minutes.

FOLD TO DEGAS After 20 minutes of bulk fermentation.

PRESHAPE Oval.

FINAL PROOF In the freezer for about 30 minutes, then at 1°C (35°F) for 12 hours.

TURNING (TOURAGE) Degas the dough. Encase the dry butter in the dough. Make one single turn and one double turn *(see page 14)*.

REST At 1°C (35°F) for about 45 minutes.

PRESHAPE Using a dough sheeter, roll out the dough to a thickness of 2.5 millimeter (1/16 to 1/8 inch), then into a 44 × 41-centimeter (17 × 1/2 16-inch) rectangle.

REST In the freezer for about 15 minutes.

CUT TO SIZE Cut out twelve 3.4 × 44-centimeter (1 3/8 × 17-inch) strips **(1)**.

SHAPE Moisten the strips **(2)**, then fold them to make four loops **(3)**. Place the folded strips inside the crescent-shaped molds **(4)**, then pipe 16 grams (5/8 oz) of pastry cream into each pastry **(5)**.

FINAL PROOF At 27°C (80°F) for about 2 hours.

PREBAKE PREP Pipe raspberry cream into each loop **(6)**.

BAKE In a convection oven at 170°C (340°F) for 15 minutes.

TO FINISH Brush with neutral syrup **(7)**.

COOL On a wire rack.

1

2

3

4

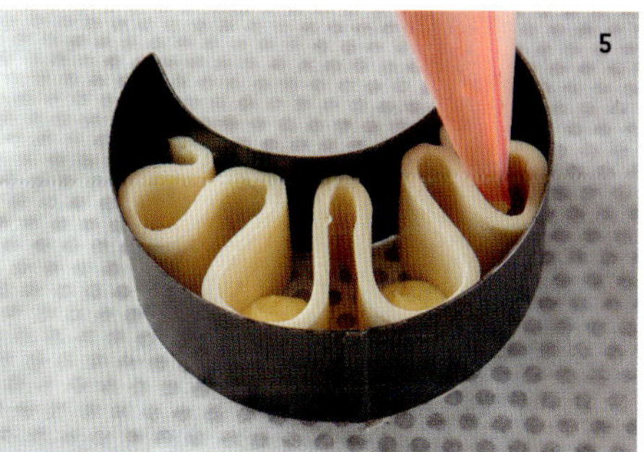
5

6

7

BERRY NESTS

MAKES 12 PASTRIES

PLAIN BRIOCHE DOUGH

(see page 184)	**600 G (1 LB 6 ⅛ OZ)**

HONEY CRÈME BRÛLÉE

Milk	**110 G (3 ⅞ OZ)**
Whipping cream 35% fat	**110 G (3 ⅞ OZ)**
Egg yolks	**60 G (2 ⅛ OZ)**
Hawthorn honey	**50 G (1 ¾ OZ)**

JELLIED FRUIT FILLING

Frozen red currants	**110 G (3 ⅞ OZ)**
Frozen blueberries	**110 G (3 ⅞ OZ)**
Superfine sugar	**80 G (2 ⅞ OZ)**
Pectin NH	**2.5 G (1/16 OZ)**

TO FINISH

Blueberries	**AS NEEDED**
Red currants	**AS NEEDED**
Neutral syrup	**AS NEEDED**

FOR THE HONEY CRÈME BRÛLÉE

Combine the egg yolks and honey, then stir in the milk and cream.
Let rest at 3°C (35°F) for 12 hours, then pour into 6-centimeter (2 ½-inch)-diameter silicone molds **(1)**.
Bake in a convection oven at 90°C (195°F) for about 45 minutes. Set aside in the freezer.

FOR THE JELLIED FRUIT FILLING

Combine the sugar and pectin. In a saucepan, cook the red currants and blueberries over medium heat for about 3 minutes, then add the dry ingredients.
Continue to cooking for about 1 minute, still over medium heat.
Pour the mixture into 6-centimeter (2 ½-inch)-diameter silicone molds **(2)**. Set aside in the freezer.

METHOD

WEIGHT Twelve 50-gram (1 ¾-oz) dough pieces.
SHAPE Gently shape into balls.
REST At 3°C (35°F) for about 45 minutes.
PRESHAPE Use a rolling pin, roll out the dough into disks about 8 centimeters (¼ oz) in diameter **(3)**. Use the end of the rolling pin to flatten the center of the disks **(4)**.
SHAPE Place a disk of frozen crème brûlée in the bottom of each greased 12-centimeter (4 ¾-inch)-diameter fluted mold **(5)** and cover with a brioche disk **(6)**.
FINAL PROOF At 27°C (80°F) for about 2 hours.
BAKE In a convection oven at 145°C (295°F), or 180°C (355°F) in a deck oven, for about 15 minutes
TO FINISH While still hot, place a frozen jelly disk on each crème brûlée **(7)**.
COOL On a wire rack.
TO FINISH Brush the disks with neutral syrup **(8)**. Decorate each pastry with one blueberry and three red currants.

1

2

3

4

5

6

7

8

PAINS AU CHOCOLAT 3.0

MAKES 12 PASTRIES

PLAIN LEAVENED LAMINATED DOUGH

Croissant dough *(see page 186)*	**600 G (1 LB 6 ⅛ OZ)**
Dry butter *(see page 10)*	**200 G (7 OZ)**

COCOA CROISSANT DOUGH

Croissant dough *(see page 186)*	**100 G (3 ½ OZ)**
Unsweetened cocoa powder	**10 G (⅜ OZ)**
Milk	**10 G (⅜ OZ)**
Butter	**5 G (3/16 OZ)**

FILLING

8 × 1-cm (3 ¼ × ⅜-inch) chocolate sticks *(see page 31)*	**24**

TO FINISH

Neutral syrup	**AS NEEDED**

FOR THE COCOA CROISSANT DOUGH

In a stand mixer fitted with the paddle attachment, beat all the ingredients on speed 1 until smooth. Bulk ferment about 40 minutes, then rest at 1°C (35°F) for 12 hours.

FOR THE ALMOND AND HAZELNUT PRALINE CHOCOLATE STICKS

Melt the chocolates and praline together, then stir. Pour into 8 × 1-centimeter (3 ¼ × ⅜-inch) silicone molds. Set aside at 3°C (35°F) for 1 hour.

METHOD

TURNING (*TOURAGE*) Degas the plain dough. Encase the dry butter in the dough. Make two single turns.

REST At 1°C (35°F) for about 1 hour.

PRESHAPE Roll out to a thickness of 8 millimeters (5/16 inch), then into a 15 × 40-centimeter (6 × 15 ½-inch) rectangle. Cut out 5-millimeter (3/16-inch)-wide strips, then place them on the moistened dough **(1, 2)**. Using a dough sheeter, roll out the cocoa croissant dough to a thickness of 2 millimeter (1/16 inch), then cut out 3-millimeter (3/16-inch)-wide strips **(3)**. Moisten the surface of the dough, then lay the strips across it diagonally **(4, 5)**.

CUT TO SIZE Using a dough sheeter, roll out the dough to a thickness of 2.7 millimeter (⅛ inch), then into a 29 × 60-centimeter (11 ½ × 23 ½-inch) rectangle. Cut out twelve 9 × 15-centimeter (3 ½ × 6-inch) rectangles **(6)**, then turn them over.

SHAPE Place two praline chocolate sticks at each end of the rectangles and shape into pains au chocolat **(7, 8, 9)**. Place on baking sheets lined with parchment paper.

FINAL PROOF At 27°C (80°F) for about 2 hours 30 minutes.

BAKE In a convection oven at 170°C (340°F) for about 17 minutes.

FINISH Brush with neutral syrup **(10)**.

COOL On a wire rack.

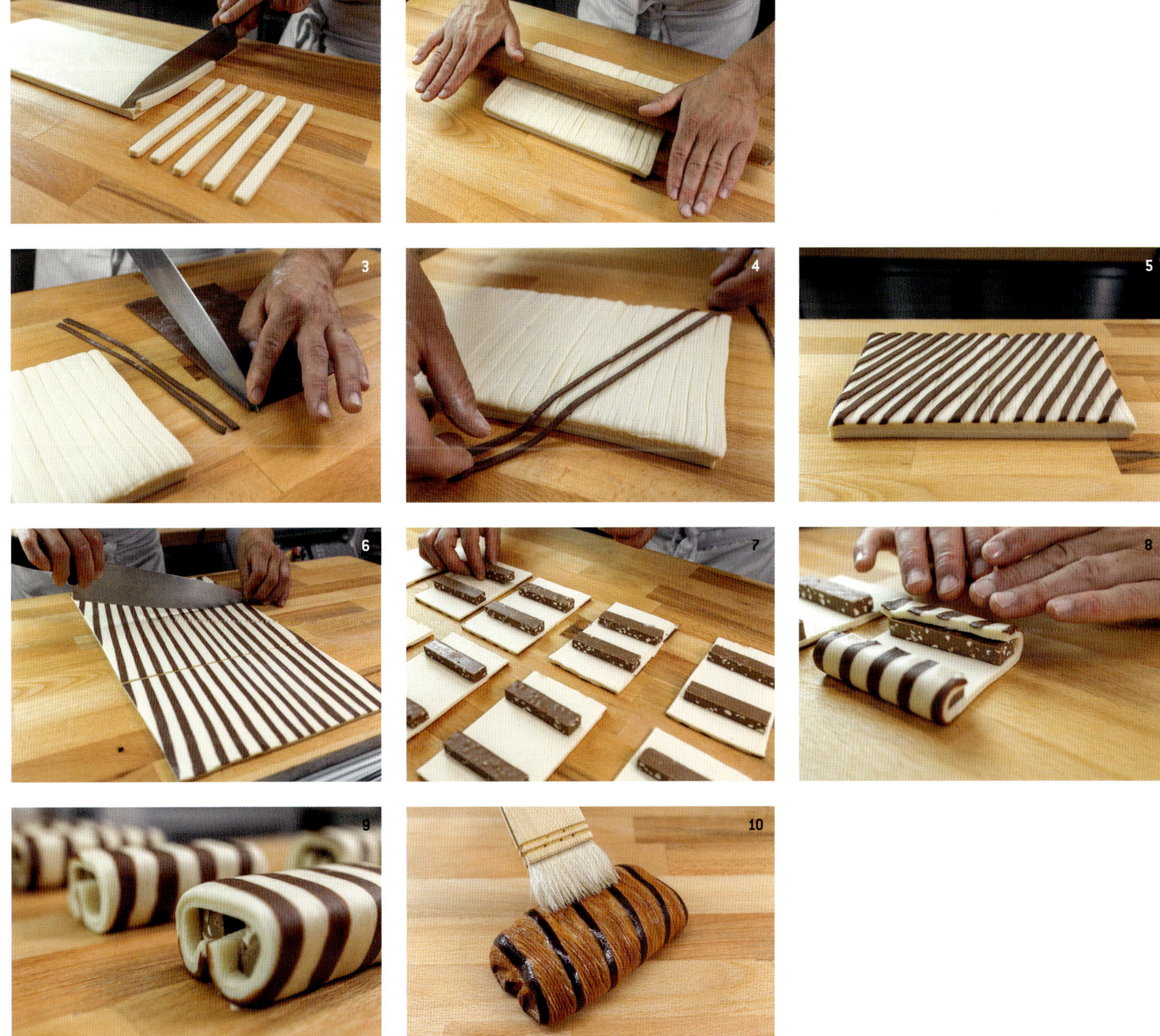
1
2
3
4
5
6
7
8
9
10

LEMON AND LIME SPIRALS

MAKES 12 PASTRIES

LEAVENED LAMINATED DOUGH

Croissant dough *(see page 186)*	**700 G (1 LB 8 ¾ OZ)**
Dry butter *(see page 10)*	**200 G (7 OZ)**

COCONUT AND LEMON FILLING

Butter	**60 G (2 ⅛ OZ)**
Superfine sugar	**60 G (2 ⅛ OZ)**
Shredded coconut	**60 G (2 ⅛ OZ)**
Egg	**50 G (1 ¾ OZ)**
Candied lemon and lime, diced and chopped	**75 G (2 ⅝ OZ)**

LEMON CREAM

Lime juice	**100 G (3 ½ OZ)**
Lemon juice	**35 G (1 ¼ OZ)**
Milk	**60 G (2 ⅛ OZ)**
Butter	**12 G (⅜ OZ)**
Eggs	**62 G (2 ⅛ OZ)**
Superfine sugar	**90 G (3 ⅛ OZ)**
Cornstarch	**18 G (⅝ OZ)**
Pectin NH	**8 G (¼ OZ)**

TO FINISH

Neutral syrup *(see page 31)*	**AS NEEDED**
Lime, zest only	**AS NEEDED**
Lemon, zest only	**AS NEEDED**
Confectioners' sugar	**AS NEEDED**

FOR THE COCONUT AND LEMON FILLING

In a stand mixer fitted with the paddle attachment, cream the butter and sugar, then add in the shredded coconut. Beat in the egg, then the chopped candied lemon and lime. Pipe 25 gram (7/8 oz) into 4-centimeter (1 1/2-inch)-diameter round silicone molds **(1)**. Set aside in the freezer.

FOR THE LEMON CREAM

Bring the lime juice, lemon juice, milk, and butter to a boil. Cream the remaining ingredients. Combine the two mixtures and boil for 1 minute. Pipe 25 grams (7/8 oz) of cream into 4-centimeter (1 1/2-inch)-diameter silicone hemisphere molds **(2)**. Set aside in the freezer.

METHOD

TURNING (*TOURAGE*) Degas the dough. Encase the dry butter in the dough. Make two single turns *(see page 14)*.

REST At 1°C (35°F) for about 1 hour.

PRESHAPE Roll out to a thickness of 8 millimeters (5/16 inch), then into a 15 × 40-centimeter (6 × 15 1/2-inch) rectangle. Cut out 5-millimeter (3/16-inch)-wide strips, then place them on the moistened dough. Roll out to a thickness of 3 millimeter (1/8 inch), then into a 40-centimeter (15 1/2-inch) square.

CUT TO SIZE Cut 3 × 34-centimeter (1 1/4 × 13 1/2-inch) strips in the direction of the puff pastry **(3)**, then cut one end off each strip diagonally **(4)**. Roll out the scraps to a thickness of 1 millimeter (1/32 inch), then set aside at 1°C (35°F).

SHAPE Join a lemon and a coconut insert together, then place the double insert at the end of the strip. Roll it up, leaving the tip free **(5, 6)**. Cut 4-centimeter (1 1/2-inch)-diameter disks from the rolled-out scraps. Place the disks in greased 12-centimeter (4 3/4-inch) brioche molds, then top with the spirals **(7)**.

FINAL PROOF At 27°C (80°F) for about 2 hours 30 minutes.

BAKE In a convection oven at 170°C (340°F) for about 17 minutes.

FINISH Brush with neutral syrup, then sprinkle with lemon and lime zest **(8, 9)**.

COOL On a wire rack.

FINISH Using a curved bowl scraper, dust the diagonal ends of the pastries **(10)** with confectioners' sugar.

1
2
3
4
5
6
7
8
9
10

COFFEE BREAKS

MAKES 12 PASTRIES

PLAIN BRIOCHE DOUGH

(see page 184)	660 G (1 LB 7 ¼ OZ)

STAR ANISE PASTRY CREAM

Milk	100 G (3 ½ OZ)
Superfine sugar	25 G (⅞ OZ)
Egg yolk	18 G (⅝ OZ)
Custard powder	4 G (⅛ OZ)
Unsweetened cocoa powder	4 G (⅛ OZ)
Ground star anise	1 G (1/32 OZ)

COFFEE CRÈME BRÛLÉE

Whipping cream 35% fat	240 G (8 ½ OZ)
Coffee beans	24 G (⅞ OZ)
Egg yolks	72 G (2 ½ OZ)
Superfine sugar	48 G (1 ⅝ OZ)

CIGARETTE BATTER

Butter, softened	50 G (1 ¾ OZ)
Confectioners' sugar	50 G (1 ¾ OZ)
Egg whites at room temperature	50 G (1 ¾ OZ)
Unsweetened cocoa powder	30 G (1 OZ)
Strong flour	30 G (1 OZ)

FOR THE STAR ANISE PASTRY CREAM

Stir the sugar, egg yolk, custard powder, cocoa powder, and star anise together. Stir in the milk.
Microwave for about 2 minutes.
Whisk and cool in a blast chiller. Set aside at 3°C (35°F).
Using a pastry bag fitted with a D6 star tip, pipe pastry cream stars into 6-centimeter (2 ½-inch)-diameter silicone molds **(1)**.

FOR THE COFFEE CRÈME BRÛLÉE

In a saucepan, heat the cream and coffee and let infuse for 15 minutes. Strain.
Stir the egg yolks and sugar together, then stir in the infused cream. Let rest at 3°C (35°F) for 12 hours.
Pour the pastry cream around the stars **(2)** in the silicone molds. Bake in a convection oven at 90°C (195°F) for about 45 minutes. Set aside in the freezer.

FOR THE CIGARETTE BATTER

Stir the butter and confectioners' sugar together.
Stir in the warm egg whites, then the cocoa powder and flour.
Spread the batter over the small Greek frieze relief strips placed directly in the 10-centimeter (4-inch)-diameter circles **(3)**.

METHOD

WEIGHT	Twelve 55-gram (2-oz) dough pieces.
SHAPE	Gently shape into balls.
REST	At 3°C (35°F) for about 30 minutes.
SHAPE	Using a rolling pin, roll out the dough into 8-centimeter (3 ¼-inch)-diameter disks **(4)**, then use the end of the rolling pin to make a cavity in the center of each disk **(5)**. Place the disks in the ring molds **(6)**.
FINAL PROOF	At 27°C (80°F) for about 2 hours.
GLAZE	Whisked egg.
PREBAKE PREP	Add the frozen crèmes brûlée inserts **(7, 8)**.
BAKE	In a convection oven at 145°C (295°F), or in a deck oven at 180°C (355°F), for about 15 minutes.
COOL	On a wire rack.

1

2

3

4

5

6

7

8

TROPICAL FLAKY FLOWERS

MAKES 12 PASTRIES

LEAVENED LAMINATED DOUGH

Croissant dough *(see page 186)*	**720 G (1 LB 9 3/8 OZ)**
Dry butter *(see page 10)*	**180 G (6 3/8 OZ)**

MANGO AND PASSION FRUIT JELLY DISKS

Passion fruit puree	**240 G (8 1/2 OZ)**
Mango puree	**60 G (2 1/8 OZ)**
Raspberry pieces	**60 G (2 1/8 OZ)**
Superfine sugar	**90 G (3 1/8 OZ)**
Pectin 325 NH 95	**3.5 G (1/8 OZ)**
Xanthan gum	**2 G (1/16 OZ)**

MACERATED PITAHAYA

Pitahaya (dragon fruit)	**1**
Black currant puree	**100 G (3 1/2 OZ)**

TO FINISH

Neutral syrup *(see page 31)*	**AS NEEDED**

FOR THE MACERATED PITAHAYA

The day before, peel the pitahaya, then cut it lengthwise with a 7-centimeter (2 ¾-inch)-diameter plain round pastry cutter **(1)**.
Let the pitahaya macerate in the black currant puree at 3°C (35°F) for about 12 hours **(2)**.
Before baking, rinse the pitahaya and cut into 12 thin slices using a mandoline **(3)**.

FOR THE MANGO AND PASSION FRUIT JELLY DISK

Sprinkle the raspberry pieces into the bottom of 6-centimeter (2 ½-inch)-diameter silicone molds **(4)**.
Combine the sugar, pectin, and xanthan gum.
Bring the fruit purees to a boil and add the dry ingredients. Cook over medium heat for 1 minute. Pour the mixture into the 6-centimeter (2 ½-inch)-diameter silicone molds **(5)**.
Set aside in the freezer.

METHOD

TURNING (*TOURAGE*) Degas the dough. Encase the dry butter in the dough. Make two double turns *(see page 14)*.

REST At 1°C (35°F) for about 45 minutes.

PRESHAPE Using a dough sheeter, roll out the dough to a thickness of 4 millimeters (3/16 inch), then into a 39 × 29-centimeter (15 ½ × 11 ½-inch) rectangle.

REST In the freezer for about 15 minutes.

CUT TO SIZE Using a *petit beurre* pastry cutter, cut out 12 shapes **(6)** and place on baking sheets lined with parchment paper.

GLAZE Egg **(7)**.

FINAL PROOF At 27°C (80°F) for about 2 hours.

GLAZE Whisked egg.

PREBAKE PREP Gently degas the dough in the area that will be filled. Add the frozen jelly disks **(8, 9)**, then top with a slice of pitahaya **(10)**.

BAKE In a convection oven at 170°C (340°F), or a deck oven at 200°C (390°F), for about 17 minutes.

TO FINISH Brush the edges of the leavened laminated dough **(11)** with neutral syrup.

COOL On a wire rack.

1
2
3
4
5
6
7
8
9
10
11

LITTLE VANILLA AND ORANGE PILLOWS

MAKES 12 PASTRIES

BRIOCHE DOUGH 800 G (1 ¾ LB)

ORANGE ALMOND PASTE

Almond paste 50%	450 G (15 ⅞ OZ)
Vanilla bean	1
Orange, zest only	1
Candied orange peel	100 G (3 ½ OZ)

TO FINISH

White velvet spray	AS NEEDED
Small, dark chocolate balls	60

FOR THE ORANGE AND ALMOND PASTE

In a stand mixer fitted with the paddle attachment, beat all the ingredients until smooth. Using a dough sheeter, roll out the dough to a thickness of 4 millimeters (3/16 inch) between two guitar sheets **(1)**. Set aside in the freezer.

METHOD

PRESHAPE Using a dough sheeter, roll out the dough to a thickness of 4 millimeters (3/16 inch), then into a 30 × 35-centimeter (11 3/4 × 14-inch) rectangle.

REST At 1°C (35°F) for about 20 minutes.

CUT TO SIZE Using an 8-centimeter (3 1/4-inch)-square pastry cutter, cut out 12 squares. Using a dough sheeter, roll out the dough scraps to a thickness of 1 millimeter (1/32 inch), then cut into twelve 8-centimeter (3 1/4-inch) squares. Using a 7-centimeter (2 3/4-inch)-square pastry cutter **(2)**, cut out squares of orange almond paste.

SHAPE Place an almond paste square on a square rolled out to 4 millimeters (1/8 inch), then top with another 1-millimeter (1/32-inch) square **(3)**.

Seal the edges of the two dough squares **(4)**, then turn them over.

Using a dowel, press the dough squares from corner to corner, then press again into squares **(5, 6)**. Place the pillows on baking sheets lined with parchment paper, then place a greased 9-centimeter (3 1/2-inch)-square baking frame around each one **(7)**.

FINAL PROOF At 27°C (80°F) for about 2 hours 30 minutes.

BAKE In a convection oven at 145°C (295°F) for about 17 minutes.

COOL On a wire rack.

FINISH Chill in the freezer for 30 minutes. Spray the pastries with velvet spray, then place a chocolate ball where the indented lines intersect **(8, 9)**.

1
2
3
4
5
6
7
8
9

MINI ICE CREAM CUPS

MAKES 12 PASTRIES

PLAIN BRIOCHE DOUGH

(see page 184)	**680 G (1 ½ LB)**

CHOCOLATE FONDANT

Dark couverture chocolate 55%	**115 G (4 OZ)**
Butter	**95 G (3 ⅜ OZ)**
Eggs	**88 G (3 ⅛ OZ)**
Superfine sugar	**69 G (2 ⅜ OZ)**
Cornstarch	**14 G (½ OZ)**
Fleur de sel	**1 G (1/32 OZ)**

MANGO AND PASSION FRUIT JELLY FILLING

Mango puree	**60 G (2 ⅛ OZ)**
Passion fruit puree	**60 G (2 ⅛ OZ)**
Superfine sugar	**30 G (1 OZ)**
Pectin NH	**2.2 G (1/16 OZ)**
Lime, zest only	½

CHOCOLATE GLAZE

Glucose	**75 G (2 ⅝ OZ)**
Superfine sugar	**75 G (2 ⅝ OZ)**
Sweetened condensed milk	**50 G (1 ¾ OZ)**
Water	**50 G (1 ¾ OZ)**
Dark couverture chocolate 55%	**75 G (2 ⅝ OZ)**
Water	**35 G (1 ¼ OZ)**
Gelatin powder	**5 G (3/16 OZ)**

TO FINISH

Chopped toasted almonds	**AS NEEDED**
Gold leaf	**AS NEEDED**

FOR THE CHOCOLATE FONDANT

In a microwave, melt the chocolate and butter. Stir the eggs, sugar, starch, and fleur de sel together. Stir the two mixtures until smooth. Pour 30 grams (1 oz) of the mixture into 8-centimeter (3 1/4-inch)-diameter silicone hemisphere molds, then cook in a bain-marie for 18 minutes **(1)**.
Set aside in the freezer.

FOR THE MANGO AND PASSION FRUIT JELLY FILLING

Whisk the cold purees, zest, and dry ingredients, then bring to a boil **(2)**. Set aside in a pastry bag at 3°C (35°F).

FOR THE CHOCOLATE GLAZE

Soak the gelatin in the 35 grams (1 1/4 oz) of cold water. Heat the remaining ingredients except for the dark couverture chocolate, and when the mixture boils, whisk in the gelatin and the dark chocolate couverture, then bring to a boil again **(3)**.
Gently mix the glaze, being careful not to incorporate any air.
Cover with plastic wrap in direct in contact and set aside at 3°C (35°F). Use at 35°C (95°F).

METHOD

WEIGHT One 440-gram (15 1/2-oz) dough piece and one 240-gram (8 1/2-oz) dough piece **(4)**.

PRESHAPE Using a dough sheeter, roll out the 440-gram (15 1/2-oz) dough piece to a thickness of 2.5 millimeters (1/16 to 1/8 inch), and roll out the 240-gram (8 1/2-oz) dough piece to a thickness of 0.5 millimeter (1/64 inch).

REST In the freezer for about 15 minutes.

CUT TO SIZE Cut out 12 "ice-cream cups" and twelve 3-centimeter (1 1/8-inch)-disks from the 440-gram (15 1/2-oz) dough piece **(5)**, and cut out 12 large "ice-cream cups" from the 240-gram (8 1/2-oz) dough piece **(6)**.

BAKE Using an ice-cream cone waffle maker, precook the large "cups" **(7)** and immediately place them in the molds **(8)**.

SHAPE Place the pieces of raw dough in the molds **(9)**, then place a T across the top of each mold to create a cavity **(10)**.

FINAL PROOF At 27°C (80°F) for about 2 hours.

BAKE In a convection oven at 140°C (285°F), with a baking sheet on top of the molds, for about 14 minutes.

COOL On a wire rack.

FINISH Pipe mango and passion fruit jelly filling into the pastries **(11)**. Glaze the frozen chocolate fondants **(12)**, then roll the edges in the chopped almonds **(13)**. Place the fondants on the pastries **(14)** and decorate with gold leaf **(15)**.

1
2
3
4
5
6
7
8
9
10
11
12
13
14
15

TROPICAL CHOCOLATE SUNBURSTS

MAKES 12 PASTRIES

PLAIN LEAVENED LAMINATED DOUGH

Croissant dough *(see page 186)*	**620 G**
Dry butter *(see page 10)*	**180 G (6 3/8 OZ)**

COCOA CROISSANT DOUGH

Croissant dough *(see page 186)*	**100 G (3 1/2 OZ)**
Unsweetened cocoa powder	**10 G (3/8 OZ)**
Water	**10 G (3/8 OZ)**
Butter	**10 G (3/8 OZ)**

CHOCOLATE BROWNIE

Dark couverture chocolate 55%	**90 G (3 1/8 OZ)**
Butter	**90 G (3 1/8 OZ)**
Superfine sugar	**100 G (3 1/2 OZ)**
Eggs	**60 G (2 1/8 OZ)**
Strong flour	**35 G (1 1/4 OZ)**

FOR THE TROPICAL CREAM

Mango puree	**36 G (1 1/4 OZ)**
Passion fruit puree	**36 G (1 1/4 OZ)**
Superfine sugar	**18 G (5/8 OZ)**
Cornstarch	**6 G (3/16 OZ)**
Lime, zest only	1/2

TO FINISH

Neutral syrup *(see page 31)*	**AS NEEDED**

FOR THE COCOA CROISSANT DOUGH

In a stand mixer fitted with the paddle attachment, beat the ingredients for the cocoa croissant dough on speed 1 until smooth. Bulk ferment about 40 minutes, then at 1°C (35°F) for 12 hours.

FOR THE CHOCOLATE BROWNIE

In a microwave, melt the dark chocolate and butter. Combine the eggs, sugar, and flour. Combine the two mixtures until smooth. Pipe 15 grams (½ oz) of brownie batter into twenty-four 3.5-centimeter (1 ⅜-inch)-diameter sushi maki silicone molds **(1)**. Chill at 3°C (35°F) for about 1 hour, then bake in a convection oven at 150°C (300°F) for 8 minutes.

FOR THE TROPICAL CREAM

Combine the sugar and starch. Stir the cold purees, zest and dry ingredients together, then bring to a boil. Fill the centers of the cooled brownies **(2)**, pair two brownies together **(3)**, then set aside in the freezer.

METHOD

TURNING (*TOURAGE*) Degas the dough. Encase the dry butter in the dough. Make one single and one double turn *(see page 14)*. Moisten the surface of the dough, then roll out the cocoa croissant dough to the size of the folded dough **(4)**.

REST At 1°C (35°F) for about 45 minutes.

PRESHAPE Using a dough sheeter, roll out the dough to a thickness of 3.25 millimeter (⅛ inch), into a 45 × 34-centimeter (17 ½ × 13 ½-inch) rectangle.

REST In the freezer for about 15 minutes.

CUT TO SIZE Using an 11-centimeter (4 ¼-inch)-diameter pastry cutter, cut out 12 disks **(5)**. Using a template, cut 12 curves into each disk **(6)**.
Roll out the dough scraps to a thickness of 1 millimeter (1/32 inch), chill in the freezer for 10 minutes, then cut out twelve 4.5-centimeter (1 ¾-inch)-diameter disks and twelve 4-centimeter (1 ½-inch)-diameter disks.

SHAPE Place a 4-centimeter (1 ½-inch) disk on the brownie inserts **(7)**.
Place a brownie insert on each pastry disk, then fold each flap over **(8)**. Seal with the lightly moistened 4.5-centimeter (1 ¾-inch) disks. Place in greased 9-centimeter (3 ½-inch)-diameter flared molds **(9)**.

FINAL PROOF At 27°C (80°F) for about 2 hours.

BAKE In a convection oven at 170°C (340°F) for about 16 minutes.

TO FINISH Brush with neutral syrup **(10)**.

COOL On a wire rack.

1

2

3

4

5

6

7

8

9

10

CHOCOLATE AND PISTACHIO ROSETTES

MAKES 3 PASTRIES

PLAIN LEAVENED LAMINATED DOUGH

Croissant dough *(see page 186)*	**600 G (1 LB 6 1/8 OZ)**
Dry butter *(see page 10)*	**210 G (7 3/8 OZ)**

COCOA CROISSANT DOUGH

Croissant dough *(see page 186)*	**90 G (93 1/8 OZ)**
Unsweetened cocoa powder	**7 G (1/4 OZ)**
Butter	**3.5 G (1/8 OZ)**
Water	**3.5 G (1/8 OZ)**

CRÈME BRÛLÉE WITH PISTACHIO

Milk	**40 G (1 3/8 OZ)**
Whipping cream 35% fat	**40 G (1 3/8 OZ)**
Egg yolk	**15 G (1/2 OZ)**
Superfine sugar	**8 G (1/4 OZ)**
Pistachio paste	**8 G (1/4 OZ)**

CHOCOLATE BROWNIE

Butter	**80 G (2 7/8 OZ)**
Dark couverture chocolate 63%	**80 G (2 7/8 OZ)**
Superfine sugar	**80 G (2 7/8 OZ)**
Egg	**50 G (1 3/4 OZ)**
Strong flour	**30 G (1 OZ)**

TO FINISH

Neutral syrup *(see page 31)*	**AS NEEDED**

FOR THE COCOA CROISSANT DOUGH

In a stand mixer fitted with the paddle attachment, beat the ingredients for the cocoa croissant dough on speed 1 until smooth. Bulk ferment for about 40 minutes, then at 1°C (35°F) for 12 hours.

FOR THE CRÈME BRÛLÉE WITH PISTACHIO

In a saucepan, bring the cream, milk, and pistachio paste to a boil, then let infuse until completely cool.
Cream the eggs yolk and sugar a little. Stir in the milk, cream, and pistachio paste infusion. Set aside at 3°C (35°F) for 12 hours.
Pour 35 grams (1 ¼ oz) of the mixture into 6-centimeter (2 ½-inch)-diameter silicone molds **(1)**. Bake in a convection oven at 90°C (195°) for about 45 minutes. Set aside in the freezer.

FOR THE CHOCOLATE BROWNIE

Melt the butter and chocolate. Gently cream the eggs and sugar, then add the flour. Combine the two mixtures.
Pour 25 grams (⅞ oz) of the batter into 5-centimeter (2-inch)-diameter hemisphere silicone molds **(2)**, then pour 80 grams (2 ⅞ oz) of the batter into greased 12.5-centimeter (5-inch)-diameter savarin molds **(3)**. Bake in a convection oven at 150°C (300°F) for about 15 minutes.
Unmold the rings and hemispheres 5 minutes after removing them from the oven **(4)**. Set aside in the freezer.

METHOD

TURNING (*TOURAGE*) Degas the dough. Encase the dry butter in the dough. Make one single and one double turn *(see page 14)*. Moisten the surface of the dough **(5)**, then roll out the cocoa croissant dough to the size of the folded dough **(6)**.

REST At 1°C (35°F) for about 45 minutes.

PRESHAPE Using a rolling pin, roll out the dough to a thickness of 3.5 millimeters (3⁄16 inch), then into a 65 × 21-centimeter (25 ½ × 8 ¼-inch) rectangle.

REST At 1°C (35°F) for about 15 minutes.

CUT TO SIZE Cut three 20-centimeter (8-inch) diameter disks.

SHAPE Using a template, cut eight curves into each disk, being careful to keep the chocolate facing downward **(7, 8)**. Turn the disks over and place a frozen brownie ring **(9)** in the center on each one. Bring each tip to the center and fold it over the brownie ring **(10, 11)**. Place the pastries in greased 14-centimeter (1 ½-inch)-diameter springform pans **(12)**.

FINAL PROOF At 27°C (80°F) for about 2 hours 30 minutes.

PREBAKE PREP Place a hemisphere of frozen brownie **(13)** in the center of each pastry and top with a disk of frozen pistachio crème brûlée **(14)**.

BAKE In a convection oven at 170°C (340°F) for about 15 minutes, then at 120°C (250°F) for about 10 minutes.

TO FINISH Brush with neutral syrup.

COOL On a wire rack.

1
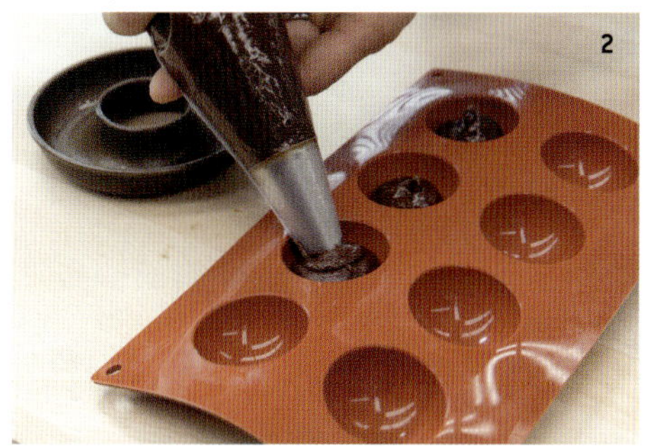
2

3

4

5

6

7

8

9

10

11

12

13

14

SUNLIGHTS

MAKES 12 PASTRIES

LEAVENED LAMINATED DOUGH

Croissant dough *(see page 186)*	600 G (1 LB 6 1/8 OZ)
Dry butter *(see page 10)*	150 G (5 1/4 OZ)

PINEAPPLE AND COCONUT FILLING

Butter	60 G (2 1/8 OZ)
Superfine sugar	60 G (2 1/8 OZ)
Shredded coconut	60 G (2 1/8 OZ)
Eggs	60 G (2 1/8 OZ)
Custard powder	5 G (3/16 OZ)
Dried pineapple, chopped	150 G (5 1/4 OZ)

TO FINISH

Neutral syrup	AS NEEDED
Shredded coconut	AS NEEDED

FOR THE PINEAPPLE AND COCONUT FILLING

In a stand mixer fitted with the paddle attachment, cream the butter and sugar, then add the shredded coconut and custard powder. Whisk in the eggs, then the chopped dried pineapple **(1)**. Set aside in a pastry bag.

METHOD

TURNING (*TOURAGE*) Degas the dough. Encase the dry butter in the dough. Make two double turns *(see page 14)*.

REST At 1°C (35°F) for about 45 minutes.

PRESHAPE Using a dough sheeter, roll out the dough to a thickness of 3.5 millimeters (3/16 inches), then into a 42 × 32-centimeter (16 1/2 × 12 1/2-inch) rectangle.

REST In the freezer for about 15 minutes.

CUT TO SIZE Cut out 14 × 8-centimeter (5 1/2 × 3 1/4-inch) rectangles.

SHAPE Pipe the pineapple and coconut filling down the middle and along the length of each rectangle **(2)**. Moisten the lower part of each rectangle **(3)**, then fold in half lengthwise **(4)**. Using a knife, make six cuts **(5)**, then join the two ends to form circles **(6)**. Seal, then place on baking sheets lined with parchment paper.

GLAZE Whisked egg.

FINAL PROOF 2 hours at 27°C (80°F).

GLAZE Whisked egg.

BAKE In a convection oven at 170°C (340°F), or a deck oven at 200°C (390°F), for about 17 minutes.

FINISH Brush with neutral syrup **(7)**, then sprinkle the outer edges with shredded coconut **(8)**.

COOL On a wire rack.

1
2
3
4
5
6
7
8

MARRON DRUMS

MAKES 12 PASTRIES

PLAIN BRIOCHE DOUGH

(see page 184)	**650 G (1 LB 7 OZ)**

COCOA BRIOCHE DOUGH

Brioche dough *(see page 184)*	**86 G (3 OZ)**
Cocoa powder	**7 G (1/4 OZ)**
Water	**7 G (1/4 OZ)**

CHOUX PASTRY

(see page 29)	**205 G (7 1/4 OZ)**

MARRON CREAM

Pastry cream *(see page 30)*	**200 G (7 OZ)**
Chestnut (marron) cream	**150 G (5 1/4 OZ)**
Grand-Marnier®	**5 G (3/16 OZ)**

TO FINISH

Confectioners' sugar	**AS NEEDED**

FOR THE COCOA BRIOCHE DOUGH

In a stand mixer fitted with the paddle attachment, beat the brioche dough with the cocoa-water mixture on speed 1 until smooth. Bulk ferment for about 30 minutes. Gently fold to degas the dough, then proof at 3°C (35°F) for 12 hours.

FOR THE MARRON CREAM

Stir all the ingredients together. Set aside in a pastry bag at 3°C (35°F).

FOR THE CHOUX PASTRY

Prepare the choux pastry *(see page 29)*.
Line twelve 4.5-centimeter (1 ¾-inch)-diameter, 4.5-centimeter (1 ¾-inch)-deep *nonette* molds with microperforated silicone matting, and place on a baking sheet lined with a microperforated silicone mat. Place 17 grams (⅝ oz) of choux pastry in each mold **(1)**. Cover the molds with a microperforated silicone mat and a baking sheet.
Bake in a convection oven at 170°C (340°F) for about 45 minutes. Unmold them as soon as they come out of the oven. When cool, pipe the marron cream into the choux pastries **(2)** and set aside at 3°C (35°F).

METHOD

WEIGHT One 400-gram (14-oz) plain brioche dough piece, one 250-gram (5 ¼-ox) plain brioche dough piece, and one 100-gram (3 ½-oz) cocoa brioche dough piece.

PRESHAPE Using a dough sheeter, roll out the 250-gram (5 ¼-oz) plain brioche dough to a thickness of 2 millimeters (1/16 inch). Set aside in the freezer.
Using a rolling pin, roll out the 400-gram (14-oz) plain brioche dough and the cocoa dough into 20 × 25-centimeter (8 × 9 ¾-inch) rectangles. Moisten the plain brioche dough **(3)** and place the cocoa dough **(4)** on top.

REST In the freezer for about 15 minutes.

ROLL OUT Using a dough sheeter, roll out the bicolored dough into a 32 × 42-centimeter (12 ½ × 16 ½-inch) rectangle.

REST In the freezer for about 15 minutes.

CUT TO SIZE Cut out twelve 5.5 × 20-centimeter (2 ⅛-inch) rectangles **(5)**, then cut each rectangle into eight identical rectangles **(6)**. Place in a checkerboard pattern on 5.5 × 20-centimeter (2 ⅛ × 8-inch) microperforated silicone mats **(7)**.

FINAL PROOF 2 hours at 27°C (80°F).

PREBAKE PREP Using a 6.5-centimeter (2 ⅝-inch)-diameter pastry cutter, cut 12 disks from the frozen 2-millimeter (1/16-inch) dough **(8)**.
Place them on baking sheets lined with parchment paper, then place a 6.5-centimeter (2 ⅝-inch)-diameter, 6-centimeter (2 ½-inch)-deep ring mold on each pastry disk.
Wrap the checkerboards around the choux pastry cylinders using the microperforated silicone mats to help you **(9)**.
Place the wrapped cylinders in the ring molds **(10)**.
Cover the pastries with parchment paper and a stainless steel rack **(11)**.

BAKE In a convection oven at 150°C (300°F) for about 18 minutes. Turn the cylinders over after baking.

COOL On a wire rack.

FINISH Using a stencil, dust with confectioners' sugar **(12)**.

1
2
3
4
5
6
7
8
9
10
11
12

LEMON AND BLACK CURRANT SPINNING TOPS

MAKES 12 PASTRIES

LEMON BRIOCHE DOUGH

Brioche dough *(see page 184)*	750 G (1 LB 10 ½ OZ)
Ground turmeric	4 G (⅛ OZ)
Lemon, zest only	½

BLACK CURRANT BRIOCHE DOUGH

Brioche dough *(see page 184)*	100 G (3 ½ OZ)
Black currant powder	10 G (⅜ OZ)
Water	10 G (⅜ OZ)

LEMON SPONGE CAKES

Butter	65 G (2 ¼ OZ)
Superfine sugar	65 G (2 ¼ OZ)
Egg	40 G (1 ⅜ OZ)
Strong flour	65 G (2 ¼ OZ)
Baking powder	2 G (1/16 OZ)
Almond flour	20 G (¾ OZ)
Lemon zest	15 G (½ OZ)
Black currants, frozen	30 G (1 OZ)

LEMON SYRUP

Water	80 G (2 ⅞ OZ)
Superfine sugar	80 G (2 ⅞ OZ)
Lemon juice	20 G (¾ OZ)

FOR THE LEMON BRIOCHE DOUGH

In a stand mixer fitted with the paddle attachment, beat the brioche dough, turmeric, and lemon zest on speed 1 until smooth. Bulk ferment for about 30 minutes. Gently fold to degas the dough, then proof at 3°C (35°F) for 12 hours.

FOR THE BLACK CURRANT BRIOCHE DOUGH

In the stand mixer fitted with the paddle attachment, beat the brioche dough and black currant powder-water mixture on speed 1 until smooth. Bulk ferment for about 30 minutes. Gently fold to degas the dough, then proof at 3°C (35°F) for 12 hours.

FOR THE LEMON SPONGE CAKES

In the stand mixer fitted with the paddle attachment, gently cream the butter and sugar, then add the egg. Gently fold in the sifted dry mixture. Fold in the lemon zest, then the frozen black currants **(1)**.
Place 25 grams ($\frac{7}{8}$ oz) of the batter in 5-centimeter (2-inch)-diameter silicone hemisphere molds. Bake in a convection oven at 150°C (300°F) for about 15 minutes. Flatten the surface of the cakes a little. Set aside in the freezer.

FOR THE LEMON SYRUP

Bring the water and sugar to a boil, then add the lemon juice. Set aside at 3°C (35°F).

METHOD

WEIGHT One 500-gram (1 lb 2-oz) lemon brioche dough piece and one 250-gram (5 $\frac{1}{4}$-oz) lemon brioche dough piece. One 120-gram (4 $\frac{1}{4}$-oz) black currant brioche dough piece.

PRESHAPE Using a rolling pin, roll out the 500-gram (1 lb 2-oz) lemon brioche dough and the black currant brioche dough into 25 × 15-centimeter (11 $\frac{3}{4}$ × 6-inch) rectangles. Moisten and put one on top of the other **(2)**.
Roll out the 250-gram (5 $\frac{1}{4}$-oz) lemon brioche dough to a thickness of 2 millimeters ($\frac{1}{16}$ inch).

REST In the freezer for about 15 minutes.

PRESHAPE Using a rolling pin, roll out the bicolored dough into a 45 × 22-centimeter (17 $\frac{1}{2}$ × 8 $\frac{3}{4}$-inch) rectangle.

REST In the freezer for about 15 minutes.

CUT TO SIZE Cut 12 identical strips lengthwise. Cut tip of each strip to obtain a 45-degree angle **(3)**, then use the rolling pin to flatten 4 centimeter (1 $\frac{1}{2}$ inches) at end of each one **(4)**.
Using a 9-centimeter (3 $\frac{1}{2}$-inch)-diameter pastry cutter, cut 12 disks from the 250-gram (5 $\frac{1}{4}$-oz) brioche dough **(5)**.

SHAPE Line 8.5-centimeter (3 $\frac{3}{8}$-inch)-diameter flared molds with the disks **(6)**.
Roll the bicolored strips around frozen lemon currant cake domes, starting with the pointed end at the top and working your way down and around **(7, 8)**, ending with the flattened part that should be tucked under sponge cakes **(9)**.
Place in the lined molds **(10)**.

FINAL PROOF At 27°C (80°F) for about 2 hours.

BAKE In a convection oven at 145°C (295°F) for about 12 minutes.

TO FINISH Brush with the lemon syrup.

COOL On a wire rack.

1
2
3
4
5
6
7
8
9
10

TZARINES

MAKES 12 PASTRIES

LEAVENED LAMINATED DOUGH

Plain croissant dough *(see page 186)*	700 G (1 LB 8 ½ OZ)
Dry butter *(see page 10)*	210 G (7 ⅜ OZ)

CRAQUELIN

Strong flour	40 G (1 ⅜ OZ)
Butter, softened	45 G (1 ½ OZ)
Superfine sugar	40 G (1 ⅜ OZ)
Almond flour	40 G (1 ⅜ OZ)
Salt	1 G (1/32 OZ)

CHOUX PASTRY

Choux pastry *(see page 29)*	180 G (6 ⅜ OZ)
Vanilla pastry cream *(see page 30)*	360 G (12 ⅝ OZ)

MACARONADE

Almond flour	50 G (1 ¾ OZ)
Superfine sugar	50 G (1 ¾ OZ)
Egg white	30 G (1 OZ)

TO FINISH

Confectioners' sugar	AS NEEDED

FOR THE CRAQUELIN

In a stand mixer fitted with the paddle attachment, beat all the ingredients until smooth.
Roll out the dough between two sheets of guitar paper to a thickness of 1.5 millimeters (1/32 inch). Set aside in the freezer.
Using a 4-centimeter (1 1/2-inch)-diameter pastry cutter, cut out 12 disks. Using a 3-centimeter (1 1/4-inch)-diameter pastry cutter, cut out 12 disks **(1)**.

FOR THE CHOUX PASTRY

Prepare the choux pastry *(see page 29)*.
Pipe twelve 10-gram (3/8 oz) and twelve 5-gram (1/8 oz) of choux pastry onto a microperforated silicone mat **(2)**.
Top each large choux puff with a large craquelin disk **(3)**. Top each small choux puff with a small *craquelin* disk **(4)**.
Bake in a convection oven at 170°C (340°F) for about 20 minutes.
When cool, fill the choux with the vanilla pastry cream: 20 gram (3/4 oz) for the large choux puffs,
10 gram (3/8 oz) for the small ones **(5)**.

FOR THE MACARONADE

Stir all the ingredients together. Set aside at 3°C (35°F).

METHOD

TURNING (TOURAGE) Degas the dough. Encase the dry butter in the dough. Make one single and one double turn *(see page 14)*.

REST At 1°C (35°F) for about 45 minutes.

PRESHAPE Using a dough sheeter, roll out the dough to a thickness of 3.5 millimeters (3/16 inch), then into a 42 × 32-centimeter (16 1/2 × 12 1/2-inch) rectangle

REST In the freezer for about 15 minutes.

CUT TO SIZE Using a 10-centimeter (4-inch)-diameter pastry cutter, cut out 12 disks. Using a template, cut six curves into each disk **(6, 7)**.

SHAPE Place a large choux puff **(8)** in the center of each disk and fold the tips toward the center **(9, 10)**.
Place in greased 8-centimeter (3 1/4-inch)-diameter springform pans.

FINAL PROOF At 27°C (80°F) for about 2 hours 30 minutes.

PREBAKE PREP Using a pastry bag, pipe the macaronade in the gaps as well as on top **(11)**, then place a small choux puff on top of the pastry **(12)**.

BAKE In a convection at 170°C (340°F) for 15 minutes.

COOL On a wire rack.

TO FINISH Sprinkle with confectioners' sugar.

1

2

3

4

5

6

7

8

9

10

11

12

SW
EET

BAK
ED ·
· GO
ODS

LEMON POUND CAKE

MAKES 9 CAKES

INGREDIENTS

Strong flour	750 G (1 LB 10 ½ OZ)
Baking powder	12 G
Superfine sugar	600 G (1 LB 6 ⅛ OZ)
Invert sugar	200 G (7 OZ)
Lemons, zest only	4
Limes, zest only	2
Eggs	600 G (1 LB 6 ⅛ OZ)
Whipping cream	200 G (7 OZ)
Rum	20 G (¾ OZ)
Salt	1 G (1/32 OZ)
Brown butter	350 G (12 ⅜ OZ)

LEMON SYRUP

Superfine sugar	130 G
Water	90 G (3 ⅛ OZ)
Lime juice	40 G (1 ⅜ OZ)
Lemon juice	90 G (3 ⅛ OZ)

LEMON GLAZE

Confectioners' sugar	800 G (1 ¾ LB)
Lime juice	80 G (2 ⅞ OZ)
Lemon juice	180 G (6 ⅜ OZ)
Rum	20 G (¾ OZ)

FOR THE LEMON SYRUP

Wash, zest, and squeeze the lemons and limes. Bring the water and sugar to a boil. Add the zests, cover with plastic wrap, and set aside in the refrigerator. Add the lemon and lime juices to the cold syrup.

FOR THE LEMON GLAZE

Mix all the ingredients together.

METHOD

Sift the flour and baking powder.
In a stand mixer fitted with the whisk attachment, whisk the sugar, invert sugar, and lemon and lime zests.
Add the eggs and whisk together.
Add the cream, rum, and salt.
Add the brown butter.
Gently whisk in the flour and baking powder.
Pour 300 grams (10 ½ oz) of batter into each buttered 24 × 5 × 5-centimeter (9 ½ × 2 × 2-inch) loaf pan.
Bake in a convection oven at 155°C (310°F) for about 20 minutes.
Soak the cakes with the lemon syrup.
Let the cakes cool on a wire rack.
Frost the cakes with the lemon glaze.
Dry the lemon glaze in a convection oven, with the vent open, at 90°C (195°F) for about 4 minutes.

BORDEAUX CANELÉS

CANELÉS ARE BELIEVED TO DATE BACK TO 1519 TO THE ANNONCIADES CONVENT IN BORDEAUX. ACCORDING TO LEGEND, THE NUNS MADE PASTRIES WITH FLOUR THEY SALVAGED FROM THE DOCKS, RUM FROM THE FRENCH COLONIES, AND UNUSED EGG YOLKS FROM WINEMAKERS WHO ONLY USED THE WHITES TO CLARIFY THEIR WINE. THEIR CAKES AND PASTRIES WERE THEN DISTRIBUTED TO THE POOR. THEIR RECIPE WAS PERFECTED BY A PASTRY CHEF FROM BORDEAUX IN 1830, BECOMING THE REGIONAL SPECIALTY THAT WE KNOW TODAY: A DELICIOUS BITE-SIZE DESSERT WITH A CRISP, GOLDEN EXTERIOR AND A SOFT, DELICATELY RUM-FLAVORED INTERIOR.

MAKES 24 CANELÉS

INGREDIENTS

Vanilla beans	**2**
Milk	**1 KG (2 LB 3 1/4 OZ)**
Unsalted butter	**50 G (1 3/4 OZ)**
Strong flour	**180 G (6 3/8 OZ)**
Superfine sugar	**500 G (1 LB 1 5/8 OZ)**
Egg yolks	**100 G (3 1/2 OZ)**
Eggs	**100 G (3 1/2 OZ)**
Rum	**50 G (1 3/4 OZ)**

GREASING

Unsalted butter	**200 G (7 OZ)**
Beeswax	**100 G (3 1/2 OZ)**

FOR GREASING

Melt the butter and wax together.
Grease the molds.

METHOD

Scrape out the vanilla seeds. Bring the milk, butter, and vanilla seeds to a boil.
Stir in the flour and sugar, then add the eggs, egg yolks, and rum.
Pour the warm milk gradually into the flour mixture while stirring.
Let the batter rest at 3°C (35°F) for 12 to 24 hours.
Fill the molds to within 5 millimeters (3/16 inch) from the top.
Bake in a convection oven, with the vent open, at 185°C (365°F) for about 45 minutes.
Let cool in the molds, then turn out onto a wire rack.

PEANUT BUTTER
COOKIES

THESE COOKIES WERE INVENTED BY CHANCE BY RUTH GRAVES WAKEFIELD IN 1930 AT HER TOLL HOUSE INN IN MASSACHUSETTS. ONE DAY, WHILE PREPARING A BATCH OF BUTTER COOKIES, SHE ADDED SMALL PIECES OF NESTLÉ® CHOCOLATE TO THE DOUGH, THINKING THEY WOULD MELT INTO THE COOKIES. THIS WAS NOT THE CASE: THE CHOCOLATE PIECES KEPT THEIR SHAPE AND CONSISTENCY AFTER BAKING, MUCH TO THE DELIGHT OF HER CUSTOMERS! THIS PRODUCT WAS SO SUCCESSFUL THAT NESTLÉ® SAW ITS SALES BOOM IN THE AREA, AND, IN EXCHANGE FOR A LIFETIME SUPPLY OF CHOCOLATE FOR RUTH, THEY MARKETED THE NEW RECIPE.

MAKES 20

INGREDIENTS

Strong flour	**300 G (10 ½ OZ)**
Baking powder	**5 G (3/16 OZ)**
Unsalted butter	**225 G (8 OZ)**
Superfine sugar	**200 G (7 OZ)**
Brown sugar	**220 G (7 ¾ OZ)**
Salt	**3 G (⅛ OZ)**
Eggs	**100 G (3 ½ OZ)**
Peanut butter	**300 G (10 ½ OZ)**
Chocolate chips (64% cocoa)	**90 G (3 ⅛ OZ)**

METHOD

Sift the flour and baking powder.
In a stand mixer fitted with the paddle attachment, cream the butter, superfine and brown sugars, and the salt.
Add the eggs while mixing.
Add flour and baking powder.
Add the peanut butter, then mix in the chocolate chips.
Shape into 70-gram (2 ½-oz) balls.
Place the balls on baking sheets lined with parchment paper.
Gently press on the balls to flatten them slightly.
Bake in a convection oven at 170°C (340°F) for about 12 minutes.
Cool on the baking sheets for 15 minutes, then on a wire rack.

CRÊPES

THE ORIGIN OF THE CRÊPE DATES BACK TO 7,000 BCE, WHEN IT WAS SIMPLY A LARGE, THICK PANCAKE COOKED ON A HOT, FLAT STONE. CRÊPES FIRST APPEARED IN BRITTANY IN THE THIRTEENTH CENTURY, WHEN THEY WERE MADE WITH BUCKWHEAT INTRODUCED BY THE CRUSADERS. THE INTRODUCTION OF WHITE WHEAT FLOUR IN THE EARLY TWENTIETH CENTURY GAVE RISE TO THE CRÊPES WE ARE FAMILIAR WITH TODAY. THEY ARE TRADITIONALLY ASSOCIATED WITH CANDLEMAS AND MARDI GRAS, ALSO KNOWN AS SHROVE TUESDAY.

MAKES ABOUT 24 CRÊPES

INGREDIENTS

Vanilla bean	**1**
Strong flour	**500 G (1 LB 1 5/8 OZ)**
Salt	**5 G (3/16 OZ)**
Superfine sugar	**25 G (7/8 OZ)**
Eggs	**250 G (8 3/4 OZ)**
Milk	**1.1 KG (2 LB 5 1/2 OZ)**
Oil	**15 G (1/2 OZ)**

METHOD

Scrape out the vanilla seeds.
Whisk the flour, salt, sugar, eggs, milk, oil, and vanilla seeds.
Let the batter rest at 3°C (35°F) for at least 3 hours.
Heat a 26-centimeter (10 1/4-inch) skillet until it starts slightly smoking.
Lightly grease the pan.
Ladle about 75 grams (2 5/8 oz) of the pancake batter into the pan, enough to cover the bottom with a thin layer.
Cook each pancake for 30 seconds, then flip.
Continue cooking for 10 seconds.
Place the crêpes on a plate and stack them as they cook to keep them soft.

ALMOND CRUNCH

(*CROQUANT DE CORDES*)

THESE CRUNCHY ALMOND COOKIES ARE FROM THE CHARMING TOWN OF CORDES-SUR-CIEL IN THE TARN REGION OF FRANCE, AND THE RECIPE DATES BACK TO THE SEVENTEENTH CENTURY. BACK THEN, THERE WAS AN ABUNDANCE OF ALMOND TREES IN THE REGION, WITH SO MANY ALMONDS THAT NO ONE KNEW WHAT TO DO WITH THEM ALL. LEGEND HAS IT THAT AN INNKEEPER IN THE VILLAGE OF CORDES BAKED *COUQUES*, USING ALMONDS, SUGAR, AND EGG WHITES, WHICH HE SERVED ALONG WITH GALLIC WINE, GIVING RISE TO THIS CRUNCHY, DELICATE, GOLDEN CARAMELIZED MARVEL.

MAKES ABOUT 30 COOKIES

INGREDIENTS

Raw almonds	**125 G (4 ³/₈ OZ)**
Egg whites	**70 G (2 ¹/₂ OZ)**
Superfine sugar	**230 G (8 ¹/₈ OZ)**
Bread flour (T65)	**50 G (1 ³/₄ OZ)**

METHOD

Coarsely chop the almonds.
Mix together the almonds, egg whites, sugar, and flour.
Shape the dough into 15-gram (¹/₂-oz) balls of dough and place on silicone mats on baking sheets.
Bake in a convection oven at 170°C (340°F) for about 15 minutes.
Let cool.
Remove from the silicone mats.

FAR BRETON

FAR BRETON IS AN EMBLEMATIC SPECIALTY OF BRITTANY'S CUISINE. ORIGINALLY A DISH EATEN BY THE POOR, IT CONSISTED OF A SAVORY PORRIDGE THAT BRETONS ATE PRACTICALLY EVERY DAY. BUT FOR FESTIVITIES TODAY, IT IS DRESSED UP AND SWEETENED WITH FRUIT (PRUNES, APPLES, OR RAISINS) OR OTHER FLAVORS (RUM, ORANGE BLOSSOM, VANILLA, ETC.). MAKING IT WITH PRUNES IS DEFINITELY THE MOST POPULAR RECIPE.

MAKES 3 CUSTARD CAKES

INGREDIENTS

Vanilla bean	**1**
Strong flour	**150 G (5 ¼ OZ)**
Eggs	**150 G (5 ¼ OZ)**
Superfine sugar	**100 G (3 ½ OZ)**
Milk	**500 G (1 LB 1 ⅝ OZ)**
Prunes	**180 G (6 ⅜ OZ)**

METHOD

Scrape out the vanilla seeds. Whisk together the flour, eggs, sugar, and vanilla seeds.
Gradually whisk in the milk.
Set aside at 3°C (35°F) for at least 12 hours.
Generously butter three 15 × 10-centimeter (6 × 4-inch) dishes.
Arrange 60 grams (2 ⅛ oz) of prunes evenly over the bottom of each dish.
Mix the batter gently with a whisk, then pour it into the dishes, being careful to avoid moving the prunes.
Bake in a convection oven at 165°C (330°F) for about 25 minutes, then at 200°C (390°F) for 8 minutes.
Let cool in the dishes.

NANTAIS CAKES

PART AND PARCEL OF THE HISTORY OF THE CITY OF NANTES AND ITS PORT, THIS CAKE IS A TRIBUTE TO THE MARITIME TRADE AND EXCHANGES BETWEEN NANTES AND THE WEST INDIES. SAID TO HAVE BEEN INVENTED IN ABOUT 1820 BY A MASTER BAKER, HIS RECIPE INCLUDED CANE SUGAR AND RUM FROM FRANCE'S CARIBBEAN ISLANDS. THIS IS A SOFT DESSERT WITH EXOTIC FLAVORS THAT KEEPS WELL—UP TO A MONTH, IF WELL WRAPPED AND STORED IN A COOL PLACE.

MAKES 18 CAKES

INGREDIENTS	
Strong flour	120 G (4 1/4 OZ)
Baking powder	10 G (3/8 OZ)
Unsalted butter	380 G (13 3/8 OZ)
Superfine sugar	450 G (15 7/8 OZ)
Almond flour	300 G (10 1/2 OZ)
Eggs	450 G (15 7/8 OZ)
Rum	90 G (3 1/8 OZ)

ICING	
Confectioners' sugar	390 G (13 3/4 OZ)
Water	60 G (2 1/8 OZ)
White rum	5 G (3/16 OZ)

FOR THE ICING

Mix all the ingredients together.

METHOD

Sift the flour and baking powder.
In a stand mixer fitted with the paddle attachment, cream the butter and sugar.
Add in the almond flour, then the eggs.
Add the flour and baking powder and beat.
Add the rum.
Pour 100 grams (3 1/2 oz) of the batter into each greased 10-centimeter (4-inch)-diameter round mold.
Bake in a convection oven at 180°C (355°F) for about 20 minutes.
Cool the cakes on a wire rack.
Coat each Nantais cake with 25 grams (7/8 oz) of icing.

WAFFLES

WAFFLES ARE ONE OF FRANCE'S OLDEST PASTRIES. IN MEDIEVAL TIMES, THESE WERE THIN, ROUND, CRISP WAFERS BAKED BETWEEN TWO HEATED METAL PLATES, CALLED *OUBLIES* IN FRENCH, WHICH COMES FROM THE LATIN *OBLATA*, MEANING "OFFERED," AS IN AN OFFERING TO GOD. AT AROUND THE SAME TIME, A BLACKSMITH CAME UP WITH A MOLD INSPIRED BY THE HONEYCOMB PATTERN MADE BY BEES. THIS NATURAL DESIGN WAS CALLED *WALFRE,* MEANING "HONEYCOMB" IN OLD FRENCH, AND FROM THAT WORD WE GET BOTH THE WORD "WAFFLE" IN ENGLISH, AS WELL AS THE FRENCH WORD *GAUFRE*.

MAKES 15 WAFFLES

INGREDIENTS

Eggs	**200 G (7 OZ)**
Bread flour (T65)	**600 G (1 LB 6 1/8 OZ)**
Superfine sugar	**150 G (5 1/4 OZ)**
Brown butter	**200 G (7 OZ)**
Milk	**1 KG (2 LB 3 1/4 OZ)**
Baking powder	**20 G (3/4 OZ)**
Salt	**1 G (1/32 OZ)**

TO FINISH

Confectioners' sugar	**AS NEEDED**

METHOD

Separate the egg yolks and whites.
Combine all the ingredients except the egg whites.
Beat the egg whites.
Fold the beaten egg whites into the batter.
Mix the batter.
Preheat large-cavity waffle makers to 220°C (430°F).
Pour 140 grams (5 oz) of the waffle batter on the waffle makers.
Close and turn them over.
Cook for about 1 minute and turn over again.
Cook for about 2 minutes.
Sprinkle with confectioners' sugar and serve.

SPICE BREAD

SPICE BREAD HAS A LONG HISTORY! ALTHOUGH THE ANCIENT EGYPTIANS, GREEKS, AND ROMANS WERE FAMILIAR WITH A BREAD MADE WITH HONEY AND SPICES, THE TRUE ANCESTOR OF TODAY'S SPICE BREAD IS THOUGHT TO BE FROM CHINA. IT IS SAID TO HAVE BEEN EATEN BY THE HORSEMEN WHO FOUGHT FOR GENGHIS KHAN, AND DURING THOSE CAMPAIGNS IT BECAME KNOWN TO THE ARABS. IT WAS DISCOVERED BY EUROPEAN CRUSADERS IN THE HOLY LAND, WHO BROUGHT BACK NOT ONLY SPICES, BUT ALSO THE RECIPE FOR THIS BREAD. SPICE BREAD BECAME POPULAR IN GERMANY AND ALSACE, WHERE THERE IS STILL A GREAT TRADITION OF MAKING IT. IN FRANCE, BY THE FIFTEENTH CENTURY, THE MAKERS OF SPICE BREAD WOULD EVEN ENJOY THEIR OWN GUILD.

MAKES 1 LOAF

INGREDIENTS

Bread flour (T65)	**270 G (9 1/2 OZ)**
Sorbitol	**15 G (1/2 OZ)**
Baking soda	**5 G (3/16 OZ)**
Salt	**1 G (1/32 OZ)**
Ground cinnamon	**6 G (3/16 OZ)**
Ground ginger	**3 G (1/8 OZ)**
Ground allspice	**2 G (1/16 OZ)**
Milk	**150 G (5 1/4 OZ)**
Honey	**320 G (11 1/4 OZ)**
Brown butter	**150 G (5 1/4 OZ)**
Orange, zest only	**1**

ORANGE SYRUP

Honey	**25 G (7/8 OZ)**
Orange juice	**100 G (3 1/2 OZ)**

FOR THE ORANGE SYRUP

Bring the honey and orange juice to a boil.

METHOD

Sift together the flour, sorbitol, baking soda, salt, cinnamon, ginger, and allspice.
Heat the honey to 45°C (115°F).
Combine the milk, honey, brown butter, and orange zest.
Stir the liquid and dry mixtures together.
Pour 900 grams (1 lb 15 3/4 oz) of batter into a buttered 30 × 8 × 8-centimeter (11 3/4 × 3 1/4 × 3 1/4-inch) baking pan.
Bake in a convection oven at 155°C (310°F) for about 40 minutes.
When cool, soak the top of the spice bread with the warm orange syrup.

SCONES

ORIGINATING IN SCOTLAND BUT MUCH APPRECIATED BY THE BRITISH, SCONES ARE PERFECT FOR BREAKFAST OR IN THE AFTERNOON WITH A CUP OF TEA. THEY CAN BE EATEN PLAIN, STUDDED WITH RAISINS, OR SPLIT IN HALF HORIZONTALLY AND TOPPED WITH BUTTER AND JAM, OR JAM AND A THICK SET CREAM . . . OR ALL THREE!

MAKES 25 SCONES

INGREDIENTS

Bread flour (T65)	**1 KG (2 LB 3 1/4 OZ)**
Baking powder	**50 G (1 3/4 OZ)**
Salt	**10 G (3/8 OZ)**
Unsalted butter	**160 G (5 5/8 OZ)**
Superfine sugar	**180 G (6 3/8 OZ)**
Eggs	**210 G (7 3/8 OZ)**
Acidified milk	**300 G (10 1/2 OZ)**

TO FINISH

Egg yolks	**AS NEEDED**

METHOD

Sift together the flour, baking powder, and salt.
In a stand mixer fitted with the paddle attachment, cream the butter and sugar.
Add the eggs and acidified milk.
Add the dry ingredients and stir.
Let the dough rest for 5 minutes.
Roll out the dough to a thickness of 13 millimeters (1/2 inch).
Cut into 6-centimeter (2 1/2-inch)-diameter disks and place upside down on baking sheets lined with silicone mats.
Glaze the top with beaten egg yolk, then repeat again 5 minutes later.
Bake in a deck oven at 200°C (390°F) for about 15 minutes.

SPÉCULOOS

A TRADITIONAL COOKIE FROM NORTHERN EUROPE—IN PARTICULAR, NORTHERN BELGIUM—SPÉCULOOS ARE TRADITIONALLY EATEN ON ST. NICHOLAS DAY. ORIGINALLY, THEY WERE MADE IN THE SHAPE OF THE SAINT, BUT THAT TRADITIONAL FORM HAS BEEN ABANDONED TODAY IN FAVOR OF SIMPLER, NONFIGURATIVE ONES. NOW EATEN ALL YEAR ROUND, EVERYONE CAN ENJOY THEIR CRUNCHY TEXTURE AND THE FLAVORS OF CINNAMON AND BROWN SUGAR. THEY HAVE BECOME A HIT ALL OVER THE WORLD.

MAKES 120 COOKIES

INGREDIENTS

Bread flour (T65)	**1 KG (2 LB 3 ¼ OZ)**
Baking powder	**15 G (½ OZ)**
Cloves	**10**
Brown sugar	**750 G (1 LB 10 ½ OZ)**
Unsalted butter, softened	**500 G (1 LB 1 ⅝ OZ)**
Ground cinnamon	**50 G (1 ¾ OZ)**
Salt	**1 G (1/32 OZ)**
Eggs	**150 G (5 ¼ OZ)**

METHOD

Sift the flour and baking powder.
Crush the cloves with the flat of a knife.
In a stand mixer fitted with the paddle attachment, cream the brown sugar, softened butter, cinnamon, cloves, and salt.
Add the eggs one by one.
Add the flour and baking powder and mix.
Roll out to a rectangle 4 centimeters (1 ½ inches) thick and 10 centimeters (4 inches) wide.
Wrap in plastic wrap and refrigerate for at least 2 hours.
Cut slices every 4 millimeters (⅛ inch) to obtain 4 × 10-centimeter (1 ½ × 4-inch) rectangles.
Place the rectangles on baking sheets lined with parchment paper.
Bake in a convection oven at 170°C (340°F) for about 15 minutes.
Cool the spéculoos on a wire rack.

· L A
· M I
N A T
E D ·

DO
UGH

APPLE TURNOVERS

MAKES 12 TURNOVERS

YOUR CHOICE OF LAMINATED DOUGH

Five-turn laminated dough (*see* Basics)	**1 KG (2 LB 3 ¼ OZ)**

APPLE COMPOTE

Apples, diced	**800 G (1 ¾ LB)**
Superfine sugar	**120 G (4 ¼ OZ)**
Water	**40 G (1 ⅜ OZ)**
Vanilla bean	**1**

TO FINISH

Egg yolks	**AS NEEDED**
Neutral syrup	**AS NEEDED**

FOR THE APPLE COMPOTE

Cook the apples, sugar, water, and vanilla bean over low heat for about 20 minutes, or until the apples are translucent. Remove the vanilla bean.

Blend half of the apple mixture, then stir into the remaining cooked apples. Set aside at 3°C (35°F).

METHOD

Roll out the dough to a thickness of 2 millimeters (1/16 inch).

Using a 17 × 12.5-centimeter (6 ¾ × 5-inch) oval pastry cutter, cut out 12 pieces.

Let the dough rest at 3°C (35°F) for at least 1 hour.

Using a pastry bag, pipe 50 grams (1 ¾ oz) of apple compote in the center of the lower half of each turnover.

Lightly moisten the edges, then close and seal.

Turn the turnovers over and brush with egg yolk.

Using a knife, gently score the surface of each turnover to make your desired design, then prick them. Let rest at 3°C (35°F) for about 12 hours.

Bake in a convection oven at 175°C (345°F), or in a deck oven 190°C (375°F) for about 35 minutes.

Brush apple turnovers with neutral syrup.

Cool on a wire rack.

NEAPOLITAN TURNOVERS

MAKES 15 TURNOVERS

YOUR CHOICE OF LAMINATED DOUGH

Five-turn laminated dough (*see* Basics)	1 KG (2 LB 3 ¼ OZ)
Unsalted butter, melted	40 G (1 ⅜ OZ)
Confectioners' sugar	20 G (¾ OZ)

NEAPOLITAN TURNOVER FILLING

Raisins	135 G (4 ¾ OZ)
Rum	15 G (½ OZ)
Choux pastry *(see page 29)*	300 G (10 ½ OZ)
Pastry cream *(see page 30)*	300 G (10 ½ OZ)

TO FINISH

Confectioners' sugar	AS NEEDED

FOR THE NEAPOLITAN TURNOVER FILLING

The day before, stir the raisins into the rum and set aside at 3°C (35°F). The next day, using a stand mixer fitted with the paddle attachment, mix the choux pastry dough with the pastry cream, then add the soaked raisins.
Set aside at 3°C (35°F).

METHOD

Using a dough sheeter, roll out the dough to a thickness of 2 millimeters (1/16 inch), then into an 80 × 30-centimeter (31 ½ × 11 ¾-inch) rectangle.
Using a rolling pin, flatten the edge of one short side of the dough.
Lightly moisten the flattened part. Generously brush the remaining dough with melted butter, then sprinkle with confectioners' sugar.
Starting at the opposite end, roll it up tightly and seal with the moistened part. Cut into fifteen 2-centimeter (¾-inch)-wide slices.
Using a dough sheeter, roll out the slices to a thickness of 2 millimeters (1/16 inch), shaping them into ovals.
Using a pastry bag, pipe 50 grams (1 ¾ oz) of Neapolitan turnover filling in the center of the lower half of each turnover.
Lightly moisten the edges, then close and seal. Turn the turnovers over.
Let rest at 3°C (35°F) for about 12 hours.
Bake in a convection oven at 175°C (345°F), or in a deck oven at 190°C (375°F) for about 30 minutes.
Cool on a wire rack. Sprinkle with confectioners' sugar.

FLAN

MAKES 4 FLANS

LAMINATED DOUGH SCRAPS	
	1 KG (2 LB 3 1/4 OZ)

FLAN FILLING

Vanilla beans	2
Milk	1.2 KG (2 LB 10 3/8 OZ)
Whipping cream 35% fat	1.2 KG (2 LB 10 3/8 OZ)
Superfine sugar	470 G (1 LB 1/2 OZ)
Cornstarch	135 G (4 3/4 OZ)
Egg yolks	72 G (2 1/2 OZ)

FOR THE FLAN FILLING

Scrape out the vanilla beans. Blend the milk, cream, sugar, cornstarch, egg yolks, and vanilla beans together. In a saucepan, bring the mixture to a boil and boil for 1 minute. Pour into the prebaked laminated dough shells while hot.

METHOD

Roll out the dough scraps to a thickness of 2 millimeters (1/16 inch), then prick them.
Cut into four 26-centimeter (10 1/4-inch)-diameter disks.
Let rest at 3°C (35°F) for at least 1 hour, then line 19-centimeter (7 1/2-inch)-diameter, 4-centimeter (1 1/2-inch)-deep cake pans with the disks.
Let rest at 3°C (35°F) for at least 1 hour. Line the cavities with parchment paper and fill with pie weights.
Bake in a convection oven at 150°C (300°F), or in a deck oven at 170°C (340°F), for about 35 minutes. Remove the pie weights and parchment paper.
Bake in a convection oven at 170°C (340°F), or in a deck oven at 190°C (375°F) for an additional 10 minutes. Let cool.
Pour 700 gram (1 lb 8 3/4 oz) of the filling into each prebaked laminated pastry shell. Set aside at 3°C (35°F) for 12 hours.
Bake in a convection oven at 180°C (355°F), or in a deck oven at 200°C (390°F), for about 45 minutes. Cool on a wire rack.

GALETTE DES ROIS

MAKES 3 GALETTES

YOUR CHOICE OF LAMINATED DOUGH

Five-turn laminated dough (*see* Basics)	1 KG (2 LB 3 1/4 OZ)

FRANGIPANE CREAM

Almond cream *(see page 30)*	720 G (1 LB 9 3/8 OZ)
Pastry cream *(see page 30)*	180 G (6 3/8 OZ)

BEANS 3

TO FINISH

Egg yolks	AS NEEDED
Neutral syrup *(see page 31)*	AS NEEDED

FOR THE FRANGIPANE CREAM

In a stand mixer fitted with the paddle attachment, loosen the pastry cream and add the almond cream.
Beat until smooth and creamy. Set aside at 3°C (35°F).

METHOD

Using a dough sheeter, roll out the dough to a thickness of 1.5 millimeter (1/16 inch). Cut out six 23.5-centimeter (9 1/4-inch) diameter disks. Let the laminated dough disks rest at 3°C (35°F) for at least 1 hour.
Using a pastry bag, pipe 300 grams (10 1/2 oz) of frangipane cream into the center of three of the disks. Place one bean on each galette.
Lightly moisten the edges, then cover with a second disk and seal. Leave rest at 3°C (35°F) for at least 1 hour.
Turn the galettes over and brush with egg yolk.
Using a knife, gently score the surface of the galettes to make the desired pattern, then prick them. Let rest at 3°C (35°F) for about 12 hours.
Bake in a convection oven at 175°C (345°F), or in a deck oven at 190°C (375°F), for about 45 minutes.
Brush the galettes with neutral syrup.
Cool on a wire rack.

CLASSIC FRENCH FINE APPLE TART

MAKES 6 TARTS

YOUR CHOICE OF LAMINATED DOUGH

Five-turn laminated dough (*see* Basics)	**1 KG (2 LB 3 ¼ OZ)**

FILLING

Apples	**3.8 KG (8 LB 6 OZ)**
Unsalted butter, melted	**150 G (5 ¼ OZ)**
Brown sugar	**210 G (7 ⅜ OZ)**
Unsalted butter, melted	**150 G (5 ¼ OZ)**

FOR THE FILLING

Peel and cut the apples with an apple peeler.

METHOD

Using a dough sheeter, roll out the dough to a thickness of 1.5 millimeters (1/16 inch), then prick it.

Cut out six 23.5-centimeter (9 ¼-inch) diameter disks. Place the disks on baking sheets lined with parchment paper, then let rest at 3°C (35°F) for at least 1 hour.

Arrange 450 grams (15 ⅞ oz) of apples attractively over each disk. Brush the apples with melted butter and sprinkle with the brown sugar.

Bake in a convection oven at 175°C (345°F), or in a deck oven at 190°C (375°F), for about 25 minutes.

Remove the tarts from the oven and brush the apples with melted butter.

Bake in a convection oven at 175°C (345°F), or in a deck oven at 190°C (375°F), for an additional 25 minutes.

Cool on a wire rack.

TARTE TATIN

MAKES 6 TARTS

YOUR CHOICE OF LAMINATED DOUGH	
5-turn laminated dough (*see* Basics)	**1 KG (2 LB 3 ¼ OZ)**
CARAMEL	
Superfine sugar	**800 G (1 ¾ LB)**
Unsalted butter	**320 G (11 ¼ OZ)**

FOR THE CARAMELIZED APPLES	
Apples	**5. 8 KG (12 ¾ LB)**
Caramel	**1.02 KG (2 ¼ LB)**

FOR THE CARAMEL

In a hot saucepan, prepare a caramel, adding the sugar gradually. Stir in the finely diced butter. Pour onto a silicone mat and let cool.
In a mixer or blender, blend the caramel.

FOR THE CARAMELIZED APPLES

Peel the apples with an apple peeler and thinly slice.
Arrange 680 grams (1 ½ lb) of apple slices attractively in each 22-centimeter (8 ¾-inch)-diameter silicone mold.
Cover with 170 grams (6 oz) of processed caramel.
Bake in a convection oven at 160°C (320°F), or in a deck oven at 180°C (355°F), for about 1 hour.
Let stand for 10 minutes, then press down on the apples.
Let cool and press down again.
Set the molds aside at 3°C (35°F) or in the freezer.

METHOD

Using a dough sheeter, roll out the dough to a thickness of 1.5 millimeters (1/16 inch), then prick it.
Cut out six 23.5-centimeter (9 ¼-inch) diameter disks.
Place the disks between two baking sheets lined with parchment paper.
Let the laminated dough disks rest at 3°C (35°F) for at least 1 hour. Bake in a convection oven at 175°C (345°F), or in a deck oven at 190°C (375°F), for about 22 minutes.
Trim the edges of the baked laminated dough disks to a diameter of 22-centimeter (8 ¾ inches). Remove the caramelized apples from the molds and arrange them on the laminated dough disks.

THE · AUTHORS ·

JÉRÉMY BALLESTER

From a very young age, Jérémy had been drawn to the world of baking.
It was only natural that, at the age of fifteen, he would join the Compagnons du Devoir to learn the art of baking. There, he met exceptional educators who wholeheartedly passed on their passion for his calling. Self-demanding and tenacious, he was determined to meticulously learn everything about the profession.

At seventeen years old, with his CAP qualifications under his belt, he set off to work around France. Paris, and then Brussels, provided rewarding experiences that enabled him to quench his thirst for knowledge and, thanks to his drive, he was happy to work long hours in pursuit of his passion.

His taste for adventure and his curiosity about baking would lead him to explore beyond the borders of France, where he discovered other worlds. After a few years in Oslo, he continued his journey of initiation in New Zealand, Dubai, and England. In 2012, armed with a wealth of experience, he returned to Oslo to take up a managerial position.

He has seamlessly combined his two passions, traveling and baking. He moved to Seoul and joined the SPC Culinary Academy as an educator, where he created an entire training program on French baking, passing on his passion with precision and great generosity. His quest for knowledge led him to train at the Institute de la Boulangerie Pâtisserie (INBP), obtaining diplomas in baking and pastry making as well as culinary management in 2017.

These experiences were further shaped when he met Jean-Marie Lanio. The two hit it off, and the fruit of this friendship are three books on baking, published in Korea in 2020.

BRIAN BOCLET

The son of a baker, Brian Boclet was born in 1987 in Arras in the Hauts de France region, where he grew up in the apartment above the family bakery in Roubaix. The aromas of pastries and hot bread would spark his appetite and curiosity for baking. To keep him from getting under their feet, the bakers would give him small jobs to do in the bakery. For him, the bakery was a place of sensory and gustatory discovery. He always enjoyed dropping by the store, where he would often help his mother make sales.

When the time arrived to decide what to study, he had to choose: baking or sales. He opted to learn how to manage commercial ventures and earned a BTS MUC degree. In the following years, he gained experience abroad, most notably in Cambridge, London, and Singapore.

On his return to France, he decided to join his parents' baking business and learn the profession. After earning CAP, BP, and BM qualifications from the INBP, where his passion for baking was confimed, he then spent two years in Paris learning new techniques from leading bakers. In the southwest of France, he took over a business where he enjoyed a string of successes in local competitions (for his traditional French baguettes, butter croissants, etc.).

After six years with the company, he moved to Switzerland, where he joined Thomas Marie's team of MOF bakers at the EHL Lausanne Hospitality Business School as a practical arts educator. Thomas Marie became Brian's friend, mentoring him while he prepared for the Meilleurs Ouvriers de France (MOF) boulanger competition, for which he was a finalist. His tenacity and epicurean spirit continually inspire his creativity in the profession he so dearly loves.

Thanks to his hard work, in July 2023, Thomas Marie handed Brian the keys to the prestigious bakery at the Hospitality Business School, founded ten years earlier with Jean-Marie Lanio.

Ready for a new challenge, Brian became the head of the EHL bakery, heading up a team that has seen him grow up.

JEAN-MARIE LANIO

While on vacation when he was a high school student, Jean-Marie discovered Philippe Lanoë's bakery, which happened to be next door to his family's home in Sévérac, Loire-Atlantique. He had wanted to keep busy during the summer, but as the start of the new school year approached, it was bread that was uppermost in all his thoughts and plans. With his high school diploma under his belt, his parents and teachers finally allowed him to do an apprenticeship.

After earning CAP, BEP, and BP diplomas, he spent four years as a head baker in the Nantes region. On the strength of this experience, and eager to learn, he joined the INBP in Rouen to prepare for the culinary management diploma. After earning it, he joined their team of baking educators. For three years, he trained young French and foreign students for the CAP baker's diploma, as well as professional bakers for the baker's diploma in culinary management. He passes on to them his love of good bread.

At the end of 2012, following a call from Thomas Marie, he joined EHL, the renowned Hospitality Business School in Lausanne, for three years. He taught baking with passion, while developing his baking skills alongside Thomas. The publication of *Grand Livre de la boulangerie* brought his wonderful time in Switzerland to a close.

A new opportunity arose in 2015, and he moved to Seoul to oversee the launch of the INBP Seoul Master Class at SPC Culinary Academy, where he found it fascinating to teach Korean students about French baking.

There, he met Jérémy Ballester, and the two of them worked closely and skillfully together. In 2020, their shared passion for baking led them to write three books devoted to the baked products most loved by Koreans: the croissant, the French baguette, and the brioche.

The enriching experience offered by reaching the final of the MOF competition in 2015 and 2018 has enabled him to delve deeper into specific facets of his profession and further develop his creativity in the field of viennoiserie.

OLIVIER MAGNE

Born in France's Cantal region, Olivier Magne grew up in Polminhac in his mother's café-restaurant, *Le Berganty*.

As an adolescent, Olivier enjoyed time spent with his maternal grandparents, who owned a bakery, delicatessen, grocery store, and café in Saint-Julien-de-Jordanne. It was there that a real passion for baking was born, along with a desire to make good bread while continuing the family tradition.

At the age of seventeen, after earning a CAP diploma in baking from the IFPP in Aurillac, he took over the family business. In 2000, he earned a baker's diploma in culinary management from the École Française de Boulangerie Pâtisserie in Aurillac. For five years, he split his time between training at the EFBPA and running the family business. Numerous internships and a good deal of determination resulted in him being a finalist in the 2004 and 2007 MOF competitions. In 2009, a pivotal year, Olivier met Virginie, and the two would start a family. She encouraged him to prepare for the competition. When the opportunity arose to join the INBP in Rouen, Olivier seized it, albeit with a heavy heart—he had to close the family business for good to teach around the world. Thanks to the energy that drives him, he entered the MOF competition in 2015. All those years of preparing would earn him the most prestigious title in the profession: Meilleur Ouvrier de France.

He met Florian Argoud on a training course, and, in 2016, they decided to open a bakery together in Paris's 11th arrondissement. This was followed in 2017 by a second one, called *Farine et O,* in the 9th arrondissement. Florian and Olivier were made for each other, driven by the same values and with complementary skills.
Olivier then set up his own bakery consultancy, which has taken him to the four corners of the globe.

In 2020, Olivier and his team at *Farine et O* won third place for the best traditional French baguette in Paris.
After the publication of *Ils vont aimer* (INBP), on which he collaborated, Olivier is delighted to take part in cowriting this book with his renowned colleagues.

THOMAS MARIE

When his parents bought a bakery in Vesoul (Haute-Saône), young Thomas quickly realized that it was a sign that he was going to become a baker.

When he passed his exams in management with honors, he enrolled at the INBP in Rouen, where he successively prepared for and obtained CAP, BEP, BP, and BM diplomas in pastry making. After working in two bakeries in Nancy, he returned to the family business as a baker, where he was given free rein to use his creativity and put his stamina, meticulousness, and organizational skills to the test. At the same time, he took part in numerous competitions, winning several prestigious titles: Coupe de France de la boulangerie (bread category in 2005) and European runner-up in the team category (2006). He then joined the INBP as an itinerant educator. While he was often on the road to pass on his knowledge, he also learned a lot at the same time.

At the age of twenty-four, while constantly striving to improve, he entered the prestigious MOF competition, and for two years devoted all his free time to preparing for it. His breakthrough came in 2007, when, at the age of twenty-six, he won the blue, white, and red collar on his first attempt.

After a gap year abroad, he returned to the INBP to resume his job as an itinerant educator. In 2013, he was offered a new and exciting opportunity: the prestigious EHL Hospitality Business School in Lausanne was looking for an MOF baker to set up a bakery unit. He left the INBP and headed for Switzerland, where he continued to work as an educator.

In 2017, his path crossed that of Vaud-based Laurent Buri and took a new turn. The two men shard the same passion for gastronomy and the same exacting standards. Joining forces, they would come up with a concept aimed at restoring bread to its former glory. And so, in June 2018, the first BREAD STORE boutique in Lausanne was launched, offering French-Swiss specialties. This was soon followed by a second in Vevey, and then a third in another part of Lausanne.

Thomas is, with Sébastien Odet, the co-author of *60 Boulangerie-Pâtisserie successes (INBP)*, the *Grand Livre de la boulangerie*, the *Grand Livre de la viennoiserie*, and the *Grand Livre du snacking*.

PATRICE MITAILLÉ

Hailing from a family of artisans, including butchers, bakers, and even a top chef in California, Patrice Mitaillé would be destined to work in the food industry.

Born in Vannes, Brittany, in 1989, Patrice first explored the world of pastry making during an apprenticeship in Ploemeur and Vannes, where he successfully earned a BEP diploma, a Mention Complémentaire, and a BTM diploma.

Not content with these initial qualifications, he went on to take a BTM Chocolaterie and a BM Pâtisserie at the INBP in Rouen, where he would meet Thomas Marie and Jean-Marie Lanio (his baking instructor, whom he would meet again at the EHL Hospitality Business School in Lausanne), who would become his mentors.

His thirst for knowledge has been insatiable. He would double his efforts and take up baking, earning his CAP diploma at the INBP and finishing top of his class. What a great journey!

This was followed by eighteen months working in a bakery in Paris alongside the illustrious, world-famous head baker Eric Kayser.

When Thomas Marie called him to join his team at EHL Hospitality Business School in Lausanne, Patrice didn't give it a second thought and sped off to join him in Switzerland. After Jean-Marie Lanio left for Korea, he took his place, accompanying and passionately teaching baking to groups of French and foreign students.

Straightforward, meticulous, and precise, Patrice, who enjoys passing on his knowledge, was selected to be part of the French team at the Bakery World Cup in 2014. Some of the breads and viennoiseries he made for that event are featured in this book.

Many thanks to:

THE MANAGEMENT AT THE EHL HOSPITALITY BUSINESS SCHOOL IN LAUSANNE and **BREADSTORE SWISS** for providing equipment and ingredients,

JÉRÔME LANIER, DYLAN HALFF, and **KWANGSOO LEE** for their great work,

DENIS FATET and **ÉLISABETH MARIE** for their careful proofreading,

LAURENT BURI, THOMAS GALA, BENOIT LAAGE, NICOLAS MORET, and **THÉO VO** for help with product design,

ALAIN DUCASSE, AURORE CHAROY, and **FANNY MORGENSZTERN** for their efficiency, the high quality of their work, and the trust they placed in us,

Our wives and children: **Yunhee** and **Tae Oh Ballester; Alicia Sponton; Boyan** and **ALESSIO BOCLET; MIN YOUNG** and **AH IN LANIO; ÉLÉONORE, PÉNÉLOPE** and **VICTOR MARIE;** and **VIRGINIE SANGO, ROBIN,** and **JULIE MAGNE** for their support and invaluable presence every single day,

Our parents and grandparents:
PASCAL and **BRIGITTE BALLESTER; BERNARD** and **NELLY BOCLET; PATRICK** and **ANNIE LANIO; JACQUES** and **ÉLISABETH MARIE; PATRICK** and **CÉLINE MITAILLE; ANNE SALAT;** and **ANTONIN** and **MARINETTE SALAT** for the education they gave us and the values they have passed on to us.

We would also like to extend our warmest thanks to **ALL OUR PARTNERS**, and to all those who have worked to bring this book to fruition.

COLLECTION MANAGER

Alain Ducasse

PROJECT MANAGER

Thomas Marie

DIRECTOR

Aurore Charoy

EDITOR

Aurélie Legay, with the assistance of Valentine Lacoste

TRANSLATION

Cillero & De Motta

COPYEDITING & PROOFREADING

Sarah Scheffel

PHOTOGRAPHY CREDITS
©Jérôme Lanier (cover and pp. 35 to 39, 42 to 47, 50, 55, 58, 69, 72 to 77, 84 to 87, 101 to 107, 112, 120, 133, 141 to 143, 149, 159, 162, 167, 177, 190, 194, 215, 219, 224, 230, 235, 245, 252, 256 to 268, 278, 284, 286, 292, 294, 328, 334 to 345, 348, 353, 356 to 368, 376 to 384, 392 to 400, 408, 432 to 452, 464 to 480, 491, 496, 501, 518, 520.)
©Dylan Halff (pp. 40, 48, 53, 56, 61 to 67, 71, 78, 80, 82, 89 to 99, 109, 114 to 119, 122 to 131, 134 to 139, 146, 152 to 156, 159, 165, 168 to 175, 178, 216, 220, 223, 227, 232, 237 to 242, 325, 327, 331, 332, 346, 351, 487, 488, 492, 495, 498, 502 to 507.)
©Kwangsoo Lee (back cover and pp. 182 to 186, 192, 196 to 204, 208 to 212, 248, 250, 254, 270 to 276, 280 to 282, 288, 290, 296, 372, 388, 404, 412, 416, 428, 456, 460, 510 to 516.)
©Mathilde Anceaume (portrait p. 529)

ART DIRECTION AND GRAPHIC DESIGN
Soins Graphiques
Pierre Tachon, Camille Demaimay

PHOTOENGRAVING
Nord Compo

Printed in China by Toppan

ISBN: 978-2-37945-101-0
Legal deposit 3rd quarter 2025

Distributed in North America
by ABRAMS, New York.

Ducasse Édition
2, rue Paul-Vaillant-Couturier
92532 Levallois-Perret Cedex

FAN

CY